TEXAS AT THE CROSSROADS

TEXAS
AT THE
CROSSROADS

*People,
Politics,
and
Policy*

Edited by

Anthony Champagne and Edward J. Harpham

Texas A&M University Press
College Station

Library of Congress Cataloging-in-Publication Data

Texas at the Crossroads.
Includes Index.
1. Texas—Politics and government—1951–
2. Political participation—Texas. 3. Texas—
Economic policy. 4. Texas—Social policy.
I. Champagne, Anthony. II. Harpham, Edward J.
JK4895.T48 1987   976.4′063   87-9959
ISBN 0–89096–317–7 (pbk.)

To our fellow Texans

CONTENTS

LIST OF FIGURES

LIST OF TABLES

ACKNOWLEDGMENTS

Many people have helped to bring this book to press. The staff of the School of Social Sciences at The University of Texas at Dallas have suffered through numerous drafts of the manuscript and been a source of encouragement throughout. In particular we would like to thank Evelyn Stutts, Cynthia Keheley, Janice Moore, Marie Walls, and Sheryl Thierry for the many hours that they spent typing the manuscript. We also would like to thank Marilyn Herrick for helping to proofread the final draft of the manuscript and Melvin Letteer for assisting us on the computer.

Warren Dixon read the manuscript and provided many useful insights and suggestions that assisted the authors in revising their chapters.

Finally, we would like to thank our wives, Beatriz Champagne and Wendy Harpham, for putting up with us as we labored over the book for the past two years. We hope that they are pleased with the final result.

TEXAS AT THE CROSSROADS

INTRODUCTION

Anthony Champagne and Edward J. Harpham

Texas is a state undergoing many changes. With the passing of the Republic's Sesquicentennial, the Lone Star State finds itself in the midst of a great transition. Texas is no longer the rustic frontier state of myth and legend. It is a complex, highly urbanized society that is rapidly replacing old dreams and ways of life with new ones. Traditional beliefs still percolate throughout the state. Religion remains a powerful force. Individualism continues to dominate the Texas psyche. Entrepreneurialism is still valued by a people who crave the opportunity to "make it big." But while such values survive, the people holding them and the actual opportunities available to them have changed enormously.

Dramatic demographic and economic changes underlie Texas' great transition. While V. O. Key's description of Texans as being "concerned about money and how to make it" may still be accurate, the money to be made no longer is tied simply to the land or the minerals beneath it.[1] The growth of "high-tech" industry has generated new opportunities and lessened the state's dependence upon agriculture and extraction-based industry. But high-tech has not been a cure for all that ails the state's economy as it undergoes a fundamental transformation. High-tech has not addressed the problems confronting the poverty-plagued border economy, or the declining industries in the Beaumont-Port Arthur area, or agriculture in the Panhandle. Large portions of the population have been and will continue to be left out of the high-tech boom well into the 1990s, posing serious problems for policymakers in the new Texas in coming years.

Perhaps nothing illuminates better the transition that Texas is undergoing in the 1980s than its changing politics. When V. O. Key wrote *Southern Politics* in 1949, Texas was a state dominated by a newly rich business establishment.[2] The conservative political leadership of the state, though claiming a Democratic party affiliation, was hostile to government, taxes, and social welfare programs and was drifting away from the national party of Roosevelt and Truman. The Republican party was largely a nonentity at the state level, composed of individuals who saw value in keeping the party small so that they would be able to control and benefit from federal patronage when a Republican occupied the White House. Segregation was still law in Texas and political power for minorities was unknown. Blacks only recently had been freed from the white primary which excluded them from political participation. Hispanic voters had little influence within the political process outside of several South Texas counties where a patron system operated. Under this system powerful and corrupt political bosses controlled the Hispanic vote and traded that vote for political plums at the state level.

Antiestablishment, prosocial welfare views did exist in Texas at mid-century, but such populism did not have much of a voice at the state level. East Texas populists were well represented by Sam Rayburn and Wright Patman in the U. S. House of Representatives, but they lacked the strength to elect someone to a statewide office. A welfare-oriented governor had not occupied the governor's mansion since Jimmy Allred during the depths of the Depression. Those state politicians who used a populist rhetoric generally pursued policies no different from those who acted in behalf of the state's business community. The popular "Pappy" O'Daniel, for example, was a one-time flour salesman who skyrocketed first to the governorship and then to the Senate on a platform comprising the Ten Commandments, the Golden Rule, and a promised pension for the state's elderly. Significantly, the pension program was to be funded with a sales tax. It was a populist program with an antipopulist funding system.

Texas politics in Key's time had a style all its own. To achieve high office, one had to construct a personal political organization and canvass the entire state. The enormous size of the state required significant campaign expenditures, which encouraged politicians to depend on wealthy entrepreneurs who made up the state's business establishment. The need to be identified by voters who were unorganized by political parties, unions, or other associations required candidates to be either good old boys, clowns, or worse. "Pappy" O'Daniel's colorful radio oratory and his use of the Light Crust Doughboys band was an extreme example of such clowning, but not that unusual. Other candidates became readily known for their anticommunist rhetoric, their states' rights oratory, their fighting skills, and even their attacks on the "obscene" books used in The University of Texas English classes.

Much that Key wrote about is still characteristic of Texas politics. The state's politics continues to be heavily influenced by a conservative business establishment. Union activity remains minimal, as does the organization of poor people and minorities. Texas is still characterized by low services and low taxes. Yet there are signs of change. While all might not be dramatic and are subject to a number of conflicting interpretations, they are nevertheless indicative of one fundamental truth about the Lone Star State in the 1980s: the state's future will differ significantly from its past.

One sign of change in Texas politics has been the gradual erosion of the old-style politics chronicled by Key. Moderates have challenged the stranglehold that conservatives have held over the Democratic party. Republicans (pariahs in Texas since Reconstruction) have become acceptable and even respectable participants in state politics. But the changes being introduced into Texas go beyond ideology or party affiliation.

Over the past decade, minorities and the poor have become increasingly involved in the political process. The state's Hispanic population has been growing rapidly, comprising 21% of the total population in 1980. South Texas is under Hispanic political control. San Antonio has its first Hispanic mayor in modern times. In the 1982 gubernatorial elections, there was an 86% increase in the Hispanic voter turnout over the 1978 election. In some heavily Mexican-American counties, 90% of the Hispanic vote went to Democrat Mark White. In statewide races in which Republicans attempt to challenge seriously the Democratic nominee, Democrats need the Hispanic vote to win.[3]

Black voters, too, have begun to exert some influence in Texas politics. Although blacks makeup only 12% of the state's population and are thus less crucial for political victory than Hispanics, they are being elected to the state legislature and city councils in increasing numbers. Indeed, black political leaders are beginning to assume a pivotal role in the politics of East Texas urban areas for the first time since Reconstruction.

The full significance of minority participation in Texas politics is not yet completely clear. Though minority voters have far more influence within the state than in the past, a firm Hispanic-black alliance has not occurred in spite of similar problems with discrimination and poverty. Cultural differences have so far prevented a cementing of alliances, although similar problems do create pressures for a large state government and for expanded social services.[4] One thing has become apparent already, however. Coupled to Texas' population boom and the natural increase in the demand for services that follows from such growth, minority participation has stimulated a call for a more activist state government, a direct challenge to the traditional lethargy of Texas state government.

A limited state government dominated by business interests may have been appropriate in the past for a rural Texas that reaped the blessings of oil reservoirs so large that even low severance taxes provided sufficient sums for governmental operations. But maintaining such a system has become increasingly difficult as state leaders have tried to cope with the problems of an increasingly urbanized and industrialized state. Such problems as declining oil and gas reserves, reductions in water supply in parts of the state, a highway system in need of construction and repair, an education system in need of revamping, a welfare system in need of reform, and a prison system bursting at the seams have taxed the genius and raised questions about the effectiveness of old-style politics in Texas.

If Texas is in the midst of a great transition, it is one that is imperfectly understood by those living through it. The 1970s were boom years for the state, particularly when compared with the nation as a whole. From 1970 to 1980, per capita personal income in the nation rose from $3,945 to $9,494. When controlling for inflation, this translates into a real increase of 13.3%. In Texas, however, per capita income rose from $3,536 in 1970 to $9,439 in 1980, a real increase of 25.7%, almost twice the national increase.[5] At the same time population in the state rose from 11.2 million in 1970 to 14.2 million in 1980, an increase of 26.8%, well above the 11.4% increase in population nationally.[6] For Americans adversely affected by two major recessions and chronic inflation, Texas appeared to be a land of hope and opportunity.

Various explanations have been offered for Texas' boom years. Politicians have argued frequently that the key to Texas' economic growth has been a favorable business climate. Low taxes plus anti-union right-to-work laws have brought people, business, and prosperity to Texas. A second explanation has suggested that ultimately it was the Texas character that sparked the state's fantastic growth. The spirit of independence and self-reliance championed by Texans for generations has fostered an entrepreneurial spirit which has led to rapid economic development and population expansion.

However appealing such explanations might be, they tend to underestimate the central role played by energy in the state's economy. The boom years in Texas in the 1970s were due in large part to a worldwide energy crisis coupled with the fact that Texas sat upon some of the greatest oil and natural gas reserves in the United States. A favorable business climate and an alleged Texas spirit may have driven the state's economic engine forward, but oil and gas were the crucial lubricants that kept it functioning smoothly. Table I-1 shows how changes in population and real per capita income in the state are related to changes in the value of oil and gas produced in Texas. Significantly, Table I–1 marks out a direct and positive relationship to exist from 1950 to 1982 between population and real per capita income and the value of oil and gas produced in Texas. As the value of oil and gas produced in Texas increased, population growth and per capita income rose.

Table I–1 also identifies another fascinating feature of the Texas political economy: the relationship between the energy sector and the state budget. As the value of oil produced in Texas rose from $4.1 billion in 1970 to $21.3 billion in 1980 and the value of natural gas rose from $1.2 billion in 1970 to $10.7 billion in 1980, the state budget rose from $3.0 billion in 1970 to $10.2 billion in 1980. In constant dollars, this translates into a real increase of 65%, an astounding number in light of Texas' history of fiscal austerity.

Table I–1. The Texas Political Economy, 1950–84.

	1950	*1960*	*1970*	*1980*	*1982*	*1984*
Population[a] (millions)	7.7	9.6	11.2	14.2	15.3	16.0
Per capita income[b] ($)	1,349	1,924	3,536	9,439	11,378	12,636
Value of oil produced in Texas[a] (billions $)	2.1	2.7	4.1	21.3	29.1	25.1
Value of gas produced in Texas[a] (billions $)	0.1	0.7	1.2	10.7	13.6	13.5
State expenditures in Texas[a] (billions $)	0.5	1.2	3.0	10.2	12.1	15.0

Sources: [a] *The Texas Almanac* 1984–85 and 1986–87
   [b] *Statistical Abstract of the United States* 1986, 1974

One of the most important reasons for this relationship between the growth in the state budget and the value of the oil and gas produced in Texas is that severance taxes on oil and gas production have been a major source of state revenues over the years. The importance of severance taxes on oil and gas had declined from 20% of total tax collections in 1963 to 13% in 1973. Rising energy prices throughout the seventies and early eighties, however, touched off rapid increases in severance tax revenues. By 1982, oil and gas tax income accounted for 27.4% of state tax income and 17.7% of total state income.[7]

One of the most important consequences of the rising severance taxes in the late 1970s and early 1980s was that they enabled politicians to expend more funds on governmental programs while

not raising taxes. From 1973 to 1981, Texas politicians found themselves confronting an enviable task: how best to spend an ongoing,
often unanticipated budget surplus. Fueled by buoyant oil and gas
markets, the Texas boom economy appeared to be immune from national recessions and to be able to produce an ever-increasing flow
of dollars to meet the needs and demands of a new era in Texas history. As late as September of 1982, state revenues were projected
to increase by $3.8 billion, leaving an additional $1 billion surplus at
the end of 1983. While these spending expectations were lowered
by $3.3 billion in three subsequent revenue estimates, the state still
closed out the year with a $1.1 billion surplus.[8]

Despite a projected budgetary surplus of $143 million built into
the 1984–85 biennium, it was becoming clear to many political observers in Texas that the boom era was drawing to a close. A decline
in the oil industry, a devaluation of the Mexican peso, and a slump in
the manufacturing sector had adverse impacts upon the sales taxes
and severance taxes. By the beginning of the 1985 meeting of the
state legislature, Comptroller Bob Bullock was warning legislators of
a $1.1 billion shortfall in the 1986–87 biennium. Because the con-
stitution mandated a balanced budget based upon the comptroller's
revenue projections, state political leaders were faced with an unfa-
miliar choice: either to cut spending in certain areas or to raise taxes.
In the end, they did both.[9]

Two things about the 1985 meeting of the state legislature stood
out. First, the legislature refused to abandon some of the policy initiatives begun in earlier years to grapple with the problems of Texas'
new era of urbanization and industrialization. Such issues as promoting the development of high-tech industry in the state, enhancing
higher education, improving the public education, and upgrading social welfare programs remained close to the hearts of policymakers in
the capital who sought to address the needs and demands of a new
era in the state's history. But at the same time, legislators had refused
to entertain any fundamental rethinking of how such expanding state
programs should be financed over the longer haul. The tax increases
that were passed in 1985 ultimately were but stop-gap measures, leaving future legislatures to deal with the troubling task of balancing new
needs and demands against a revenue base that is either declining or
much more sensitive to general economic conditions in the state and
in the nation than in the past. While some experts have proposed
the institution of a state income tax to meet the problems of financing state government in this new era, most politicians have greeted
such proposals with a derision normally reserved only for electoral
campaigns.[10]

By the summer of 1986, it was becoming clear that the budgetary crisis confronting the state in the next biennium was much worse than had been anticipated in the last meeting of the legislature. Initially, it was projected that the shortfall would be $2.3 billion for the next biennium. As the summer wore on, however, the situation appeared to be even bleaker. By early July it was estimated that the deficit would be close to $2.9 billion, and that if something were not done soon, state checks would be bouncing by the end of the year.

Lying behind the growing budget crisis were serious problems in the economy. In January, the price of oil had collapsed: it hovered around $12 and $15 per barrel for most of the spring. By July, the price of oil had dropped to a little over $11 per barrel. As the price of oil fell, the oil industry went into serious decline, bringing other sectors of the state's economy down with it, including banking and real estate. But economic troubles were not limited to the oil industry. Agriculture began to show signs of stress as well. One study found that real net farm income in 1985 had declined to one-third the level earned in 1979.[11] By mid-summer, unemployment in Texas had topped 10%, among the highest in the nation, and the state that but a few years before had been holding itself up as a land of opportunity for the rest of the nation found itself in the midst of its largest recession since the Great Depression.

The initial response of state political leaders to the budget crisis was to sit it out until after the fall elections. No one was enthusiastic about making a choice between raising taxes or cutting programs, particularly when their jobs were on the line. When Governor White called upon state agencies and institutions of higher education to cut spending voluntarily by 13%, his request went largely unheeded. As the budgetary problems intensified, calls for a special session of the state legislature to address them grew. Finally, Governor White called for a special session in August to deal with the crisis. Throughout the summer, there was talk among state political leaders of ways out of crisis including a state lottery, horse racing, state employee wage freezes and cuts, reductions in state services, an increase in the sales taxes, and, though it was mentioned ever so quietly, an income tax.

The budgetary problems that confronted the state legislature in the summer of 1986 brought in to focus many of the problems facing the state in this era of transition. They also raised serious questions about the state's ability and willingness to cope with these problems in an enlightened manner. Will the state be able to develop a coherent water policy before it is too late? Can the state's highway system be expanded and repaired to meet the needs of a new urban industrial era? Can the educational system be upgraded to meet the demands of high-tech industry? Can welfare or corrections policy be tailored to meet the needs and demands of life in late-twentieth-century America?

This book represents a systematic attempt to appraise what the Lone Star State has become and where it is going. The book examines the people and politics of Texas along with several policy areas that, the editors believe, will prove to be major issues well into the next century. It is divided into two parts. In Part I, the people, economics, and politics of Texas are examined. Chapters 1 and 2 analyze the economic and demographic changes that have transformed Texas' political economy over the past three decades and continue to propel it forward into a dynamic, albeit uncertain, future. Chapter 3 investigates the changing style of Texas politics and attempts to assess the potential for change that exists in the Texas political system. In Part II, seven public policies are studied in detail. Chapters 4 and 5 discuss the current developments that are shaping water and energy policy in Texas. Chapters 6 and 7 place the current debate over educational policy in the state in a larger historical perspective. Chapter 8 considers the many problems confronting highway policy in Texas. Chapters 9 and 10 assess the ongoing attempts to grapple with the problems of crime and welfare.

There are, of course, other policy areas that could have been included in this collection. Debates over such issues as the blue laws, abortion, unemployment benefits, and indigent health care have been controversial and even rancorous in recent years. In all likelihood, they will continue to be so in years to come. To attempt to give all such issues the attention that they deserve ultimately would make a book such as this too lengthy and unwieldly for most readers. This book is not meant to be a textbook that attempts to discuss everything about politics and policy in Texas. It is, instead, a book which attempts to appraise the current condition and future prospects of the Lone Star State in light of the changing contours of its political economy. The public policy areas finally chosen for investigation were those that the editors believe have helped to define what Texas' political economy is today and will determine, in large part, what it will become tomorrow.

This book is written in the belief that there is a need to identify the nature of the state's population growth, its political changes, its economic development, and the major policy issues that face the state over the next several decades. By offering such an overview, we hope to provide an enhanced understanding of the central theme running throughout the book: that Texas stands at a crossroads. New paths of development are not new to the state. Oil booms, population shifts, droughts, floods, panics, and depressions all have shaped and reshaped the Republic since its founding in 1836. Change is once again hitting Texas from all sides, carrying with it an excitement as well as a concern over what might be held in store for the state in the future. By seeking to understand this change, this book attempts to provide readers with an insight into the challenges and opportunities that will mold Texas anew as it moves from its Sesquicentennial anniversary into the Twenty-first century.

Notes

1. V. O. Key, *Southern Politics* (New York: Vintage Books, 1949).

2. Discussions of the establishment in Texas politics can be found in George Norris Green, *The Establishment in Texas Politics: The Primitive Years, 1938–57* (Westport, Conn.: Greenwood Press, 1979); and in James W. Lamare, *Texas Politics: Economics, Power, and Policy* (St. Paul, Minn.: West Publishing Company, 1981).

3. See Houghton Mifflin Company, *State of Texas Newsletter* (Fall, 1980), 4; T. R. Fehrenbach, *Seven Keys to Texas* (El Paso: Texas Western Press, 1983), 135.

4. Fehrenbach, 133.

5. *Statistical Abstract of the United States 1986* (Washington, D.C.: Government Printing Office, December, 1985), 440.

6. *Statistical Abstract 1986*, 10.

7. *Fiscal Notes* (May, 1984), 2.

8. For a further discussion of these issues see The Texas Research League, "The 1980s: Facing Fiscal Realities," *Analysis* 5 (November, 1984).

9. Some politicians, such as Governor White, denied that taxes had been raised, claiming that fee increases were not tax increases. Such claims spawned a riddle around the state capitol. Question: When is a tax not a tax?

Answer: When it is a fee.

10. One of the clearest statements of why a state income tax was necessary was made by James W. McGrew, a retired vice-president of research for the Texas Research League. See James W. McGrew, "A New Tax Policy for Texas," *Analysis* 5, (September 1984): During the 1985 legislative session, one state legislator responded to such proposals by proposing a constitutional amendment banning a state income tax.

11. "Texas Farmers Face Bad Times: But Not as Bad as the Midwest," *Fiscal Notes* (March, 1986): 2.

PART ONE

THE SETTING

Chapter One

THE DEMOGRAPHY OF A SUNBELT STATE

Ronald Briggs

What has been happening to the Texas population? Most people are aware of its rapid growth in the 1970s, of declines in birth rates, of the in-migration of northerners, of changing age distributions, of modified racial and ethnic balances, and of redistributions within the state. But what is the exact nature of these changes? How do trends in Texas compare with those occurring elsewhere in the nation, and what are their implications for politics and policy? These are the issues which this chapter addresses.

On the surface, at least, demographic analysis is simple. Population change during some time period depends solely on four values: (1) the number of births, (2) the number of deaths, (3) the number of in-migrants, and (4) the number of out-migrants. The balance of one and two determines natural increase (or decrease) and that of three and four determines net migration. Together, natural increase (or decrease) and net migration establish whether the population of an area grows, declines, or remains stable. Unfortunately, the simplicity ends here since the four components of population change themselves are a function of a complex of interactions. In particular they are all affected by, and in turn affect in a cycle of continuous and circular causation, the basic demographic structure of the population, including the age distribution, the sex distribution, and the racial/ethnic composition. In addition, these all interrelate with the broader socioeconomic characteristics of the population, such as marital status, education, income, occupation, and place of residence.

Discussion will focus upon six elements from the above framework which are significant both because they are key components of population change and because they have significant political and policy implications for Texas. The birth rate is the primary determinant of the rate of natural increase, since it is substantially more volatile than the death rate. In-migration has been the primary factor underlying much of Texas' recent population growth. The age structure of the population, which is affected both by the birth rate and the characteristics of in-migrants, has major impacts on state policy in many critical areas. The ethnic/racial makeup of the Texas population has drawn increasing political attention, as have shifts in residential location patterns within the state. Finally, trends in income will be briefly reviewed. Emphasis will be on the extent to which current and expected future trends in these key elements of population change are consistent both with their past trajectories and with trends occurring elsewhere in the United States. Current trends will be considered as those prevailing in the late 1970s and on into the 1980s; past trends will be those from the end of World War II to the 1970s. For the most part, "elsewhere" will be the nation as a whole.

The Texas Population

The approximately 15 million residents of the State of Texas in 1985 represent a doubling of the state's population since 1950, when the census recorded 7.7 million residents (Table 1–1). The U.S. population over the same period grew only by one-third. The result was that Texas moved from sixth-largest state in 1950 (after New York, California, Pennsylvania, Illinois, and Ohio) to third-largest in 1980 (after New York and California) and is projected to surpass New York by 1990 to become the second most populous state in the Union. However, growth rates exceeding those of the nation and most other large states (excepting California) have been characteristic of Texas throughout much of the twentieth century. The uniqueness of recent events is the sharp acceleration in growth rates experienced in the 1970s and the early 1980s, especially in comparison to the nation, as well as the components of that growth.

Through the 1950s and 1960s the ratio of the growth rate in Texas to that of the nation was around 1.3. In the 1970s this increased substantially to 2.4. Even more striking is the change in the source of that growth. Whereas in the 1940s through the 1960s the great majority of growth could be attributed to natural increase, with migration at around 100,000 persons per decade, accounting for less than 10% of all growth, in the 1970s migration dramatically increased to 1.7 million, to account for over 50% of the decade's population growth. Extant projections assume that a similar pattern will prevail through the remainder of the century, with a heavy rate of net in-migration being the primary component underlying a continued rapid rate of population growth. However, the current depression in the oil industry casts very serious doubts on the validity of those projections.

Table 1–1. Population Growth in Texas and the United States.

Year	Population of Texas	% Change from Previous Decade	% Growth from Net Migration	Ratio: Texas/U.S.
1950	7,711,194	20.2	5.6	1.4
1960	9,579,677	24.2	6.1	1.3
1970	11,196,730	16.9	9.1	1.3
1980	14,228,383	27.1	58.7	2.4
1990*	17,498,200	22.5	47.3	2.3
2000*	20,739,400	18.5	49.7	2.5

Sources: U.S. Bureau of the Census, *Statistical Abstract of the U.S. 1986* (Washington, D.C.: Government Printing Office, 1986), Table 11; idem, "Provisional Projections of the Population of States by Age and Sex, 1980-2000," *Current Population Reports,* P-25, No. 937 (August, 1983).
*Projected

For the most part, Texas was quite successful in absorbing the migrants of the 1970s. Unemployment remained consistently below that of the nation, and income growth was generally higher. State government services continued without tax increases, and, although not without some significant problems, the state's local governments were able to cope without a major citizen outcry. It remains to be seen whether the same can be achieved over the next two decades. The problems the state may face become more discernible as more detailed elements of population change are examined below.

Birth Rates   In combination, birth and death rates determine a population's rate of natural increase. In both the United States and Texas, the death rate has exhibited a slow and steady decline over past decades, and this is generally expected to continue without dramatic change for the rest of the century. The birth rate, on the other hand, has been far more volatile. From a then-historical low in the 1930s, the rate at which U.S. women bore children increased, with particular rapidity in the 1950s, to a fertility rate of 3.7 children per woman in 1957, the peak of the post war baby boom.[1] The rate then declined, gradually at first and then precipitously in the early 1970s, passing the replacement level of 2.1 children in 1972, to a historical low of 1.77 in 1976. Since then it appears to have stabilized at somewhat above 1.8, a figure which is still below replacement. If maintained, once the effects of the baby boom have worked their way through the population, without foreign in-migration the U.S. population will begin to decline after 2020.[2] Although this seems a very distant date, and there are a plethora of unknowns between now and then, people currently being born will only be thirty-five years old at that time.

The Texas experience mirrors that of the nation except that the fertility rate has consistently been slightly higher, although the difference has narrowed,[3] and absolute population declines are not anticipated. The higher fertility rate relative to the nation has been the primary reason for Texas' higher population growth in the past. In the future, however, fertility in Texas is expected to equal approximately that of the nation, and any population growth will need to be generated by in-migration from elsewhere in the United States or from abroad.[4]

Although most experts expect the current relatively low rate of fertility to persist in the future, past fluctuations in fertility as well as policy responses to them should be a salutary lesson. Major changes in the rate at which people choose to have children, such as occurred in the baby boom of the 1950s and the bust of the 1970s, have implications for the size of both the total population and age groups within that population. Past fluctuations in fertility will continue to have effects well into the twenty-first century. Future changes from current fertility levels are certainly possible, and they would invalidate the population projections used in this discussion. Whatever the outcome, policymakers should be alert to the possibility of such changes occurring. On the other hand, they should also take advantage, which has not always been the case in the past, of the lead times for policy action which demographic analysis provides. If an unanticipated rise in fertility should occur, policymakers have a five-year lead time to plan for its impact on education enrollments, for example. All in all, even though migration is increasingly the major factor underlying population change, particularly at the state level, fertility should not be ignored.

Migration   In the 1970s migration took over from natural increase as the primary source of population growth in Texas. This is expected to continue in the future and generate continued population growth in the state. However, considerably more so than in the case of fertility, there is always the possibility of a shift in migration streams. In fact, in the early 1970s such an unanticipated shift occurred in migration streams between metropolitan and nonmetropolitan areas (see below). Consequently, as migration patterns are examined, although major changes are not expected, such a possibility should always be included in the calculus of policymaking. Furthermore, changes in migration patterns are not only more likely to occur than in fertility patterns, but they also provide less lead time for policy response.

Increased in-migration of families with school-age children, for example, creates an immediate need for schooling facilities, not a need five years hence, as would have been the case if fertility had increased. All in all, of the components of population change, migration needs to be the most closely monitored for policy implications.

The dramatic increase in net migration experienced by Texas in the 1970s was primarily a consequence of a rise in the number of in-migrants to the state. Out-migration from the state remained approximately equal to levels pertaining in earlier periods. Table 1–2 is based upon data from the decennial censuses of population for 1970 and 1980, in which respondents were asked their state of residence five years before. Based upon this question, the number of in-migrants over these two five-year periods increased by 57% (from 915,181 to 1,436,237) whereas the number of out-migrants, contrary to common conceptions, also increased, although it did so only by 11% (from 776,339 to 862,230), which is less than the state's population growth over this period.

These changes are even more striking when the geographical pattern of migration streams is examined (Table 1–2 and Figure 1–1). Largely because of geographical proximity, Texas' major migration exchanges (both in-migrants received and out-migrants sent) are with the South and the West. The South, for example, received 42% of all out-migrants from Texas in the 1980 period and contributed 36% of all in-migrants, figures which are considerably larger than might be expected based on the South's population alone. In keeping with common conceptions, some of the more dramatic changes have been with respect to the Northeast. In-migration from that region of the United States into Texas increased by 120% and, alone of all regions, out-migration to this area decreased absolutely. Even so, the Northeast still contributed only 13.6% of all in-migrants to Texas, and its contribution to Texas' net migration (24.6%) was comparable with its population (23.3). The Midwest experienced a similar but less extreme pattern, with in-migration increasing by 86% and out-migration remaining constant. This region did, however, become the single largest contributor of net migrants to Texas, at 39%. Although this figure was not substantially higher than the 37% it contributed for 1970, both these numbers are considerably above the region's population proportion (28%).

Part of the reason that the Midwest became the major contributor to net migration into Texas for the 1980 period was changes with respect to the South. Although in-migration to Texas from the remainder of the South did increase quite substantially (40%), out-migration also increased. Apparently, in the 1970s the South became

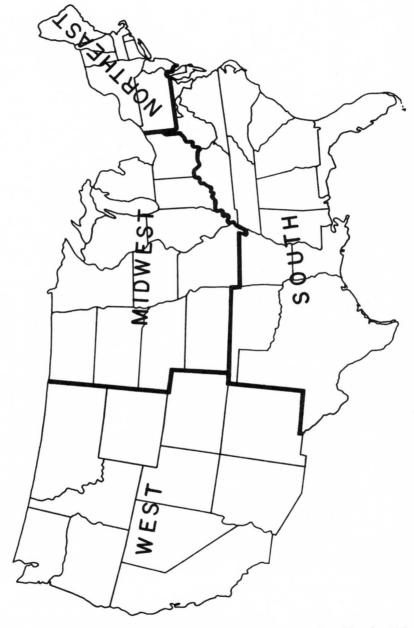

Figure 1–1. Standard Regions of the United States as Defined by the U.S. Bureau of the Census.

Table 1–2. In-Migrants and Out-Migrants for Texas (Persons 5 Years of Age and Older).

Type of Migrant		% of Migrants				
		Northeast	Midwest	South	West	Total
In-migrants						
	1980	13.6	25.9	36.3	24.2	100
	1970	9.6	16.2	33.1	29.1	100
Out-migrants						
	1980	6.3	17.3	42.3	34.1	100
	1970	7.6	19.1	40.0	34.3	100
Net migrants						
	1980	24.6	38.8	27.2	9.3	100
	1970	21.4	36.5	50.4	−8.3	100
% of population						
	1980	23.3	27.6	28.8	20.2	100
	1970	25.6	29.4	26.9	18.1	100
		% Change				
In-migrants		120.5	86.5	40.0	36.6	56.9
Out-migrants		−8.8	0.2	20.6	10.5	11.1

Sources: U.S. Bureau of the Census, *State of Residence in 1975 by State of Residence in 1980*, 1980 Census of Population, Supplementary Report, PC80-S1-9 (Washington, D.C.: U.S. Government Printing Office, 1983), Table 1. U.S. Bureau of the Census, *Mobility For States and the Nation*, 1970 Census of Population, Subject Report PC (2)-2B (Washington, D.C.: U.S. Government Printing Office, 1973), Table 44.
Note: Percentages may not add to 100 because of rounding.

a substantially more attractive migration destination than it had been in the past for Texas residents, as it did for residents of the United States in general. In addition, Texas apparently became a considerably more attractive migration destination for residents of the West. Although out-migration to this region from Texas did increase by 10%, in-migration expanded by 36%. The result was that the net migration loss that Texas experienced with the West for 1970 (the only such loss) changed to a gain.

Overall, on a regional basis the Midwest has become the dominant source of new Texans, although the Northeast's contribution is increasing rapidly. The South has slipped substantially as a supplier, with the contribution of the West being small but growing. However, there is no certainty that these patterns will prevail in the future.

Certainly, migrants add directly to population numbers, but they also have significant demographic implications because of their age

structure. Figure 1–2 shows that the migration stream to Texas is typical, being highly concentrated in the twenty to thirty age bracket.
Generally, these people have yet to complete their child bearing,
thus they will elevate the state's birth rate and add to future population numbers. Furthermore, they are also in their most productive
years economically, contributing both to the state's labor force and
to consumer income and purchasing power.

Despite recent attention, elderly migration into Texas is relatively
unimportant on a statewide basis. Only 3.0% of all in-migrants were
sixty years old or over compared with 13.3% of the resident population, and these in-migrants constituted only 2.3% of the state's
elderly population.[5] Furthermore, although the absolute number of
elderly in-migrants to the state increased between the 1970 and 1980
periods (by 11.3%), in-migration as a whole increased even more (by
56.9%), thus elderly migration has become relatively less important
over time. This is not to deny, however, the existence of pockets of
elderly migration which have substantial local importance, particularly
in the Rio Grande Valley, the Austin area, and East Texas.[6]

Although not formally considered as migration, nonpermanent
residents have also occupied increasing attention. It is argued that official Census Bureau population counts seriously understate the number of persons in the state because of the presence of relatively large
numbers of persons who report out-of-state permanent residences,
such as migrant agricultural workers and "sunbirds" who move to the
state for the winter months and return "home" to the north for the
summer. Although Texas has the fourth-largest nonresident population of all states, these persons still add less than 0.2% to the state's
population. This ratio of 1.7 nonresidents per thousand residents
pales in comparison to those of Florida (25.9) and Arizona (14.4) and
is little different from the average for all states.[7]

Again, however, there are significant local concentrations of
nonresidents (Table 1–3). These are either in the major metropolitan
areas (Harris, Bexar, and Dallas counties) or in the Rio Grande Valley
(Cameron, Hidalgo). The region of usual residence for these persons suggests that two distinct subpopulations are involved. In the
metropolitan areas, nonresidents are primarily from the South, reflecting relatively short-distance moves probably in search of employment
opportunities. In the Valley, nonresidents are predominantly from the
Midwest, suggesting seasonal movements from severe winters in the
Plains States. Only in the Valley, however, are the numbers of nonresidents significant relative to the local population, and even here the
largest value (8.5 nonresidents per thousand residents for Hidalgo
County) does not approach the figures for Florida or Arizona.

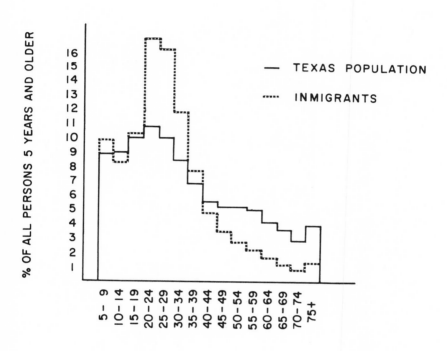

Figure 1–2. Age Structure of In-Migrants to Texas Compared with the Texas Population as a Whole.

Table 1-3. The Nonpermanent Resident Population of Texas, 1980.

Counties with more than 500 Nonresidents	No. of Nonresidents	Nonresidents per 1,000 Residents	Region of Usual Residence*							
			Northeast		Midwest		South		West	
			No.	%	No.	%	No.	%	No.	%
Bexar	2,714	2.7	185	8.2	326	14.5	1,442	63.9	302	13.4
Cameron	1,217	5.8	50	4.6	811	74.6	179	16.5	47	4.3
Dallas	590	0.4	125	31.0	98	24.3	145	36.0	35	8.7
Harris	2,234	0.9	125	8.0	145	9.3	1,205	77.3	84	5.4
Hidalgo	2,422	8.5	64	2.9	1,705	78.4	283	13.0	125	5.7
Nueces	749	2.8	66	10.2	178	27.4	332	51.1	73	11.3
Travis	872	2.1	4	0.8	43	8.1	440	82.6	45	8.5
Texas	24,765	1.7	989		5,868		10,800		1,410	

Source: U.S. Bureau of the Census, "Nonpermanent Residents by State and Selected Counties and Incorporated Places," 1980 Census of Population, Supplementary Reports, PC80-S1-6 (Washington, D.C.: Government Printing Office, 1982), Table 1.
* Numbers do not sum to state total because usual residence not reported in all cases.

There is little doubt, however, that of all demographically related policy issues, illegal immigration has generated the greatest debate, especially in Texas. Estimates of the number of illegal immigrants in the state have ranged from 50,000 to 1.75 million, with the most recent and thorough assessment placing the number at around 750,000.[8] If, as the same study estimates, 300,000 of these illegals were actually counted in the 1980 census, those omitted increase the total population by about 3% and the Hispanic population by around 15%.

Age Structure   The age structure of a population affects demands for goods and services in both the public and private sectors (for example, education, housing, health care), because it influences the ability to provide those services through the size of the labor force, and because it has an impact on the components of population change (birth, death, and migration rates), which in turn determine future population levels and age structures. On average, Texans, with a median age of 28.2 years, are younger than the U.S. population as a whole. In fact, only six states had a lower median age in 1980 than Texas.[9] Nevertheless, the state population has been aging and the gap between the median age of Texans and the nation's people has been narrowing through much of this century, from a difference of 4.2 years in 1900 to 1.7 years in 1970. However, the gap increased to 1.8 in 1980. Although the Texas population itself is expected to continue to age throughout the remainder of the century, the new trend relative to the nation is expected to continue, with the state's population becoming progressively younger relative to that of the nation.

The age/sex pyramid in Figure 1–3 illustrates dramatically some of the recent changes in the state's population. Between 1970 and 1980 the number of Texans increased at all age levels (with one exception), but the change was greatest in the fifteen to forty age categories. This reflects both the post war baby boomers (whose births peaked between 1955 and 1960) moving from their teens in 1970 to their twenties in 1980, as well as the influx of migrants in their twenties (see above). This temporal coincidence of two essentially independent trends resulted in an unprecedented 58% increase in the number of Texans between the ages of twenty and thirty-nine over the 1970 to 1980 period (Table 1–4). From constituting approximately one-quarter of the Texas population in 1970, this group came to constitute one-third by 1980.

Because the two major influences on the Texas population (the 1950s boom in births and the 1970s migration) will not again influ-

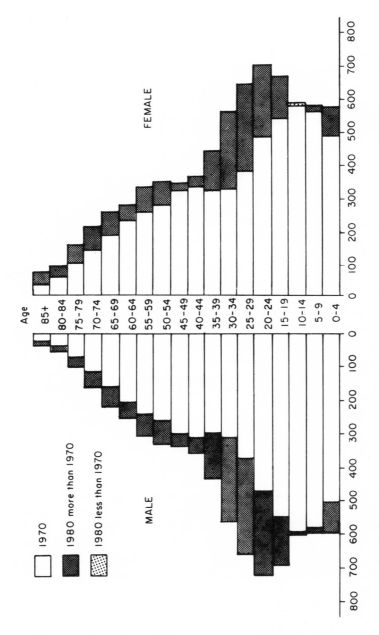

Figure 1–3. Composition of the Texas Population by Age and Sex, 1970 and 1980.

ence the same age group simultaneously, changes of this magnitude are not anticipated in the future. However, the baby boomers will continue to have an effect on the population well into the twenty-first century. For example, a 48% increase is projected in the forty to fifty-nine age group between 1990 and 2000 (Table 1–4). As this group reaches retirement in the first two decades of the twenty-first century, its size will have significant implications for a variety of policy concerns.

Table 1–4. Changing Age Structure of the Texas Population.

Age	Population in Thousands				
	1960	1970	1980	1990	2000
0–19	3,919	4,421	4,871	5,670	6,675
20–39	2,552	2,993	4,727	5,900	6,084
40–59	2,032	2,344	2,728	3,540	5,249
60–80	962	1,226	1,640	1,974	2,169
>80	115	182	263	417	563
	% Change from Previous Decade			
	1960–70	1970–80	1980–90	1990–2000
0–19	12.8	10.2	16.4	17.7
20–39	17.3	57.9	24.8	3.1
40–49	15.4	16.4	29.8	48.3
60–80	30.6	30.6	20.4	9.9
>80	58.3	44.5	5.9	35.0
	% of Total Population				
	1960	1970	1980	1990	2000
0–19	40.9	39.5	34.2	32.4	32.2
20–39	26.6	26.7	33.2	33.7	29.3
40–59	21.2	20.9	19.2	20.2	25.3
60–80	10.0	11.2	11.5	11.3	10.5
>80	1.2	1.6	1.8	2.4	2.7

Sources: U.S. Bureau of the Census, *1980 Census of Population, General Population Characteristics*, Texas, PC 80-1-B45 (Washington D.C.: Government Printing Office), Table 20; idem, "Provisional Projections of the Population of States by Age and Sex, 1980–2000," *Current Population Reports*, P-25, No. 937 (August, 1983).

One of the key issues revolving around a population's age structure is the ratio of the economically active population to that of the dependent population, the young and the elderly. The dependency ratio (the number of younger persons, under twenty, plus older persons, sixty and above, for each one thousand persons in the productive age group, twenty to fifty-nine) increased somewhat during the 1950s and 1960s, primarily because of the baby boom, but began to decline in the 1970s, a trend which is expected to hold for the rest of the century. In other words, the number of Texans of working age available to support the dependent population will increase through the rest of the century.

Although the overall trend is positive, there are some potential problems evolving from changes in the makeup of the dependent population. The proportion of young persons in the dependent population is declining whereas that of the elderly is increasing. Consequently, the number of elderly for every one hundred children will increase from about thirty-eight in 1960 to an expected forty-one in 2000, with a substantial increase from 2010 onwards as the 1950s baby boom moves into its retirement years. This "graying" of the dependent population has considerable policy significance since demands on government resources will shift, primarily from educational to income-support needs. Programs must have the flexibility to permit this transition. Situations where a fixed portion of a tax base is dedicated to education, for example, could be problematic. Also, income support is considerably more controversial than education, leading to the possibility of more legislative conflict.

While these trends in the age structure of the Texas population suggest some potential future problems for the state, their seriousness is far less than for the nation. The dependency ratio for the nation as a whole is expected generally to increase in the future, whereas in Texas it will decrease, and the elderly will become a far larger portion of the nation's dependent population than of Texas'. By 2000, for example, the United States is expected to have about sixty-one elderly for every hundred children, whereas the Texas figure is only expected to be forty-one.[10] These national figures should be treated as more than just comparisons. The future expectations regarding the age structure of Texas are based upon population projections which presume that the historically high rates of migration which pertained in the 1970s will continue in the future. Since migration is the major component of population growth, any moderation in these rates will result in the Texas experience paralleling more closely that of the nation.

Racial/Ethnic Composition Despite their centrality in U.S. society, consistent and comparable data on the racial/ethnic composition of the population are less available than might be expected. The problem evolves primarily from the difficulty of defining the partially racial/partially ethnic concept of "Hispanic," and the changing methodologies used to identify this population. In the 1980 census of population respondents were asked in separate questions to identify their race and then to indicate if they were of Hispanic origin. Combining

the results of these questions shows that 66% of the Texas population considered themselves to be Anglo (white, but not of Hispanic
origin), 12% black, 21% Hispanic, and 1% other. These are reasonably definitive numbers for 1980. However, different methodologies
were used in the 1970 census, and the Bureau of the Census has not
issued population projections by race. The result has been widely
conflicting expectations as to the future racial/ethnic makeup of the
Texas population (Table 1–5).

After declining from 30% in 1870 to 12.7% in 1950, blacks as
a proportion of the Texas population have declined only marginally
since that time, to 11.9 in 1980, a figure which is identical to that
for the nation as a whole. On the other hand, although the exact
values depend upon definitional issues, Hispanics have been consistently increasing as a proportion of the population as a consequence
of both their higher fertility and in-migration. Since 20% of the nation's Hispanics resided in Texas in 1980, the composition of the
Texas population, with 21% Hispanic and 67% Anglo, is considerably
different from that of the nation, which is around 80% Anglo and only
6% Hispanic.

In the future, blacks and Anglos will most likely make up a decreasing proportion of the population, whereas the Hispanic proportion will expand. They have a younger age structure with relatively
large cohorts going through their child-bearing years; even though it
has declined, their fertility is still substantially above that of the population as a whole; and migration, both legal and illegal, appears to be
continuing. Although the figure in Table 1–5 of 40% of the Texas population by the year 2000 seems high, it is not impossible should Hispanic in-migration continue, particularly if Anglo in-migration slows
down. On the other hand, if political action is taken to slow the rate
of foreign in-migration from Mexico, continued Anglo in-migration
from elsewhere in the United States could offset the higher Hispanic
birth rate, resulting in little change in Hispanics as a proportion of the
Texas population.

To a considerable degree, however, these overall proportions
have little real meaning since blacks and Hispanics are far from evenly
distributed over the state. Some 80% of the state's black population resides in East Texas (Figure 1–4). East of a line from Sherman,
through Fort Worth and Austin to Victoria, virtually every county has
at least a 10% black population, with the highest (Waller County)
having 42%. West of that line no county has more than a 10% black
population, with sixty-seven having less than one hundred blacks and
ten having none.[11] As might be expected, the Hispanic population is
primarily located along the Mexican border in South and West Texas,

Table 1–5. Scenarios for the Future Racial/Ethnic Composition of the Texas Population.

U.S. Bureau of the Census (thousands)				
	Anglo*	Black	Hispanic	Total
1980	9,554	1,693	2,986	14,229

Texas Department of Health (% of total)				
	Anglo	Black	Hispanic	Total
1970	73.2	13.2	13.6	100
1980	67.1	11.9	21.0	100
1990	60.1	10.3	29.6	100
2000	51.6	8.4	40.0	100

Texas 2000 Commission (% of total)				
	Anglo	Black**	Hispanic	Total
1970	68.7	13.2	18.1	100
1979	69.7	13.2	17.1	100
1990	66.8	14.4	18.8	100
2000	64.7	14.8	20.5	100

Sources: Texas Department of Health, Population Data System, Computer-Based File, 1983; Mary Young, "The Future of Texas' Population: One Scenario," in *Texas Past and Future: A Survey* (Austin: Texas 2000 Commission, Office of the Governor, 1981), Table 1–7.

 * Includes "other" nonblack non-Hispanic
** Includes "other" nonblack non-Hispanic

although concentrations extend northward in West Texas up into the Panhandle (Figure 1–5). Hispanics are somewhat more evenly distributed than blacks in that all counties have at least some Hispanics and only ten have less than one hundred, but there are also local concentrations where the incidence of Hispanics is far higher than is found for blacks. For example, there are four counties (Starr, Webb, Jim Hogg, and Maverick) where 90% or more of the residents are Hispanic.

Residential Location and Regional Change

In the United States as a whole, residential shifts have been occurring on three spatial scales.[12] At the regional level there has been the relative shift out of the old industrial "heartland" of the Northeast and

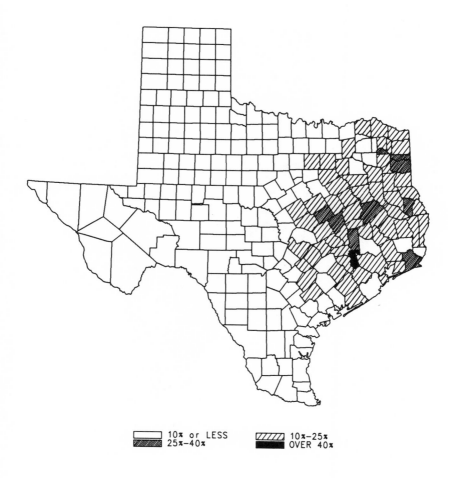

Figure 1–4. Black Population Percentages, 1980.

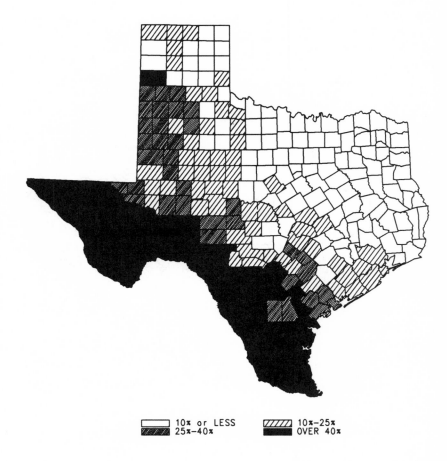

Figure 1–5. Spanish Heritage Population Percentages, 1980.

North Central regions to the "peripheral" areas of the South and West, a trend which accelerated substantially during the 1970s. At a second level there has been population redistribution among metropolitan areas in which century-old trends of net movements from non-metropolitan to metropolitan areas and from smaller to larger centers were reversed in the 1970s. At a third level, continued decentralization within metropolitan areas resulted for the first time in an absolute decline in the central city population of U.S. metropolitan areas as a whole in the 1970s. What have been the implications of these changes for Texas and to what extent has Texas itself experienced them?

The rapid population growth experienced by Texas in the 1970s was part of the general shift of the U.S. population to the peripheral regions of the nation. It was certainly not unique to Texas. Indeed, nine other states grew at a faster rate than Texas, and California added more absolutely to its population. Also, all regions of the state did not experience population growth. Although a much higher proportion of Texas counties experienced growth in the 1970s than in past decades, most counties in West Texas continued their historical pattern of population loss. Gains were primarily concentrated elsewhere in the state (Figure 1–6).

Contrary to common conceptions, Texas is an urban state today, although this is a recently achieved status. The United States had more urban than rural residents beginning in 1920, yet it was not until 1950 that the same was true of Texas. Since that time the urban population of the state has grown rapidly so that now 80% of the population is classified as urban compared with 74% for the nation as a whole. However, between 1970 and 1980 there was little change in these figures for either the nation or Texas, suggesting that the long-standing historical trend of increasing urbanization may be coming to an end (Table 1–6).

The same conclusion holds when metropolitan areas are examined. In contrast to the urban population, which counts persons living in concentrated settlements of twenty-five hundred or more, the metropolitan population comprises residents of counties containing places with fifty thousand or more residents together with adjacent counties which are linked by substantial commuting. This concept better reflects today's far-flung metropolitan complexes in which residents have moved from the denser core areas to suburban and even low-density "exurban" areas. Again the data suggest that while the proportion of the population living in these areas increased steadily through the 1950s and 1960s, it changed little in the 1970s. The reason is found in the historical reversal of residential location trends

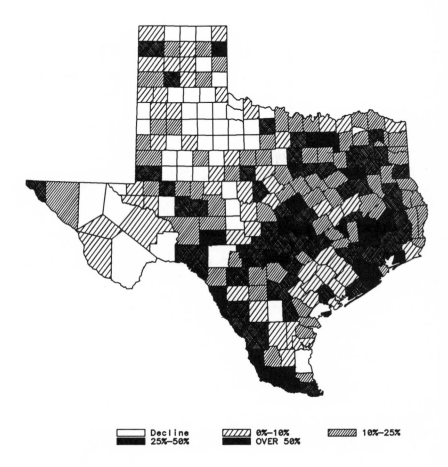

Figure 1-6.   Population Change Percentages, 1970–80.

Table 1–6. Trends in Urbanization and Metropolitanization.

Year	% Urban		% Metropolitan	
	U.S.	Texas	U.S.	Texas
1950	64.0	62.7		
1960	69.9	75.0		
1970	73.5	79.7	75.6	78.4
1980	73.7	79.6	74.8	80.0

Source: U.S. Bureau of the Census, *Statistical Abstract of the U.S. 1982-83* (Washington, D.C.: Government Printing Office, 1982), Tables 19, 22, 23.

which occurred in the 1970s. In the 1960s, and for decades previously, metropolitan areas grew faster than nonmetropolitan regions. In the 1970s, in the United States, this pattern was reversed: metro growth slowed to 10.2%, whereas nonmetro growth accelerated to 15.1%, exceeding metropolitan growth for the first time ever. In Texas, nonmetropolitan growth accelerated remarkably from a decline of 2.1% in the 1960s to an increase of 17.1% in the 1970s, although in contrast to the nation it remained below that of metropolitan areas, which grew by 29.8% in the 1970s and 23.5% in the 1960s.

Because Texas cities grew at considerably faster rates than cities in the nation as a whole, they have generally figured among the fastest growing in the nation over the last several decades. Houston and Dallas were among the ten fastest growing of the one hundred largest metropolitan areas in the nation between 1960 and 1970, as were Houston and Austin between 1970 and 1980. There has, however been a clear shift in the locus of growth among different size classes of cities. In the United States, larger metropolitan areas generally grew at faster rates than smaller metropolitan centers until the late 1960s and 1970s, when the pattern reversed. Indeed, many of the very largest metropolitan areas (even when suburban and exurban portions were included) began to experience absolute population losses in the 1970s, especially those in the Northeast. The large Texas metropolitan areas are marked exceptions to this pattern, particularly Houston, which was by far the fastest growing large metropolitan area in the nation in the 1970s, growing by 45% to almost three million. The next largest fast-growing area, Denver, was half Houston's size and grew by only 30%. Nevertheless, as in the nation, the locus of growth in Texas also shifted; small and medium-size metropolitan areas definitely accelerated, and growth in some larger areas (Dallas, for example) slowed. If the Texas pattern is moving toward that prevailing in the nation as a whole, as these data would seem to suggest, there are significant implications, particularly for the larger metropolitan centers in the state, whose future growth would be expected to slow substantially.

The third national location trend, decentralization from central cities to suburbs, has also occurred in Texas. However, the magnitude of this shift has been masked and its impact softened in Texas by the political structure of metropolitan areas. Because of development at earlier dates, together with differences in annexation laws, the incorporated city forming the core of the metropolitan areas of the Northeast and Midwest (the "central city") most commonly is geographically smaller and consequently constitutes a considerably smaller portion of the population of the metropolitan area than is typical in Texas. Since data on suburbanization are usually based upon movement out of the central city, much of the movement from the center to the edge of Texas cities goes unrecorded because it remains within the jurisdictional boundaries of the central city. Consequently, although Texas central cities have remained stable or grown in population, in contrast to those in many other parts of the nation, at the same time they have experienced marked shifts within their boundaries from the center to the periphery.

This structuring of metropolitan areas has been a substantial benefit to Texas since cities have been able to retain the tax base of the affluent suburbanite within their boundaries. This has been a primary reason why Texas cities have not had to face the fiscal crises common to many cities in the Northeast. On the other hand, data comparing Texas' central cities with those elsewhere in the nation, not only on suburbanization trends, but also on such items as unemployment, minority population, education, poverty, crime, and so on, can be most deceptive since different functional entities are involved. In Texas, the data reflect both the disadvantaged city core and the affluent suburban fringe, whereas elsewhere only the core is involved. The situation is particularly problematic if the distribution of federal funds is based upon these measures, as has increasingly been the case. It also accounts for some major differences in the politics of Texas central cities compared to those elsewhere in the nation.

Income

Although not strictly a demographic issue itself, income and demographics are certainly interrelated. As Table 1–7 shows, shifts in trends in the 1970s occurred in income as they did in demographics. Most marked was an acceleration in income growth, which elevated state

Table 1–7. Income Trends in Texas, 1949-79.

Median Family Income

Year	Texas	Ratio: Texas/U.S.	Ratio: Rural/Texas NonFarm	Farm	Ratio: Minority*/All
1979	$19,618	.98	.91		.66
1969	8,490	.88	.81	.76	.63
1959	4,884	.86	.77	.62	.53
1949**	2,680	.87	.86	.63	.51

Source: U.S. Bureau of the Census, *Census of Population, Vol. 1 Detailed Characteristics of the Population* (Washington, D.C.: Government Printing Office, National Summary, 1980, Table 297; 1970, Table 250; 1960, Table 225; 1950, Table 56. Texas Volume: 1980, Table 238; 1970, Table 57; 1960, Table 139; 1950, Table 30.

* Black in 1979 and 1969, nonwhite in 1959 and 1949.

** Ratios based on income for families and unrelated individuals; all other data are for families only.

incomes almost to the level of those prevailing in the nation as a whole; in contrast, in the 1950s and '60s, although absolute income levels increased substantially, they changed little relative to the nation, hovering around 87% of the national figure. A similar convergence occurred within the state between rural and urban incomes in the 1970s. Although rural farm incomes showed growth relative to incomes in the state as a whole in the 1960s, this was not true of the 1950s nor was it true in either decade for rural nonfarm incomes. However, by 1979 rural incomes had expanded to over 90% of the urban figure from around 80% in 1969. On the other hand, income convergence did not characterize all segments of society in the 1970s. Minorities, whose income grew relative to whites in the 1960s, experienced little relative improvement in the 1970s. Blacks continued to receive only about sixty cents for every dollar earned by a white family, and Hispanics were little better off, receiving around sixty-five cents (Table 1–8).

It is even more difficult to predict future trends in income than in population. However, the convergence between Texas and the United States and between rural and urban trends is likely to continue. Although advantageous from a purchasing-power perspective, income convergence does remove one of the factors, namely, lower labor and living costs, which helped fuel development and associated in-migration in the 1970s. This suggests that the high migration rates characteristic of the 1970s may not be sustained in the future. The likely future for minority income levels is even more difficult to assess. Fundamentally, it will be a function of public and private attitudes and policy, and the action which goes with them. These have seen dramatic changes over the last twenty years and the visibility and income of many individuals in minority groups has risen substantially, although that has not been translated into income equality for minorities as a whole. They still earn substantially less than their white counterparts.

Table 1–8. Income by Racial/Ethnic Characteristics, 1969 and 1979.

| | Income | | | |
| | Texas | | U.S. | |
Ethnic Group	1969	1979	1969	1979
White	$8,930	$20,955	$9,958	$20,835
Black (ratio to white)	.60	.62	.61	.60
Spanish (ratio to white)*	.63	.66	.76	.71

Source: U.S. Bureau of the Census, *Census of Population, Vol. 1 Detailed Characteristics of the Population* (Washington, D.C.: Government Printing Office, National Summary: 1980, Table 297; 1970, Table 250; 1960, Table 225; 1950, Table 56. Texas Volume: 1980, Table 238; 1970, Table 57; 1960, Table 139; 1950, Table 30.
* Because of changes in the methodology for identifying the Hispanic population, data are not strictly comparable between 1969 and 1979.

Conclusion

We have focused here on demographic trends in Texas. To a substantial degree, trends of the recent past are different from those which Texas had experienced earlier, as well as from those which pertain to the nation as a whole. What are the key implications for policy? Of the elements discussed above, the age structure is probably the most critical. More implications for the socioeconomic and political systems follow from the age structure than from any other single facet of demographics. This is a lesson being learned belatedly from the monumental societal effects of the baby boom that followed World War II. The baby boom not only swamped school systems in the 1960s and contributed to housing inflation in the late 1970s, but it also was a major factor behind fluctuations in such apparently unrelated issues as crime rates and automobile accidents, both of which are strongly age-related. Along with the in-migration of the 1970s, which itself was highly age-selective, the baby boom will continue to influence the Texas population far into the future. Most critical may be its impact on social security and Medicare demands as the age bulge moves into retirement in the second and third decades of the next century. Furthermore, behind the baby boom is a baby bust. The decade of the 1970s witnessed historically low birth rates. What are the implications of this for the future? At the very least, we must be sure that any policies and programs put in place to accommodate expanding numbers can readily contract as numbers decline.

Although the very nature of population structures allows us to make some fairly definite statements about the likely future, there are still a series of unknowns. In particular, migration patterns are difficult to predict, as are women's decisions regarding childbirth. The very fact that trends today are different from those experienced in the past should warn us against necessarily assuming that current trends will continue into the future. We have certainly been surprised before, the fluctuations in the birthrate being the prime examples. Our most intelligent response is to monitor change as closely as possible and build maximum flexibility into policies and programs.

We have focused here on Texas and recognized some key differences from trends in the nation as a whole. This should not lead us to assume that Texas can be analyzed and understood in isolation. The state is increasingly tied to the nation, and trends there cannot be ignored even if our focal interest is Texas. Migration is the primary determinant of future population growth in Texas and it is very much a function of conditions elsewhere in the nation, indeed, in the world. Should in-migration to Texas slow, which appears very definitely to be the case, the population projections implicit in much of the discussion here will overstate growth in Texas. Again, up-to-date information and policy flexibility are the key. We should begin to monitor demographic indicators as closely as we follow economic indicators.

Indeed, evidence has already appeared of changes in migration patterns. State-level population estimates (for July 1, 1985) issued by the U.S. Bureau of the Census indicate a resumption of growth in the Midwest and a relative slowing of growth in Texas, and these figures do not reflect the effect of the precipitous decline in the price of oil in early 1986.[13] If these are precursors of future patterns, as seems likely, then the scenario of continued rapid population growth in Texas through the remainder of the century will change dramatically. Furthermore, the battles in the state legislature, where budget deficits constitute another new trend, could have a potentially compounding effect. If Texas' image in the nation is tarnished in an area such as education, for example, then the state may become increasingly unattractive as a destination for migrants who are themselves typically above average in education, as well as to firms seeking an educated labor force. These are particularly critical considerations as the state attempts to transform its economy from the traditional reliance on oil and agriculture to a high-technology base.

Notes

1. The fertility of a population can be measured in several ways. The birth rate counts the number of births per one thousand population over some time period. This is the key measure for natural increase over that period. However, as an indicator of underlying fertility trends in the population, it can be deceptive since its magnitude is influenced by the population's age structure; large numbers of elderly, for example, will create low values for the birth rate. The total fertility rate totals the number of births relative to the number of women in each child-bearing age group. It is the best indication of the rate at which women are bearing children at a particular time. A value of 2.1 is required for a population to remain stable in size over the long run, although short-run growth can continue because of past fertility rates in excess of this value.

2. U.S. Bureau of the Census, "Projections of the Population of the United States: 1982 to 2050," *Current Population Reports*, Series P-25, No. 922 (October, 1982).

3. J. P. Marcum and F. D. Bean, "Texas Population in 1970: #9. Trends in Fertility, 1950–70," *Texas Business Review* (November, 1973):252–58.

4. U.S. Bureau of the Census, "Projections of the Population of the United States: 1982 to 2050."

5. U.S. Bureau of the Census, *Census of Population, 1970: Detailed Characteristics of the Population* (Washington, D.C.: Government Printing Office), 1974 PC(1) D1, Table 196; PC(1) D45, Table 145. Idem, *Census of Population, 1980: Characteristics of the Population* (Washington, D.C.: Government Printing Office) 1984 PC80–1, Table 200.

6. Thomas R. Plaut, "Migration Trends of the Elderly in the United States and the Southwest," *Texas Business Review* (May–June, 1981): 105–108.

7. The number of nonpermanent residents could be underestimated in these data, however. Only persons present on Census Day (April 1) are counted. Also, the data are restricted to persons in housing units occupied entirely by nonresidents. Excluded are persons in a residence occupied by a permanent resident, and persons in hotels, motels, campgrounds, and similar settings. See the source cited in Table 1–3 for more details.

8. Frank G. Bean et al., "Estimates of the Number of Illegal Migrants in the State of Texas," Texas Population Research Center Papers, No. 4,001 (Austin: University of Texas at Austin, 1982).

9. R. L. Skrabanek and S. H. Murdock, "The Age Composition of the Texas Population," *Texas Business Review* (May–June 1983): 143–48.

10. U.S. Bureau of the Census, "America in Transition: An Aging Society," *Current-Population Reports*, Series P-25, No. 128 (Washington D.C.: Government Printing Office) 1983.

11. R. L. Skrabanek and Steve H. Murdock, "The Black Population of Texas," *Texas Business Review* (May/June, 1982): 141–46; R. L. Skrabanek, "Population Characteristics of Texas," in *Texas Almanac 1984–85*, 337–39; R. L. Skrabanek, Steve H. Murdock, and Patricia K. Guseman, "The Population of Texas: An Overview of Texas Population Change, 1970–1980" (Austin: Texas State Data Center, 1985).

12. B. J. L. Berry and Donald C. Dahmann, "Population Redistribution in the United States in the 1970s," in B. J. L. Berry and Lester P. Silverman. eds., *Population Redistribution and Public Policy* (Washington, D.C.: National Academy of Sciences, 1980), 8–49.

13. Steve H. Murdock and Sean-Shong Hwang, "The Slowdown in Texas Population Growth: Post-1980 Population Change in Texas Counties" (Austin: Texas State Data Center, 1986).

Chapter Two

ADVANCED INDUSTRIAL DEVELOPMENT

Donald A. Hicks

In recent years the growth and development of the Texas economy have succeeded in capturing the attention of the nation and the world. Against the backdrop of a stagnant U.S. economy in the early 1980s, lingering distress in a handful of older manufacturing industries whose adjustments are as painful as they are visible, and intense competitive pressures from abroad, the business environment offered by Texas has often been judged to be a model for other states and the nation. The massive shift of population and employment growth to Texas during the 1970s was in sharp contrast to the experiences of many other states, particularly those in older industrial regions, and it continued unabated through the back-to-back recessions of the early 1980s.[1]

Continued growth and prosperity can no longer be taken for granted. Today, many of the factors which accelerated Texas' recent economic ascendance have changed their pace and/or direction. Population growth and immigration have slowed, key industrial sectors such as energy and the regional economies tied to them have stagnated, cost differentials with other parts of the nation have disappeared, and the political friction accompanying public taxation and spending has increased dramatically. Nothing so effectively concentrates public attention on the importance of economic growth as the realization that it must be actively earned rather than passively experienced.

This chapter is about economic growth in Texas. It will attempt to describe the structure of that growth and its implications for industries, cities, and the citizens who live here. But it is also about change, especially Texas' complex transition from an older to a new economic structure. As a result, wealth creation will be portrayed as a process forever dependent on a variety of critical resources and their changing combinations. Texas will be seen to be slowly shifting its dependence from what are commonly believed to be "natural" resources tied to the land and energy toward its human resources. And a key assertion will be that the distinction between natural and human resources is as misleading as it is artificial. Neither have inherent value; their development only comes to be justified by the discovery of new ways in which they can be used and the resultant rising levels of demand. At that point development becomes conscious and calculated. As Texas' economy continues its transit and its dependence shifts from its physical to its human capital, it is well to consider carefully the ways in which private and public sector activities can best be orchestrated to ensure that the new foundations of growth can be made to serve us at least as well as those we are leaving behind.

As we have come to realize, however, growth entails mixed blessings. The new pressures on infrastructure (for example, highways, utilities), natural resources (for example, air quality and water reserves), land use and mobility patterns, schools and the service capacities of local governments amply illustrate the sobering "other side" of growth. Moreover, growth has been distributed far from uniformly causing regional distinctions within the state to emerge as marked as any between multistate regions in the United States.[2]

Ultimately, we care about economic growth and development because of their ability to redistribute investment and opportunity among industries, occupations, localities, and social groups within the state. Which Texas industries are growing and which are contracting? What kinds of employment opportunities will the future hold, and how will job skills in demand match the skills possessed by Texas residents? Where in the state will the new jobs be located? And what, if any, state and local government initiatives constitute a wise adjustment policy as the Texas economy restructures? These are but a few of the questions that invite consideration as we explore growth and development trends in Texas.

Growth and Development: Differing Perspectives

Growth and development are distinct processes which can be usefully distinguished from one another.[3] While either may take place in the absence of the other, in Texas both have and will continue to take place simultaneously. Economic growth is generally, though not exclusively, indicated by rising levels of population, retail sales, personal income and construction growth; an expanding labor force; and output growth in industries throughout the state. Development, by contrast, indicates how that growth is distributed across and within localities throughout the state. Moreover, development implies that industries or parts of industries are growing at uneven rates, a pro-

cess which leads to an eventual reshaping of employment opportunities, sources of wealth creation, and even settlement patterns.
Whether a particular industry is expanding or contracting, whether
output growth is accompanied by employment growth, the direction
and rate of change relative to other industries in the state, and the
geographic location of these changes are all crucial aspects of the
development process. Ultimately, the overall health and competitiveness of Texas' economy, and of localities around the state, are
more closely tied to how economies at both levels are developing
than to whether or not they are simply growing.

The Texas Economy in Transition

A century ago, Texas was a rural state dominated by an agricultural
economy with nearly 70% of all employment tied directly to the labor
needs of Texas' farms and ranches. Today, Texas has become a largely
urbanized and industrialized state. Eighty percent of all Texans live in
approximately two dozen metropolitan areas, and the economy reveals considerable and increasing industrial diversity. Texas has a civilian labor force of slightly over 8 million with total employment at 7.6
million (May, 1984). Texas' major urban areas have had widely vary-
ing degrees of success in nurturing economic growth in recent years.
As a result, the building economic differences among regions within
the state will command as much attention in the future as will Texas'
emerging role in the larger national and international economies.

Today, following a century of industrial development, the structure of the Texas economy spans the full range of economic eras from
the preindustrial to the postindustrial. Texas is still the fourth-leading
agricultural state in the United States, yet modern agriculture is increasingly mechanized and employs less than 3% of all Texans.[4] Likewise, employment estimates for the so-called high-technology sector,
whose prospects for future employment are currently receiving widespread attention, reveal that it too has only a modest employment
share of slightly more than 5%, though estimates vary depending on
the definition of the sector.[5]

The emergence of a global economy and the interdependencies
among modern nation-states have several implications for Texas. The
dominance of the energy sector in Texas exposes the entire state,
and selected localities in particular, to both abrupt shocks and extended lulls in the world oil market. The convergence of the state
economy with that of the entire nation implies a heightened vulner-

ability to business-cycle movements that affect the nation and from which Texas has been largely immune until recently. Yet, the unevenness of recent growth across different industrial sectors and substate regions will increasingly segment the state economy. In the process, metropolitan areas anchored to different parts of the evolving Texas economy will continue to share unequally in the overall growth of the state. Therefore, trajectories of major industries in the state economy, together with those of the specialized local and regional economies tied to them, promise to further redefine Texas' economic base in the years ahead.

A Setting for Business and Employment Growth

In recent years, the Texas economy has been getting larger faster. The growth rate in personal income was in double digits all through the 1970s, until it fell off during 1982–83. Future growth is expected to proceed at a slower pace than we have seen for some time. The Texas economy has sustained its net growth not only by incubating new business births, but through the secondary expansion and retention of existing business as well. Beneath the surface, the growth and development taking place within Texas have been turbulent. Unavoidably, employment growth is accompanied by selective employment loss. Resulting net growth can obscure the respective gains and losses that have occurred beneath the surface. Between 1969 and 1976, for the nation as a whole the addition of one hundred new jobs was accompanied by the loss of eighty existing jobs for a loss-gain ratio of 0.80. In Texas over the same period, the ratio of jobs lost through business failure and out-migration to jobs gained through business formation and immigration was 0.72. The loss-gain ratio resulting from the contraction and expansion of existing businesses was only 0.61. So important was the latter source of net employment growth that the overall loss/gain ratio for whatever reason was also 0.61. Only nine other states succeeded in expanding their net employment more efficiently during 1969–76 than did Texas.[6]

It is important that net employment growth in Texas has been tied not only to the retention of existing businesses and employment, but also to the capacity of overall state and local economies to attract and incubate new businesses. Of states with the fastest growing companies in the United States in 1982, Texas ranked second (tied with New York) with fifteen companies, just behind California with seventeen.[7] These rapidly growing companies were noted as sharing the qualities of innovation, youth, high productivity, and healthy product line. Moreover, Texas has repeatedly been identified as offering either the best or second-best "business climate" (behind Florida) in the nation. With the lure of significant locational advantages, including relatively cheap and abundant land and labor, market expansion riding the tide of population growth, low living costs, weak unions, and relatively light tax burden (no individual or corporate income taxes), Texas has often been the recipient of potential growth that has been displaced, as well as of a much smaller number of established businesses that have been dislodged from elsewhere around the country. However, Texas' economic surge in recent years has been fueled principally by new firm births and secondary expansion of existing businesses rather than by the relocation of businesses from elsewhere.

As is the case with comparative advantages, as they are exercised and exploited, they begin to erode. Higher-than-average increases in the cost of living, land and housing prices, and labor costs are common responses to rapid growth. These trends, together with the common perception that public sector responses to present and future growth trends are frequently inadequate, may threaten to reduce the attractiveness of the state and especially of the flagship metropolitan economies of Dallas-Fort Worth and Houston, which together prospered so magnificently during the 1970s.

In the future as the Texas economy evolves, new comparative advantages must either emerge unaided and be identified or be developed and promoted in a more deliberate way. While land and land-based natural resources have provided the backbone for the dominant agricultural and later energy industries, a new mix of growth industries has rapidly shifted Texas' dependencies from natural to human resources. It is far from certain that Texas is prepared to exploit this shift. Yet, inevitably, this shift has begun and will continue to stimulate debate concerning the most appropriate roles for state and local government in the economic future of the state.

New Resources for a New Economy

Heated debate amid nagging uncertainty over how to respond to present and future growth and development are especially evident in Texas' metropolitan areas and reveal a characteristic ambivalence concerning the proper role of government in state and local affairs. The physical development of the state as illustrated by the rapid expansion of urban infrastructures above and below ground has both led and reinforced patterns of residential, commercial, and industrial growth. However, in a transforming economy, wherein new employment growth will depend as much or more on the quality of human capital (skills acquired through continuing education and training) as on the quality of physical capital, a reconsideration of the historical roles of government in the overall development of the state will be required.[8] Texas faces the task of reassessing the roles of state and local governments in providing the social infrastructure for creating a wide array of human resources and thereby sustaining and distributing economic opportunities in a changing state economy. An educated and educable citizenry and labor force will be of far greater importance to Texas' new economic base than to the one that is now receding. Will the state opt to retain its traditional emphasis on maintaining an environment for business growth that is as unfettered by government as possible? Or will it respond with an array of incentives and subsidies to encourage the growth of targeted industries in selected locations? Will it emphasize the role of venture and expansion capital or will it assign priority to the education, training, and retraining of workers? These are but a few of the questions around which debate will center as the role of government in Texas' economic transition to a new economy is reconsidered.

Natural Resources and the Land-based Texas Economy

Land is the oldest basis for an economy, and in Texas a land-based economy has been dominated by crops and livestock as well as by oil and gas production, each in its own time. The twentieth century has witnessed employment and output, two traditional measures of economic activity, moving in different directions for each of these two industries. There has always seemed to be something secure and permanent about land. And for obvious reasons, there has been a tendency to comprehend Texas in terms of its vast land and land-based resources. Somehow, land and the "natural" resources including "good" soil, water, and minerals distributed across and beneath the land's surface seem to represent an enduring basis for economic prosperity. Today, however, evidence is accumulating which suggests that such a perspective is increasingly dated and deceiving. Ironically, a preoccupation with the quantity, or even the quality, of land or land-based resources may obscure their more profound significance to the economy. A closer look reveals that these resources are anything but "natural" and permanent. One could hardly find a better example of the "plastic" nature of these resources than by examining the historical development of the Texas economy.

A crucial distinction demarcates the preindustrial economy of the state tied to a ten-thousand-year-old agricultural economy based on food and fiber production and the relatively new energy economy which developed during this century. Before the twentieth century, the average Texan's link to the larger economy was the land and the expanding uses to which it could be put. With the rise of world markets and the discovery of oil and gas in Texas, no longer was land valued solely for the agricultural activities that could be arrayed across its surface. Land came to be viewed as a gateway to vast reservoirs of wealth and opportunity whose value was increasingly determined by an industrializing world beyond our borders. With the twentieth century came the realization that the value of land and land-based resources is neither fixed nor inherent, but created and variable. The current economic malaise along the Texas Gulf Coast and in West Texas reveals the vulnerability of portions of the state economy tied closely to industries in which natural resources are being revalued in a shifting global economy.

Texas' original endowments of topsoil and water, and their quality, quantity, and distribution, are obscured today by the way in which large portions of the state now support a thriving agriculture. Production on farms and ranches reflects as much the way often-marginal resources have been reorganized and enhanced by a succession of new and applied technologies (for example, irrigation, crop rotation and related soil management strategies, fertilizers, new plant varieties and livestock breeds, and scale economies) as the way they have been changed by any "natural" characteristics of the land itself. Likewise, the Texas energy industry was born when the once-worthless oil and gas deposits in Texas were endowed with soaring value by an oil-thirsty industrial world as the twentieth century began. New secondary and tertiary recovery technologies and extensive refining capacities have sustained oil- and gas-related industries until now, but new shifts in global supply and demand are currently dampening the prospects for the industry which has long been assumed to have an unlimited horizon.

Texas' Agricultural Economy   In 1880, Texas employment was centered in agriculture; there was no oil and gas industry in Texas, and mining was minuscule. A century later, agriculture has retained its importance to the state even though it accounts for less than 3%

of total employment. While the long-term employment contraction within agriculture has been dramatic, the rate of contraction has been uneven. In 1900, nearly two-thirds (62.4%) of employment was in agriculture, and on the eve of World War I, the majority of jobs were in this sector. As late as World War II, approximately a third (30.3%) of all employment was still to be found on farms or ranches. Since 1940, however, this sector's employment share has been halved every decade up to the present. Increased mechanization has caused the pace of the industrialization of agriculture to be particularly rapid in recent decades. The reorganization of land resources and related production inputs, which has resulted in rising agricultural productivity, is reflected in the changing number and scale of Texas' farms. Between 1950 and 1980, the number of farms dropped from 345,000 to 159,000.[9] The substitution of capital for labor not only has reduced significantly the need for labor in this sector, but has redefined the nature of agricultural work as well. In output terms, as measured by contribution to gross state product, the agricultural share is approximately 5%. Nonetheless, the significance of this sector to the state is understated by both employment and output shares. Agriculture constitutes a smaller share of the Texas economy than it does of the national economy. However, since the largest portion of the nation's exports is composed of agricultural goods and services, the wider importance of the sector to the state's growth prospects in global economy cannot be overlooked.

Texas' Energy Industry The twentieth century was just a few weeks old when in 1901 an oil well named Spindletop located near the Upper Gulf Coast town of Beaumont in East Texas came in a gusher. An infant industry crucial to the industrial world had found a home in Texas. During the next two decades the scene was repeated often, and soon East Texas became the cradle of the world's oil industry. Then, with the success of a rig named Santa Rita No. 1 in 1923, the oil industry was born in West Texas. And for the next three decades, the oil and gas industry in Texas grew and prospered. Employment expanded in the developing oil and gas extraction, oil field machinery, petroleum refining, and chemicals and allied products industries. East and West Texas jockeyed for regional dominance as drilling technologies and techniques matured, as the skills of trained industry professionals developed, and as the income generated by the industry created wave after wave of new employment and general prosperity.

During the half-century from 1923 to 1973, the nation's economy grew increasingly dependent on Texas' oil and gas fields, and the state's economy likewise became dependent on rising levels of demand for its "liquid gold." Estimates provided by the Texas 2000 Commission indicate that a quarter of all energy produced in the nation since the 1920s, including 40% of the nation's oil, gas, and gas liquids, has come from Texas. (It is also estimated that 80% of the reserves remain locked in Texas land; but their form and mix make them either technologically or otherwise economically inaccessible for the time being.)

Yet, that bond between Texas and the outside world showed early signs of unraveling by mid-century. Since 1950, the oil and gas industry has become an increasingly mature industry. Gradually, the technologies and supporting human capital developing in the geosciences and petroleum engineering and dedicated to exploration, recovery, transshipment, and refining permitted the development of the industry in once-inaccessible locations, such as the Middle East, Alaska, and later in offshore locations near Venezuela, Norway, Scotland, and the coasts of the United States. The geography of oil and gas production soon extended to locations on and off shore around the world.

The long-term rise in oil production in Texas peaked in 1972 and began what is now expected to be a long-term decoupling of the State economy from the energy sector. By 1975, according to the Texas Energy and Natural Resources Council, the state began to import more crude oil than it exported as the state's capacity to produce crude oil began to lag behind its capacity to refine it. Between 1972 and 1982, oil and gas production declined 21% and 26%, respectively. The restructuring of supply accompanying oil field and refinery development around the world was accompanied by a restructuring of demand during the 1970s. Temporarily rising prices after the 1973 embargo spurred greater energy efficiency within the transportation sector and among other industry and residential users as well.[10]

The true size of the energy sector in Texas is not accurately portrayed in official analyses of broad industry sectors. Its impact has long been registered more in terms of output than of direct employment. Throughout the twentieth century, the oil and gas industry has never employed more than 5% of the state's work force, yet estimates indicate that this sector accounts for slightly more than one-tenth of total state output. Direct employment estimates obscure the far larger energy-related employment distributed throughout the manufacturing, construction, transportation, utilities, and selected service sectors.

Sometime in the 1990s, Texas is expected to become a net energy importer. Also, as the energy era slowly recedes in Texas, questions abound concerning what new growth sectors will emerge to take its place. As a result, attention is shifting to other goods-production industries (especially manufacturing) and service-provision industries and their potential for compensating for the slow contraction of the energy sector.

The Rise of Industrial Texas

Since World War II, Texas has rapidly industrialized and developed an increasingly diversified economy. While Texas' industrialization has been under way for a century and more, it has always lagged behind the nation. In recent years, however, that gap has been narrowing in important ways. Since 1962, total nonagricultural employment in Texas has more than doubled from 2.6 million to 6.3 million in mid-1984, a 139% increase. While population expanded by half over the same period, from 10.1 million to over 15 million, all but one industry sector doubled or even tripled in employment. The services increased 212%; finance, insurance, and real estate (FIRE) by 169%; construction by 148%; mining by 141%; wholesale and retail trade by 130%; manufacturing by 113%; and transportation and public utilities by only 78%. Growth in the government sector lagged only slightly behind total employment, expanding 120%.

The structure of the state economy has slowly come to conform to that of the nation and has been increasingly integrated with the global economy as well. Today, the construction, mining (oil and gas), wholesale and retail trade, and transportation, communication, and utilities sectors are overrepresented in the state economy relative to the national economy while agriculture, manufacturing, most services, and the public sector are underrepresented. By the end of the century, despite the expected slowdown in aggregate population and employment growth rates, the Texas economy will have developed in such a way that it will have become *more* industrialized than the national economy. As will be apparent below, the spread of manufacturing into and through the state is expected to provide the principal impetus for this development.

The Industrialization of Texas: 1880–1980　In 1880, the Texas economy comprised one dominant sector and several smaller ones. As Table 2–1 indicates, 68.8% of total employment was in the primary

Table 2–1. The Restructuring of the Texas Economy: Employment Shares, 1880–1980.

Sector	% of Employment										
	1880	1890	1900	1910	1920	1930	1940	1950	1960	1970	1
Agriculture Agriculture, forestry, fishing	68.8	61.9	62.4	59.9	46.2	38.4	30.3	15.9	8.8	4.6	
Extractive Oil, gas, and mining	0.0	0.2	0.3	0.5	1.8	1.6	2.9	3.2	3.0	2.4	
Transformative Manufacturing, construction	5.8	8.3	7.4	11.8	15.6	17.5	15.2	21.6	23.7	25.0	
Distributive services Transportation, communication	2.6	6.0	4.3	5.4	7.2	7.4	6.6	8.2	7.3	6.6	
Trade services Wholesale and retail trade	4.0	4.1	5.9	8.7	13.2	15.7	18.0	20.9	21.1	21.5	
Producer, consumer and nonprofit services Finance, insurance, real estate	0.1	0.9	0.6	0.8	1.1	1.4	2.7	3.1	4.1	4.9	
Domestic and other services	14.8	14.1	14.8	8.1	7.9	10.5	14.1	11.5	11.5	9.8	(
Professional services	2.5	3.6	3.6	3.6	4.4	5.7	6.5	7.9	11.1	16.1	(
Government services Government and military	1.4	0.9	0.7	1.2	2.6	1.8	3.7	7.7	9.4	9.0	
Total	100.0	100.0	100.0	100.0	100.0	100.0	100.0	100.0	100.0	99.9	1

Source: U.S. Department of Commerce, Bureau of the Census, *Census of Population* (Washington, D.C.: Government Printing Office, various dates). Adapted from Table II, in *Texas: Past and Future: A Survey* (Austin: Office of the Governor, Texas 2000 Commission, 1981).
Notes: Changes were made in census classifications, particularly in services, which prevented exact matches of some employment sectors.
* The percentage is the 1980 estimate for the domestic and other and professional services categories combined.

or agricultural sector. The services sector was defined somewhat differently than it is today; nevertheless, historical census figures indicate that approximately 14.8% of Texas' employment was in domestic and related services while another 2.5% was in professional services. The remaining sectors made only minute contributions to total employment.

Manufacturing and construction together have come to be regarded as the bellwether sector of an industrialized economy. Table 2–1 illustrates the overall industrialization of the state wherein this sector's share of employment increased from only 5.8% in 1880 to 24.5% in 1980. The biggest surge in growth across the two sectors came in the decade following World War II, and since then the continued diversification of the state economy has been tied to the capacity of the state to attract, retain, and incubate manufacturing growth. Despite the absolute growth of manufacturing employment, over the ten-year period 1974–84 the manufacturing employment share declined from 19.1% to 15.5%, a mirror image of the expanding share of services (excluding trade) employment from 16.9% to 19.0%. Evidently, as has long been the case with agriculture, the industrialization of Texas has and will be characterized by a gradual decoupling of employment from output growth in manufacturing. Even though the state will continue to add manufacturing jobs in the future, it is estimated that manufacturing will account for a declining share of total employment even as its share of total state output is expected to surge over the next quarter-century from 18.6% in 1982 to 23.5% in 2007.[11]

An estimated three hundred thousand new manufacturing jobs have been added in Texas since 1970. And the increasing importance of manufacturing to the state economy is reinforced by a rate of output growth expected to exceed that in all other sectors. Job growth during the 1970s was particularly robust in computers, electronics, transportation equipment, aerospace, and communication products. While a sizable proportion of the new firms in these industries are quite small, new employment growth came largely from the expansion of older and larger firms in high-growth manufacturing industries. Moreover, much of the growth in these industries was dispersed throughout the state. This has been particularly evident in the electronics industry. Radiating outward from Dallas and Austin, in particular, the electronics industry established footholds in small cities around the state during the 1970s. Lubbock, Abilene, Midland/Odessa, Waco, San Marcos, Temple, and Seguin are among the many localities to have benefited from its dispersion to every corner of the state. For example, in the corridor along the Texas-Mexico border, which laces together El Paso, McAllen, Laredo, and Corpus Christi, it is estimated that there are nearly one hundred electronics assembly plants. The recent business cycle downturn tended to slow this dispersion, however, and branch plant activities have been scaled back.

The New Service Economy in Texas

Despite the importance of manufacturing to the overall Texas economy, any employment growth in this sector when combined with
the expected contraction in the energy sector heightens speculation
concerning where the new jobs in Texas will come from. In recent
years, service sector growth in Texas has compensated for the shrinking manufacturing and energy employment share in aggregate terms
only. Service employment growth will not and cannot compensate
the same people and places that have been affected by this restructuring of the state economy. There is widespread concern that a "shift-
to-services" may not so much hinder the state's continued industrialization as transform the way in which the state's residents participate
in it. In part, this concern reflects the view that there is no compelling
reason to expect that the service sector itself is somehow immune
to the decoupling of employment growth from output growth that
has taken place in agricultural and other goods-producing industries.
It may also reflect the lingering, albeit mistaken, perception that the
service sector is largely ancillary and subordinate to goods production and therefore constitutes a far less dependable economic base
for the future than what we have had in the past.[12]

While it is premature to evaluate the implications of an increasingly services-oriented economy on Texas' advanced industrial development, Table 2–1 reveals that the service sector is itself the setting
for major restructuring. Changes in the role of the services sector in
the Texas economy can be expected to flow as much from its internal
development and its relationship to the rest of the economy as from
its overall growth. The services sector is an amalgam of several important economic activities, as Table 2–1 indicates. From an employment
perspective, it is clear that wholesale and retail trade constitute the
dominant service activities in the state economy, rivaling the combined employment capacities of manufacturing and construction. In
1880, wholesale and retail trade accounted for only 4.0% of state
employment; it only exceeded 10% during the World War I period.
After 1920, the expansion of its employment share was steady and
uninterrupted until leveling off after 1950 at approximately a one-fifth
share. Its growth resumed in the 1970s, reflecting, no doubt, the
rapid population increases being experienced throughout the state.
Today, the trade services account for roughly a quarter of the state's
employment.

Producer, consumer, and nonprofit services can be categorized
in many ways.[13] The FIRE group has slowly increased its employment
share over the past century, reaching 5.6% by 1980. Consumer-

oriented services include those domestic and related localized services for which final demand most often originates from individuals. It is these service industries whose defining characteristics most closely color the nation's perception of the services economy. However, this grouping has been steadily retreating in significance in the larger state economy as it has in the national economy since before World War II. The transformation of the service economy has involved the eclipse of consumer services by a group of so-called professional or producer services whose outputs have become essential intermediate inputs in the production of other goods and services. As such, they reveal the increasing complexity, and function to sustain the dominance, of goods production in Texas' advanced industrial economy despite the shift of employment away from traditional goods production. The steady expansion of the professional services revealed in Table 2–1 reflects this shift toward advanced services whose provision typically requires a professionalized labor force with special skills and training.

The public sector too, may be viewed as constituting a major contributor to the services sector. Government-related employment, both civilian and military, has been of steadily increasing importance in Texas all through the past century. It is estimated that by mid-1984, public sector employment in Texas accounted for 16.9% of total employment and 10.6% of the state's total output. In actuality, the full measure of its importance is probably more clearly revealed in the flow of government monies into Texas than in the rising employment share per se. This will be examined in more detail below.

Spatial Patterns of Industrial Development in Texas

The growth and development that are at present restructuring the Texas economy have been the consequence both of key sectors of the economy growing at unequal rates over time and of the tendency for employment growth to be decoupled from output growth for selected industries as Texas continues to industrialize. The even geographic distribution of this growth throughout the state has dramatic implications for the way in which the state is now and will be settled in the future. In order to examine this more closely, let us consider the major metropolitan area economies throughout Texas.

Population is relatively concentrated in Texas. Not only are Dallas, Houston, and San Antonio now three of the nation's ten largest cities, but more than 40% of the state's population and two-thirds of its nonagricultural employment are located in the sprawling metropolitan areas which these three major cities anchor. In all, more than 85% of the state's nonagricultural employment is located in Texas' twenty-five largest metropolitan areas.

While metropolitan employment has expanded, considerable economic diversity has developed and been retained as a result. A clear division of labor is reflected in the distinctive economic structures of Texas' metropolitan areas. Much can be learned about their differing vulnerabilities to larger business cycle movements and about their prospects for sharing in the newly emerging economy by examining these differences in more detail.

Metropolitan Economic Trends and Industry Profiles   Economic activities that involve transforming raw materials into finished products have come to be considered the traditional cornerstones of an industrial economy. Trends in manufacturing and construction can help us monitor the industrialization of a metropolitan economy. As Table 2–2 indicates, the industrialization of Texas as reflected in the growth of manufacturing in recent decades has been registered most clearly in El Paso, Beaumont-Port Arthur-Orange, Waco, Longview-Marshall, and Sherman-Denison. In each of these economies, the manufacturing employment share exceeds 20%. Manufacturing employment shares in nine Texas metropolitan areas exceeds that for the state as a whole. The variation in employment share for contract construction across metropolitan areas is much less than it is for manufacturing. Ten metropolitan economies have larger employment shares in construction than does the larger state economy.

As Texas continues its slow trek away from its historical dependence on the energy sector, the most dramatic impacts will be reserved for a few selected metropolitan areas. Eight metropolitan areas are more concentrated in mining, especially oil and gas extraction, than is the state as a whole. Midland, Odessa, and Abilene are most heavily committed to the fortunes of the oil and gas industry. Not directly indicated in Table 2–2, however, is the substantial dependence of the Beaumont-Port Arthur, Houston and Galveston-Texas City areas on the energy industry, given the heavy concentration of the state's petrochemical, petroleum refining, and energy administrative activities in these areas.

The distribution of services employment across metropolitan areas is likewise displayed in Table 2–2. Transportation, communication, and utilities (TCU) employment shares vary only moderately across Texas' metropolitan economies and are concentrated more heavily in ten metropolitan areas than in the larger state economy. In general, a defining feature of a metropolitan-scale economy is a relatively large commitment to trade, as is evidenced by the low variability in trade employment shares across all metropolitan economies. A dozen areas have more than a quarter of their employment in the wholesale and retail trade sectors, while in eighteen areas the combined trade sector is the area's largest employment sector; this is also true for the overall state economy.

Finance, insurance, and real estate (FIRE) services are uniformly only a third or a fourth the size of the combined services in employment terms. In only seven metropolitan economies is the employment share in FIRE as large or larger than it is in the state economy; four of those seven are the state's most populated metropolitan areas. The remaining services, when aggregated, constitute the second-largest private employment sector in eighteen of the twenty-five metropolitan areas. Likewise, in eighteen areas this collection of remaining services is associated with a larger employment share than is the respective manufacturing sector in the area. Taken together, it is apparent that, despite the misgivings by some that the "shift-to-services" is largely an employment phenomenon, a growing service economy in Texas has been and will continue to be the mainstay of Texas' metropolitan residents.

Approximately 16.9% of Texas' nonagricultural employment in late 1983 was located in the public sector, or government services. This sector's employment share varies dramatically across metropolitan areas. While government employment is relatively underrepresented in the state's two largest metropolitan areas, Dallas-Fort Worth and Houston, other locations including Austin, Bryan-College Station, San Antonio, and Killeen-Temple, which host major state universities and/or state governmental activities or U.S. military bases, have in their metropolitan economies relatively high proportions of public sector employment. In thirteen areas, public employment shares exceed those in the services; in seventeen areas, public employment exceeds manufacturing employment.

Metropolitan Migration Trends   In the era after World War II, population increases which exploded during the 1970s shifted their dependence from natural increase to migration from other states. It has been estimated that 93.9% of the population increase experienced in the 1950s was attributable to an excess of births over deaths while only 6.1% was due to interstate immigration. Roughly the same structure of population growth persisted through the 1960s. However, during the 1970s, only 41.7% of the increase was attributable to natural increase, while 58.3% was due to immigration from other states.

Table 2–2. Nonagricultural Wage and Salary Employment, Structure and Population for Texas and Twenty-five Texas Metropolitan Areas.

Texas Metropolitan Economies	Total Employment (in thousands)	Employment Structure (Oct. 1983)[a]			
		Manufac-turing %	Mining %	Construction Communication Public Utilities %	Transpor-tation %
TEXAS	6,208.6	16.3	4.6	6.2	6.2
Dallas-Fort Worth	1,596.6	19.5	2.0	5.5	6.2
Houston	1,548.9	14.5	6.7	8.7	6.9
San Antonio	439.3	11.2	0.8	6.7	4.4
Austin	274.2	12.3	0.3	5.6	2.8
El Paso	165.3	23.2	—	4.8	6.4
Beaumont-Port Arthur-Orange	145.0	23.2	1.6	6.8	8.6
Corpus Christi	133.2	11.3	6.6	9.0	5.5
Lubbock	90.2	11.6	0.8	4.7	5.3
Amarillo	79.8	13.9	2.4	4.0	8.3
McAllen-Pharr-Edinburg	77.5	11.7	2.1	7.6	8.4
Waco	73.3	20.9	—	5.0	4.4
Galveston-Texas City	69.7	15.1	1.1	7.5	9.3
Longview-Marshall	67.9	23.4	6.6	6.5	5.6
Killeen-Temple	62.6	13.7	—	5.8	5.3
Abilene	60.9	9.9	8.4	5.9	5.4
Brownsville-Harlingen-San Benito	59.1	14.8	0.2	5.8	5.8
Odessa	56.5	10.6	14.5	9.2	5.1
Tyler	56.5	19.3	5.5	4.2	5.0
Midland	54.6	7.9	24.0	7.7	5.9
Wichita Falls	54.1	17.2	6.1	4.1	5.5
Texarkana	46.3	18.1	0.4	5.4	4.5
Bryan-College Station	44.9	6.9	3.3	6.5	4.5
San Angelo	36.0	15.3	1.7	5.6	10.0
Sherman-Denison	33.5	33.1	0.6	3.9	6.9
Laredo	30.0	5.7	3.7	4.0	11.0
Total	5,355.9				
Total Nonagricultural Employment	6,208.6				
Metropolitan Employment Share	86.3%				

[a] Adapted from *Texas Labor Market Review* (November, 1983), Texas Employment Commission, Austin,

[b] U.S. Census data. M/PF Research Population Estimates, Texas State Health Department, Adapted from Business Development Group, Dallas Chamber of Commerce, February, 1983.

[c] The first percentage in each pair is for the City of Dallas, the second is for the City of Fort Worth.

Wholesale and Retail Trade %	FIRE %	Services and Misc. %	Government %	Metropolitan Net Migration Trends[b]			
				Annual Migration Rate		Migration % of Total Population Change	
				1970–80 %	1980–82 %	1970–80	1980–82
24.9	6.0	19.0	16.9	—	—	—	—
27.1	7.7	20.3	11.7	1.5	1.4	55, 63[c]	39, 57[c]
23.7	6.6	21.3	11.6	3.1	1.1	68	43
26.1	6.9	21.8	22.3	0.7	0.4	36	24
22.9	6.3	19.8	29.8	2.6	2.1	68	65
24.2	4.7	16.4	20.3	1.4	−0.3	42	−23
23.4	3.9	18.4	14.0	—	0.2	11	16
24.2	5.0	18.2	20.3	—	0.7	−3	31
29.5	5.8	19.3	23.1	0.4	—	23	−2
30.3	5.4	18.7	17.0	1.0	—	49	−4
30.7	4.1	12.9	27.5	2.9	0.3	52	11
24.4	6.0	22.8	16.6	1.0	0.4	66	38
18.7	6.3	14.6	27.4	0.7	0.6	43	35
25.2	4.3	16.8	11.6	1.7	0.3	67	29
22.2	3.7	18.4	31.0	1.1	−1.1	32	−144
25.9	5.3	23.3	15.9	0.5	0.3	39	28
29.6	4.9	17.9	21.0	2.5	1.0	51	32
27.3	4.1	15.8	13.5	1.1	1.4	44	43
26.5	5.7	19.8	14.0	2.4	−0.2	75	−38
21.6	6.6	17.2	9.2	1.5	4.3	56	72
25.0	4.8	17.0	20.1	0.7	—	−436	−4
24.2	3.5	16.0	27.9	0.5	−0.3	−40	−70
20.5	4.2	13.4	40.8	4.8	5.0	79	80
24.4	4.2	20.3	18.6	1.2	1.1	62	53
20.9	3.6	17.0	14.0	0.5	0.1	65	22
31.3	5.0	16.3	23.0	1.0	−0.6	35	−45

Table 2-3. Central City Population and Industrial Employment as a Percentage of Standard Metropolitan Statistical Area.

Major Texas Metropolitan Areas	Central City Population		Manufacturing		Retail Trade			Wholesale Trade			Selected Services		
	1980	1970	1977	1972	1977	1972	1967	1977	1972	1967	1977	1972	1967
Dallas-Fort Worth*	30.5	54.3	41.8 (62.6)	46.6 (66.6)	40.1 (57.7)	43.6 (61.5)	62.1	56.1 (69.9)	64.0 (78.1)	90.4	59.3 (73.6)	58.8 (75.3)	85.8
Houston	55.1	62.1	70.2	66.4	71.6	72.4	77.2	87.5	88.4	93.1	78.8	81.4	85.5
San Antonio	73.4	75.7	81.0	81.9	83.1	82.5	88.8	91.4	91.9	96.0	89.5	88.8	91.5
El Paso	88.7	89.7	91.4	94.2	97.2	96.7	98.2	95.7	96.6	98.3	97.3	95.9	97.0
Austin	64.8	85.2	55.6	55.0	84.3	89.4	97.9	83.6	90.6	97.6	82.7	82.4	98.8

Sources: U.S. Bureau of Census (Washington, D.C.: Government Printing Office), 1977 Census of Retail Trade: Geographic Area Series, RC 77-A, 1979; 1977 Census of Manufactures: Geographic Area Series, MC 77-A, 1980; 1977 Census of Wholesale Trade: Geographic Area Series, WC 77-A-1-52, 1979; 1977 Census of Service Industries: Geographic Area Series, SC 77-A, 1980; 1980 Census Population for Cities of 100,000 and Over by Rank Order, April, 1981; and 1970 Census of Population, General Population Characteristics, U.S. Summary (PC(1)81), Jan., 1972, Table 67.

* The figures in this row are for the City of Dallas as a percentage of SMSA; the figures in parentheses below are for the central cities of Dallas and Fort Worth combined as a percentage of SMSA for those years after the two were consolidated into a single metropolitan area.

The growth and changing structure of the Texas state economy has been accompanied, therefore, by the massive influx of new labor force participants, and not just new birth cohorts whose employment ties to a changing state economy lag up to two decades behind their arrival. In Table 2–2 net migration data are reported for both the 1970 and the 1980–82 periods. In all but five metropolitan areas, the migration rate of the early 1980s was lower than that of the 1970s. The decline was particularly marked for the Houston, Beaumont-Port Arthur-Orange, McAllen-Pharr-Edinburg, Killeen-Temple, Brownsville-Harlingen-San Benito, Tyler, and Laredo areas. In the Wichita Falls and Texarkana areas, average annual net out-migration is continuing into the second decade, while in the El Paso, Killeen-Temple, Abilene, and Laredo areas, net out-migration appears to have commenced in the 1980s.

The Restructuring of Central City Economies   At the center of each of these metropolitan areas is one or more central cities whose local economies both reflect and initiate many of the patterns of growth and development which are shaping the larger metropolitan and state economies. One feature of the advanced industrial development of Texas is the deconcentration of people and jobs away from the state's major central cities. In Table 2–3 this dynamic is illustrated for the state's five largest cities, all of which appear to be loosening their grip on key sectors of their respective metropolitan economies. Patterns of net growth typically involve the greater portion of new growth, bypassing central city locations in favor of peripheral suburban, and increasingly nonmetropolitan and rural, locations. In nearly all instances, central cities are retreating from their positions of historical dominance over employment and population through a century-long process of suburbanization and a more recent process of nonmetropolitan growth.

Yet, it is the absolute, and not the relative, dominance of the central city economy that appears to be diminished in the process. In the case of Dallas and Houston, their original central business districts appear to be in the process of becoming simply one of two or more, rather than the only, economic crossroads of their respective metropolitan areas. The emergence of multiple "downtowns" has given these cities a multinodal internal structure with which to express their expanded size and scale, rather than simply the traditional one wherein economic activities revolve around a single central city core. Large and healthy city economies like Dallas, Houston, and Austin, in particular, appear to be assuming new and more expanded roles in the information-based and advanced services sectors of both the regional and national economies. Moreover, an emerging set of international ties rooted in the export orientation of selected advanced services is developing to link these cities to a wider global economy.

Fiscal Federalism and Texas' Economic Development

Despite the fact that the aggregate size and influence of the private sector economy dwarf those of the public sector, in a mixed economy the potential influence on state and local economies of activities of the national government can be considerable. The taxing and spending relationships between a state and the federal government can influence not only the nature, quantity, and location of economic development in a state, but also the range of service assignments assumed by state and local governments.

In 1982, Texas was one of twenty states which paid more in total federal taxes than it and its constituent local governments received in federal outlays. For every $1.00 of federal aid received by the state, the state paid out $1.59 in taxes. Texas received only 84% of the average level of per capita federal spending across all states. Furthermore, Texas received proportionately less in federal spending for grants to state and local governments, salaries and wages, direct payments to individuals, and procurement than did the average state in that year.

Patterns of Defense Spending Defense spending in Texas constitutes a dramatically different situation. The Texas economy has been tied to federal expenditures for national defense since Texas first became a state. As a garrison location and training site for land and air forces, Texas has long been the recipient of defense-related expenditures. Today, a massive portion (23.3%) of federal expenditures is dispersed through the defense budget. Texas ranks third behind California and Virginia among states in receipt of defense funds with 6.6% ($12.0 billion) of the U.S. defense budget for 1982. In the competition among states for defense outlays, per capita direct defense spending for FY1982 was 21% greater and indirect defense spending was 43% greater in Texas than the average state. However, from a "balance of payments" perspective wherein the amount a state receives in defense contracts is compared to the amount its citizens pay in federal taxes destined for defense spending, Texas actually loses billions of dollars annually.[15]

Defense procurement claimed 41.6% of Texas' share of defense outlays, while pay for 255,700 civilian and military employees of the Department of Defense accounted for another 29.9%. Research and development, with the bulk of the funds targeted to manufacturing activities, accounted for another 3.8%. Only four other states (California, Florida, Hawaii, and Alaska) have more military installations than does Texas.

The flow of federal dollars for defense has a stimulative effect on economic development within both the state and selected localities. Estimates prepared by the Texas State Comptroller's Office indicate that every dollar in defense spending generates the impact of three dollars.[16] This multiplication of economic activity tied to the inflow of federal defense dollars is highly prized as a source of job creation and a further stimulus to the demand for goods and services produced by other industries throughout the state.

Defense outlays are associated with extremely uneven impacts on local economies throughout Texas. It is estimated, for example, that the Dallas-Fort Worth metropolitan economy received more than half (56.7%) of all defense contracts awarded to the state in FY1982.[17] Within the Dallas-Fort Worth metropolitan area, 178 of the 396 (44.9%) defense contractors are located in Dallas County alone; another 196 (49.5%) are located in Tarrant County. Contractors in Dallas County received 93.7% while contractors in the City of Dallas received 69.5% of the defense dollars funneled to the Dallas-Fort Worth metropolitan area. While sixty defense contractors held contracts worth more than $1 million, a single company held contracts valued at $3.5 billion, or 62.7% of the metropolitan total and 28.0% of the Texas total.

While the geographic distribution of prime or original contracts is uneven and favors states like Texas and California and counties like Dallas, round after round of subcontracts let to parts suppliers and other subcontractors in the complex production process tend to channel defense dollars back into the more industrialized regions of the United States as well as to other locations within Texas.[18] Nevertheless, defense spending may be associated with less optimistic net employment effects than is commonly realized. The technology-intensive character of modern goods and services required to maintain a formidable national defense has gradually been expressed as a shift in defense outlays away from relatively labor-intensive industries. For this reason, defense activity may no longer translate into employment growth as dramatically as it once did, nor is it tied to employment growth in the ways more direct job creation strategies are presumed to be. Every rise in the defense budget of $1 billion may actually be associated with the *loss* of up to ten thousand jobs compared with the net employment impact associated with the same level of nondefense expenditures. It has been estimated that the level of defense expenditures in 1978 was associated with the net loss of one million jobs across the nation. While Texas was one of twenty-one states to gain employment, it was estimated that there was a net increase of only 15,540 jobs in the Texas economy despite such massive defense expenditures.[19]

Advanced Technology and Industrial Development

In the 1980s, the prospects for economic growth and job creation tied to the so-called high-technology sector have received considerable attention. In the United States, three-quarters of the net increase in manufacturing jobs from 1955 to 1979 came in these industries.[20] Technology advances and the human capital they both reflect and require are increasingly regarded as the source of new industries as well the key to the renewal of older, less competitive industries. Nevertheless, while the cluster of industries including computer hardware, robotics, software and data processing services, telecommunications, advanced manufacturing computer-assisted design, biogenetics, scientific instruments, and the like appear to be the frontier for advanced industrial economies, only a small portion (less than 5%) of the nation's work force is at present employed in such industries.[21] Future employment projections do not indicate a rapid increase in that proportion either at the national or state level.

Texas appears to offer a hospitable environment for the spawning of such industries. While the number of high-technology companies does not yet exceed fifteen thousand, Texas ranks third behind California and New York as the location of more than a third of them, an increase of nearly 250% since 1978.[22] The seedbeds of high-technology growth are distributed unequally across Texas just as they are nationally. Through the 1980s, a steady 2.8% of the Texas work force has been employed in high-technology industries. Yet, both employment and sales are highly concentrated. Fully 58.0% of all Texas' high-technology workers are employed in the Dallas-Fort Worth metropolitan area alone, with another 13.2% in Houston and 5.4% in San Antonio.[23]

An examination of the high-technology sector of the Dallas-Fort Worth metropolitan area, the state's leading high-technology economy, indicates that the sector has emerged slowly during the post-war era.[24] Depending on the definition of the sector, this sector has expanded to account for as much as a fifth of metropolitan employment. The rate of expansion since 1972 has been significantly greater than the rate before that date.

Conclusion

Will Texas be able to retain its ascending position among all states in the future? Will important industrial development trends like the rise of high-technology industries ever be able to compensate directly or indirectly for the losses accompanying the emergence of a restructured economic base? How will the patterns of losses in a receding economy compare to the gains associated with the newly emerging one? These and many other questions invite attention as we look to the future.

While Texas has lagged behind other states historically in the industrialization process it has also shown the capacity to lead the way into an advanced industrial era. Thus far this role, however, has been more thrust upon the state than consciously undertaken by it. Nonetheless, as the importance of physical resources is eclipsed by human resources and created comparative advantages edge aside those tied to natural resources, business climates required for the future may well come to elevate in importance factors historically judged to have been less important, such as well-educated citizens and the school and nonschool arrangements necessary to provide them. In addition to competitive labor costs, low tax burdens on households and businesses, land availability, low cost of living and attractive residential amenities, future economic growth and development will increasingly come to depend on the availability of a flexible and appropriately skilled labor force and a network of high-quality and accessible educational facilities to which employees can turn for skill upgrading all through their careers.

In the end, Texas may be well-advised to reexamine the reigning interpretation of how its past growth and development took place originally if it is to comprehend accurately the new development that is now reshaping its economy. When it does so, it will likely discover that its past economic development has been defined continuously by the transformation of potential resources into actual ones. Today, as Texas continues to industrialize, land and the land-based resources which supported the agricultural and energy economies have begun to yield to an economy whose productive capacity is tied to new mixes of land, labor, and capital. It will be necessary to acknowledge the "created" nature of Texas' original natural resources before we can respond to the necessity to develop systematically the essential human resources so vital to the new Texas economy. Failure to do so may result in a gradual weakening of our capacity to compete with other states and our yielding our newly gained leadership position in the nation and the world.

Notes

1. John F. Long, *Population Deconcentration in the United States,* (Washington, D.C.: U.S. Department of Commerce, Bureau of the Census, November, 1981).

2. "The Texas Economy in 1984" *Fiscal Notes* (Austin: January, 1984).

3. Roger J. Vaughan, *State Taxation and Economic Development* (Washington D.C.: Council of State Planning Agencies, 1979). For the distinction between growth and development discussed at the local level, see also, Peter Libassi and Victor Hausner, *Revitalizing Central City Investment* (Columbus, Oh.: Academy for Contemporary Problems, November, 1977).

4. "The Texas Economy."

5. Susan Goodman and Victor L. Arnold, "High Technology in Texas," *Texas Business Review* (November–December 1983): 290–95.

6. Barry Bluestone and Bennett Harrison, *The Deindustrialization of America,* (New York: Basic Books, 1982).

7. *Inc.* "The Fastest Growing Companies in the United States." (1982):175.

8. For a discussion of the importance of upgraded human skills to high-growth industries such as the computer services industry throughout Texas, see Donald A. Hicks and Czi C. Pann, "Computer Software and Data Processing Services: Development Characteristics of a High-Technology Service Industry in Texas" (Dallas: Center for Policy Studies, University of Texas at Dallas; Office of the Governor, State of Texas; and Texas Computer Industry Council, July, 1984).

9. Texas 2000 Commission, *Texas Trends* (Austin: Office of the Governor, 1981), 175. For a discussion of these trends, see idem, *Texas Past and Future: A Survey* (Austin: Office of the Governor, 1981).

10. Ibid.

11. Economic forecast provided by Bureau of Business Research, University of Texas, Austin, and Data Resources, Inc., Lexington, Mass., April, 1984.

12. John M. L. Gruenstein and Sally Guerra, "Can Services Sustain a Regional Economy?" *Business Review,* (July–August, 1981):15–27; and Larry

S. Hirschhorn, "The Urban Crisis: A Post-Industrial Perspective," *Journal of Regional Science*, 9 (1979):109–18.

13. For a discussion of the changing structure of the service economy, see Thomas M. Stanback, Jr. et al., *Services: The New Economy* (Totowa, N.J.: Rowman and Allenheld, 1983).

14. Texas 2000 Commission, *Texas 2000* (Austin, 1982).

15. James B. Anderson, *Bankrupting America*.

16. "Texas Rakes in Defense Dollars," *Fiscal Notes*, (December, 1983):1–3.

17. Don-Michael Bradford, "Department of Defense Spending in the Dallas-Fort Worth Regional Economy" (unpublished, spring, 1984).

18. John Rees, "On Manufacturing Change in the Dallas-Fort Worth Area," (Dallas: Center for Policy Studies, University of Texas at Dallas, 1979).

19. Marion Anderson, "The Empty Pork Barrel," (Lansing, Mich.: Employment Research Associates, 1982).

20. U.S. Congress, Joint Economic Committee, "Location of High Technology Firms and Regional Economic Development," (Washington, D.C.: June 1, 1982). For a more detailed treatment of these issues, see Office of Technology Assessment, *Technology, Innovation and Regional Economic Development* (Washington, D.C.: Government Printing Office, July, 1984).

21. Richard W. Riche, Daniel E. Hecker, and John U. Burgan, "High Technology Today and Tomorrow: A Small Piece of the Employment Pie," *Monthly Labor Review* (November, 1983): 50–58.

22. Office of Technology Assessment, *Technology*.

23. Bob Bullock, "Texas Maintains Its Share of High Technology," *Fiscal Notes* (December, 1983):8–10.

24. Donald A. Hicks and William H. Stolberg, "The High-Technology Sector: Growth and Development in Dallas-Fort Worth Regional Economy, 1964–84," (Dallas: Center for Applied Research, University of Texas at Dallas, January, 1985).

Chapter Three

THE ELECTORATE IN TEXAS

Glenn A. Robinson

This chapter has a simple theme: Texans are rediscovering democracy. The same exuberance and confidence catapulting Texas from a colonial economy into a technologically sophisticated society are transforming Texans' expectations about politics and the way they act as citizens. A more democratic polity is in itself a desirable development, yet it also may have unintended consequences for the conduct of coherent, effective public policy.

We often reckon that the essential criterion for public policy is the "satisfaction of human wants" or, put more specifically, the resolution of pressing social and economic issues. For democracy, this is an insufficient criterion. Democracy additionally insists on the active participation and consent of the public itself, of individuals as citizens frequently and repeatedly deciding and redeciding their fates. At the very least, it means the freedom to choose among equally feasible alternatives so that participation becomes a critical ingredient in the policymaking process rather than a sporadic input into a managerially dominated exercise.

By contrast, contemporary policymaking emphasizes the hard thinking, scientific expertise, and administrative skill required to devise solutions to the intricate problems of a complex society. A premium is placed on policy coherence and feasibility with an eye towards policies which can carry Texas into the twenty-first century. The general electorate is a peripheral concern, to be educated, some would say enlightened, once hard findings from policy studies have produced a coherent plan of action. Hence the challenge: as our scientific knowledge base enhances our ability to develop effective public policies, our ability to do so democratically, routinely to engage thousands and millions of citizens in policymaking becomes increasingly difficult and demanding.

Technocracy and Democracy in Texas

For a long while, Texans told their politicians *not* to act but to keep government "at a distance and out of sight."[1] At present, Texans insist that government act efficiently as a "lean and mean" equivalent to a private corporation. This legacy has yielded state and local governments which, save for education and highways, are relatively small, disinclined to provide direct public services, and more inclined to regulate corporate and social behavior.

This has not prevented Texas Government from embracing the professionalism and technical sophistication so highly valued in the state's economic transformation. The initiative rests variously with city councils, county courts, state department heads, and, importantly, the demands of federal courts and bureaucracy. When prodded into action, the state has shown considerable ability to implement and to innovate. The term "technocracy" risks exaggerating recent developments, yet it conveys the underlying spirit: a high regard for efficient, innovative techniques; a high valuation on the uses of expert knowledge; a preference for in-house provision of public services; and a concern primarily for issues that are amenable to engineering solutions.

The democratic impulse is a more disorderly, complicated development. In the past, Texas politics involved a paradox. Texans have combined a fascination with politicians and their tricks with a disinterest in and a distaste for what government was actually undertaking.[2] Texas politics, like Friday night football, was serious business, but largely immaterial to the worldly concerns of ordinary citizens. And in much the same way they recruited football coaches, they bought efficient caretaker governments to provide essential, rather Spartan, public services.[3]

What then do greater democratic choice and participation afford Texas voters? Perhaps the immediate answer is enhanced opportunities to express and articulate sharp, often deep-seated, emotions and concerns. Rhetorical appeals and spontaneous reactions are characteristic features of democracy, from ancient Athens to contemporary Texas. They underscore the idea that public opinion is quite volatile on substantive issues and policy, readily swayed by a masterful argument and prepared to change course in light of unexpected and unfavorable development. By the same token, democracy can both reinforce and accentuate the more fundamental moral convictions variously held by citizens, values which cannot be readily incorporated into legitimate government policy.

In practice, Texas government engages Texas citizens more directly and incisively than one finds in most polities. The Texas Constitution contains no less than sixty sections requiring Texas voters to decide which candidates and which policy initiatives are to prevail.[4] Voters directly elect state and local judges, district attorneys, sheriffs, clerks, and state department heads and commissioners who elsewhere are gubernatorially appointed. Most new capital expenditures, from new schools to mass transit systems, are subject to bond elections and in many cases constitutional amendments. A constitutional section prohibiting legislative appropriation of benefits to individuals effectively debars the legislature from initiating a wide range of public programs, ranging from community economic development to augmented public assistance, without resort to a constitutional amendment.[5] In short, most policy initiatives must clear the hurdle of voter approval.

These extensive restraints on government reflect the historical importance of Texas individualism and of the inherent worth of individual opinion, eschewing, even opposing, collective expressions of interest.[6] They seem to facilitate free access and close ties between citizens and public officials, although, given the size of contemporary Texas jurisdictions, even modest opportunities for access to public officials might overwhelm the capacities of state and local governments.[7]

It is thus of some importance how the emerging democratic impulse is organized. Perhaps the most effective opportunity for the organization of individual viewpoints accompanies the emergence of articulate, coherent, disciplined political parties. In subsequent sections, I shall stress this possibility, noting how partisanship has taken root in Texas at a time where nationally it has waned. Single-issue movements, especially when focused on valence rather than material issues, afford a second organizational opportunity. These will frequently broadside public policy initiatives in reflecting the difference between deep-seated personal values and the prognoses and prescriptions of professional policy analysts. Traditional interest groups, such as trade unions and chambers of commerce, suggest a third, probably diminishing, alternative, compromised in Texas by a distaste for the "lobby" and handicapped by the declining importance of their political programs.

The dichotomy between technology and democracy risks exaggerating the problem. Policymaking is rarely a self-enclosed process unattentive to public opinion and political comment. Citizens in turn value expertise and commonly uphold professional judgments. The two cultures nonetheless diverge from one another, and Texas conditions at least suggest the *possibility* of democracy gaining the upper hand. At present, we should be far more concerned to assess the *likelihood* of such a development, as it rests on both a sea-change in the state's political climate and a reconfiguration of how Texans conduct their politics. Indications of these changes will compose the bulk of this chapter, and only in the final section will an assessment of their public policy implications be undertaken.

The Discovery of November

The critical and very recent change in Texas politics is that November general elections are more important to the electorate than the Democratic Primary. This underscores the prospects of an emerging two-party state. When taken in conjunction with the spring primaries, it multiplies the choices among candidates and their programs. Most important, it encourages sharper delineations between party programs affording the voter more programmatic, substantive choices.

During most of the century, the operative choice confronting Texas voters in November was whether or not to vote, as the Democratic Primary determined which candidate ultimately was elected. For thirty-four gubernatorial elections between 1900 and 1966, the average Democratic gubernatorial majority was 81.0%. Only twice, in 1924 and 1962, did the majority fall below 60%, to 58.9% and 54.6%, both of which are comfortable majorities. Democratic senatorial majorities over the same period averaged 78.88%. At the height of Democratic party dominance during the 30s, November majorities of greater than 90% were commonplace.

Analysis of Texas' 254 counties adds perspective to the aggregate statistics. County analysis encapsulates the heterogeneity of the state: the German Hill Country counties where Republican majorities have prevailed since the Civil War, South Texas counties continuously dominated by Mexican-Americans often subject to the extremes of machine politics, urban counties where Republicans more readily established a beachhead, and rural East Texas counties seemingly invulnerable to bipartisanship.

Table 3–1 summarizes county electoral statistics for selected Democratic primaries and general elections, comparing turnout in gubernatorial primaries with turnout in the general election. While percentage estimates for the median county serve as a bellwether, the ranges respectively for the middle 50% of counties and for all

Table 3–1. The Decline of the Democratic Primary.

*Turnout in the Democratic Gubernatorial Elections
as Percentage of Turnout in General Gubernatorial Elections.*

Election Year	Median County	Range for Middle 50% of Texas Counties	Range for all Texas Counties
1932	121.7	110.0 – 130.2	27.0 – 195.8
1942	406.3	321.0 – 466.0	34.3 – 745.3
1952	108.7	79.2 – 117.7	18.3 – 302.2
1962	114.5	96.3 – 114.5	13.4 – 217.2
1972	90.5	73.2 – 103.6	26.8 – 174.8
1974	120.2	94.7 – 152.4	29.9 – 279.7
1978	102.3	85.4 – 119.2	28.1 – 190.7
1982	64.9	49.4 – 86.9	8.4 – 131.0

Source: See Appendix.

counties reflect the diverse results one might expect. The width of these ranges can vary dramatically from one election to another, a reminder that at the local level elections are complex events, registering the impact of dozens of tenuously interlinked campaigns for office.

The 1942 results appear anomalous, but in fact register a common Texas voting pattern in nonpresidential years. In a field of six candidates in the primary, Coke Stevenson won handily with a 68.5% majority in a relatively uncontested primary election. In 244 of 254 counties, more people voted in the Democratic Primary than in the general election. In one-fourth of Texas counties, almost five times as many people voted.

The 1932 and 1952 results are more incisive. The 1932 general election not only offered Texas voters the chance to vote for Roosevelt and against Hoover, thereby reversing the state's electoral votes in 1928, it further offered a challenge to Fergusonism, inasmuch as Miriam Ferguson's campaigns were regarded by many as a recrudescence of a demagoguery distasteful to prominent citizens. Thus, the Republican gubernatorial candidate was a conservative Democrat subsequently appointed by a Democratic governor to the University of Texas Board of Regents.[8] Nonetheless, in 210 counties, primary vote exceeded general election turnout. In the median county, primary turnout was 22% above general election turnout. Similar inducements to voting in general elections emerged in 1952 when, in what remains a controversial move, statewide Democratic candidates were cross-listed on the Republican ticket to focus on the presidential race between Eisenhower and Stevenson, a race materially important to Texans because of the Tidelands offshore oil controversy.

As in 1942, the Democratic Primary contained few lively campaigns. Nevertheless, 130 counties had higher turnouts in the Democratic Primary.

The pattern from 1962 to 1978 reflects both the erosion of Democratic domination and the continued prominence of primary elections. Presidential elections after 1952 attracted more voters than respective Democratic primaries. The 1972 results are typical. In the median county, Democratic Primary turnout declined to 90% of general election turnout. This decline was sufficiently important to encourage Democratic legislators to establish four-year terms for most statewide elective offices with elections to be held in nonpresidential years. Thus, in 1974, once again the Democratic Primary was the dominant forum. Turnout in the median county was within two percentage points of median turnout in 1932. But in comparison with 1932, the range of the turnout has increased, as Table 3–1 indicates. In many counties, the role of the Democratic Primary relative to the general election increased as response to a spirited campaign by four major contenders and the indignation spurred by reactions to the Sharpstown scandal, Texas' Watergate.

Only in 1982 is it clear that the Democratic Primary had ceased to be the important election to voters. Only sixteen counties in the state had higher turnouts in primary elections. In fifty-six counties, Democratic turnout was less than 50% of turnout in general elections, including all four of the state's major urban counties (Bexar, Dallas, Harris, and Tarrant). In the median county, primary turnout was 65% of turnout in the general election.

Under ideal two-party conditions, Democratic party turnout should approach 50% of general election turnout. Assuming an equal number of Republican and Democratic voters, all of whom vote in their party's primary and who combine to vote in the general election, a truly bipartisan result for Table 3–1 would approximate the 50% line. Under one-party conditions, but where the civic obligation to vote inspires active voters, the turnout in Democratic primaries should approach 100% of general election turnout. These two standards can orient thinking about participation. Even in 1982, with a Republican gubernatorial incumbent, 188 of 254 counties voted disproportionately in the Democratic Primary. Quite possibly an unexciting 1982 primary race for governor, combined with a lively campaign featuring a personally controversial incumbent Republican governor, contributed to the dramatic change across the state in respective turnouts in 1982, as compared with 1978 and 1974. Fortuitous events aside, two trends remain: the long-term trend over the decades confirms the increasing salience of the general election; and the 1982 results confirm that Texas is a considerable way from full-scale two-party competition.

In 1984, the Texas Republican party mounted its most ambitious campaign to organize Republican primaries. Table 3–2 reflects the results. Republicans sensibly decided to forego primaries in twenty-nine counties where the costs of organizations did not warrant the effort. In ninety-six counties, less than one hundred voters participated. In many of these counties the number of voters barely exceeded the number of ballot boxes. In one-half of Texas counties, the Republican Primary attracted less than 5% of voters in the Democratic Primary. In six counties, Republican primaries attracted more voters than Democratic primaries, while in an additional eight counties (including Dallas and Harris counties) they attracted at least half of the Democratic turnout. While in these Republican enclaves, Republican primaries may have attracted voters who might otherwise have voted in Democratic primaries, for most of the state, the effects are negligible.

The statewide phenomenon of the rising importance of general elections remains. Why are traditionally active voters increasingly attracted to general elections? Why are new voters attracted for the first time?

The Attractions of Voting

Texans, like Americans, generally lack the disciplined party allegiance found in more class-oriented or cleavage-riddled societies. Over recent decades, both party identification and voter participation have steadily declined, leading thoughtful commentators to suggest the failure of the party system.[9] Thus anomalies such as increasing rates of voter participation and more durable signs of party identification beg for explanation. This section examines three factors which bear on the democratizing trend: the recovery from the era of disfranchisement; the fielding of complete party tickets; and the effects of highly visible campaigns by individual candidates.

The End of Disfranchisement In recent national elections, Texas turnout averaged 6% to 8% below national turnout.[10] To many observers, this remains a legacy of voter restrictions, notably against blacks, which Texas shared with other Southern states. Convergence of participation rates might merely reflect a catching-up exercise. All the same, a reassessment of the effects of disfranchisement is warranted.

Table 3–2. The Republican Primary, 1984.

Republican Primary Turnout as % of Democratic Primary Turnout, by County	No. of Counties
No Republican primary held	29
0 to 5	110
5 to 10	45
10 to 20	26
20 to 30	16
30 to 50	14
50 to 75	6
75 to 100	2
100 to 404*	6
Counties with fewer than 100 voters in Republican Primary	6

Source: See Appendix.

* Includes 3 urban counties (Collin, Midland, Randall) and 3 German Hill Country counties (Gillespie, Kendall, Kerr).

Disfranchisement in Texas was both a self-righteous and a short-sighted assault on the powerless and politically expendable elements in Texas society during the first two-thirds of the century. While blacks were its primary victims, two other examples help to establish the political context more meaningfully. Through 1966, all military personnel, including the Texas National Guard, were constitution-ally disfranchised or disabled from voting in Texas.[11] Few states have shown Texas' unrestrained support for the military. While the original disability was an anachronism left over from Redemption, successive amendments throughout the twentieth century allow no doubt but that legislators and voters sought to continue disfranchisement. Many Texas cities like San Antonio, Killeen, and Del Rio have high con-centrations of (primarily) out-of-state military personnel, where the military vote, like the black vote, might conceivably swing elections. During World War II, registered Texas voters on active duty over-seas encountered frequent difficulties in obtaining absentee ballots and in many cases found their ballots disallowed by election judges invoking an arcane constitutional restriction. Such disfranchisement subordinated right, not to mention common civility, to highly local-ized, short-term political gains. A similar constitutional section bars nonproperty owners from voting in bond elections.[12] While the U.S. Supreme Court has barred its use, the section remains in the state constitution.

One can discern a common thread. Soldiers shared with tenant farmers and household lodgers the qualities of being powerless and politically expendable. Unorganized for lobbying and disinclined to exercise basic rights, they resigned themselves to inequities. Once their disabilities are formally removed, they retain the same disinterest and unreadiness to organize, and participation in elections continues to be low.

This example of disfranchised, but otherwise nondiscriminated, groups sets the context for the issue of black voters. Blacks at present compose 12% of the state's population, roughly equivalent to the national average. Sheer numbers and residential housing patterns can justify black majority districts. Elsewhere, their dispersion is on a par with strength in Northern urban counties, as the figures from the 1980 census in Table 3–3 suggest.[13] Thus, in 11% of Texas counties, the local black community constitutes a potentially powerful swing vote which might under favorable circumstances elect black officials.

Table 3–3. Concentration of Blacks in Texas Counties and Northern Cities.

Percent Black	Number of Texas Counties	Equivalent Northern City
35 or more	1 (42.1%)	Philadelphia, Baltimore
30 – 35	4	Brooklyn, Bronx
25 – 30	5	Chicago
20 – 25	18	Boston

Source: Data based on U.S. Bureau of the Census, *County and City Data Book 1983* (Washington, D.C.: Government Printing Office, 1983).

Ironically, nineteenth-century Texas, when blacks composed a quarter of the population, offered greater opportunities for local black majorities, and a modest number of black officials indeed were elected. But at no point was the Texas black population sufficiently concentrated or numerically extensive enough to pose even a modest challenge to white majority rule. The white primary and the poll tax were nonetheless introduced as reform proposals to curb the corrosive impact of black bloc voting, clearly disingenuous reforms, given the zeal with which the Democratic party pursued Hispanic bloc voting in South Texas counties.

Texas disfranchisement thus has a particularistic character. It was a concession to a limited number of localities to remove a possible, but rarely immediate, threat to the political status quo, taken at the expense of a politically powerless group. In practice disfranchisement had limited effects on the size of the active electorate. The dramatic decline in Texas voting followed the political defeat of Texas populism in the 1896 election, well prior to the legal voting restrictions.¹⁴

It should be obvious that disfranchisement abetted the political powerlessness of blacks. It is much less obvious that it caused powerlessness or that its formal removal would lead, *ceteris paribus*, to substantial participation of blacks in Texas elections.

Figure 3–1 chronicles long-range trends in Texas voting, and its close interpretation raises important issues. The 1964 election serves as the legal watershed, after which the poll tax amendment and the Voting Rights Act began to affect electoral behavior in the state. The significant and permanent increase between 1966 and 1968 reflects systematic black voter registration and, to some extent, defensive white registration. The numerous court decisions and legislative measures of the 1970s to enhance minority turnout appear to have been ineffectual. Increases in registration, however, did not convert into increased turnouts in primary and general elections. Thus, women's suffrage raised the number of eligible voters in the early 1920s without appreciable rises in electoral turnout, and similar efforts among minorities during the late 1960s and '70s failed to generate voters.

If one sketches, by contrast, the trend lines of turnouts in both presidential and nonpresidential elections for the postwar period, one discovers a more gradual, permanent trend in electoral turnout. It begins prior to the civil rights revolution and is unaffected by new infusions of recently enfranchised citizens. The Democratic Primary, by contrast, ceased to be the dominant statewide forum of electoral politics as early as 1952, but unequivocally by 1960.

The end of disfranchisement, the formal removal of constitutional disabilities, and the lagged registration of blacks after 1965 appear to have played modest roles in the rediscovery of democracy.

Statewide Party Competition   One-party dominance in presidential elections was broken in 1928 when Hoover carried the state. During the following three decades, increasing numbers of voters became disaffected with the national Democratic ticket. The split ballot became indicative of Texas pragmatism at the federal level and continued loyalty to the Democratic party at the state level. At issue, however, is whether this pragmatism reflects contemporary voter sentiment or derives from restricted choices in elections.

American politics, unlike the politics of European democracies, focuses rather sharply on winning specific elections. The unopposed primary and the unopposed general election are commonplace. Often, there is only nominal opposition. Parties are thereby disinclined to field, let alone underwrite, complete party tickets for elective of-

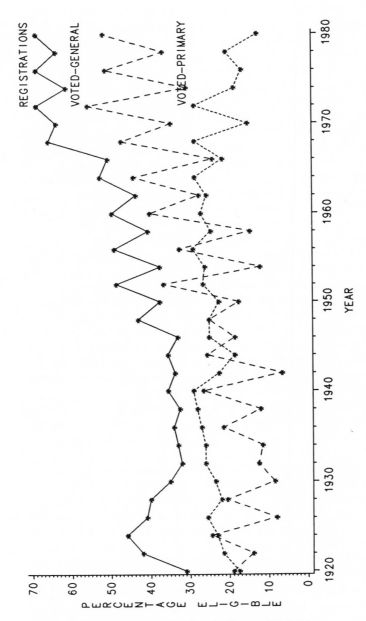

Figure 3–1   Citizen Participation in Texas, 1920–84.

fices. Yet if the invulnerability of certain candidates is everywhere a political fact of life, the absence of meaningful opposition restricts and inhibits democratic choice. This factor may be especially true in a state like Texas with a long history of one-party domination.

Hence, the questions: Are Texans pragmatic voters inclined to split-voting when their traditional Democratic loyalties are challenged occasionally? Or are Texans partisan voters with implicit party loyalties, whose explicit voting behavior has been inhibited by the lack of party competition? The answer to these questions must be based on limited evidence. Only in 1984 did the Republican party mount a statewide primary. The 1986 Republican Primary first yielded a politically interesting gubernatorial race. Partisan competition in legislative, county, and judicial races is embryonic at best. Findings thus are based on rather casual evidence and should be interpreted commensurately.

Table 3–4 addresses the issues of party voting and party competition. Texans have the option of voting a straight-party ticket, thereby simplifying the task of voting for a seemingly endless list of minor candidates. Votes accordingly register only in cases where a party has fielded a candidate for office. Thus where an election is uncontested, a voter choosing to vote a straight ticket will not vote in an election where the party has failed to mount a candidate. As gubernatorial elections generally attract the highest turnout, voting for governor can serve as a standard for voting for other offices. Statewide pluralities indicate that in 1982, no less than 28.6% of voters opted for the long ballot and split their tickets (using the railroad commissioner's race for comparison). At the other extreme, in a comparison of the gubernatorial and the unopposed associate justice elections (with 37% fewer votes), a substantial portion of these nonvotes is attributable to Republicans voting a straight ticket. This vastly exaggerates party voting, as diligent independents and Republicans are inclined to vote for an unopposed candidate.

Statewide pluralities for individual campaigns in 1982 show considerable variation. Jim Nugent's plurality in the railroad commissioner's race was the largest among statewide races. As David Prindle has persuasively demonstrated, an incumbent railroad commissioner gains significant campaign contributions and votes from the large numbers of independent oil producers and royalty holders dispersed throughout the state.[15] At the other extreme, Mark White's defeat of a Republican incumbent governor suggests that an incumbent may possess roughly a 300,000-vote edge in a campaign. Re-elected incumbents for U.S. Senate, lieutenant governor, and comptroller closely track one another. Candidates for agricultural commissioner and trea-

Table 3–4. The Effects of the Long Ballot, 1982.

Office	Statewide Vote	% of Vote for Governor	Statewide Plurality
Governor	3,191,091	100.0	231,933
U.S. senator	3,103,167	97.2	561,464
Lieutenant governor	3,137,996	98.3	558,226
Attorney general	3,093,432	96.9	584,110
Comptroller	3,088,117	96.8	546,322
Commissioner of agriculture	3,027,967	94.9	748,762
Railroad commissioner	2,999,541	94.0	863,088
Commissioner, Land Office	2,978,890	93.4	654,517
Treasurer	3,068,598	96.2	723,958
Associate justice Supreme Court, Place 1	2,884,757	90.4	442,059
Associate justice, Supreme Court, Place 2 (uncontested)	2,004,449	62.8	—
Associate justice, Supreme Court, Place 3	2,008,329	62.9	—
Combined Totals			
U.S. House of Representatives[a] (27 races)	2,819,035	88.3	881,185[a]
Texas state senator[b] (31 races)	2,508,317	78.6	841,909[b]

Source: See Appendix.

[a]Nine of the twenty-seven Congressional seats were uncontested by one of the major parties. The statewide plurality reflects the aggregation of votes in each race as if it were a statewide contest.

[b]Eighteen of the thirty-one State Senate seats were uncontested by one of the major parties. The statewide plurality reflects the aggregation of votes in each race as if it were a statewide contest.

surer, Jim Hightower and Ann Richards, respectively, ran high-profile campaigns with unusual media attention, and their efforts appear to have generated an additional 70,000 to 150,000 votes.

Towards the bottom of Table 3–4, an instructive exercise combines the state's twenty-seven races for Congress and thirty-one races for State Senate, as if these races were statewide races conducted on partisan lines. In practice, a third of all congressmen and over half of all state senators campaign without major party opposition. Tactically, these are unwinnable elections for the opposition, due to the makeup of the district or the prominence of the winning candidate. Strategically, this may be unwise, especially for the Republican party. Contested races for Congress attract 16% more votes than uncontested races, while contested races for State Senate attract 25% more votes. Very nominal costs are involved in fielding a "stalking-horse" candidate who, with no attempt to campaign, might reasonably be expected to generate a 20% share of the vote.

Yet what is merely a maneuver to reduce the mandate of an otherwise invincible candidate points up the indiscipline of Texas parties. For disciplined parties, there is a moral obligation to provide voters with an alternative. And there is a combative reason to demonstrate to opponents the limits of their support. Lacking such discipline, politicians focus on the winning of individual elections and are ill-disposed to a hopeless cause.

Specific political circumstances in postwar Texas further attenuated party loyalties and enhanced personal campaigns. Sharp hostility to the domestic programs of the New Deal forced a cleavage in the Texas Democratic party. At issue was support or nonsupport for presidential nominees in the four national elections between 1944 and 1956. Liberal and conservative groups, respectively, aligned themselves as supporters or opponents of presidential candidates. On one level, this factionalism reflected idealogical, economic-based issues.[16] On the more political level, this intraparty factionalism allowed individual candidates considerable latitude to tailor their appeals either to voters directly or to designated interest and constituency groups.

In turn, these personal appeals were consonant with a grass-roots reliance on personal networks, personal intelligence, and face-to-face contacts, as Anthony Champagne has convincingly demonstrated for the case of Sam Rayburn, who in nonelectoral politics remains the exemplar of party unity and discipline.[17]

The High-Visibility Campaign   There are few obvious distinctions between the partisan and the highly personal campaign. A personal campaign nonetheless introduces a quite different set of voter attractions to mobilize Texans, especially when individual campaigns can be rendered highly visible. In this regard, the impacts of campaign expenditures and use of the mass media may play a material role in attracting voters to the polls.

At some point, personal appeals to the voters so overwhelm party loyalties that party affiliation itself becomes a tactical choice in an individual's campaign strategy. For Phil Gramm, who switched parties midstream in 1983, this is surely the case, although one might convincingly argue that his congressional district in 1983 and prospective voters in his 1984 senatorial campaign shared much of the doctrinal zeal of the recent convert. The fate of John Connally, on the other hand, serves as a counterexample. His change of parties was never accepted; indeed, the act of conversion compromised the integrity of his earlier efforts. Thus while Connally's gubernatorial years suggest an enlightened Democratic administration, conventional opinion views him as a life-long Tory whose personal ambitions overtook the sensibilities of party.

Campaign expenditures offer a useful barometer of degrees of party organization. The costs of mounting an individual appeal to the voters will likely exceed the costs of mounting a campaign grounded in party affiliation and party loyalty. In the former case, an individual candidate must establish recognition and credentials with the voters; in the latter case, a candidate's party affiliation provides identification and support.

Table 3–5 examines campaign expenditures in congressional races in Texas and five similar polities. Conventional wisdom is confirmed: Texas campaigns are highly expensive. But comparative data suggest expenditures are comparable to polities with well-organized party systems.

The state's diverse media markets are frequently cited as a cause of high campaign expenditure. Excepting Florida, the major media markets in the states examined in Table 3–5 are more expensive than Texas markets. Texas media markets are reasonably well targeted. Unlike New Jersey, which lacks major media markets and must rely on New York or Philadelphia advertisers, Texas markets are focused towards potential voters.

Unique electoral conditions can occasion dramatically high costs: thus, the most expensive California campaign involved a popular incumbent, unfairly dislodged from renomination, who waged a successful write-in campaign. The most expensive Texas elections involve either closely contested elections, sharp intraparty competition in primaries, or nationally targeted races to dislodge a powerful incumbent.

People in Texas frequently expect personal appeals for their votes, a tradition dating back to an era where a candidate would go from farm to farm soliciting votes.[18] The modern equivalent of these appeals is the phone bank, where volunteers telephone potential sup-

Table 3–5. Campaign Expenditures in Congressional Elections: A Comparison of Six States.

Spending		Texas	California	Florida	Illinois	Pennsylvania	New York
		Combined Spending in Primary and General Elections in a District					
Average	1982	$ 517,818	$ 566,101	$ 419,863	$ 407,758	$ 362,710	$ 281,259
	1980	462,360	360,459	238,827	246,728	235,246	227,386
In Middle Five Districts	1982	386,794	387,121	387,681	302,650	288,243	180,376
	1980	237,248	191,528	219,633	160,743	161,025	120,670
In Highest Five Districts	1982	1,039,637	1,898,765	823,717	845,433	789,425	703,767
	1980	1,264,389	1,383,324	424,518	700,268	539,452	692,233
In Lowest Five Districts	1982	93,368	51,406	70,017	138,582	71,159	49,155
	1980	61,483	47,134	72,322	58,815	60,097	23,139
Range	1982	1,595,066– 66,571	3,159,674– 27,679	1,237,254– 52,322	1,583,905– 49,969	1,160,999– 51,998	880,187– 28,543
	1980	1,901,431– 21,215	2,506,524– 30,693	540,867– 52,321	1,205,542– 26,664	645,927– 23,719	1,158,186– 14,669

Source: Based on data provided in Michael Barone and Grant Ujifusa, *The Almanac of American Politics 1984* (Washington, D.C.: National Journal, 1983); and idem, *The Almanac of American Politics 1982* (Washington, D.C.: Barone and Company, 1981).

porters requesting a vote for a candidate or on an issue. Phone banks and mass-mailing campaigns can, in turn, be finely tuned to reach citizens who are especially disposed to a candidate's position on special issues.

Texas remains one of the few states where major cities retain highly competitive newspapers. Its television and radio markets are equally competitive. This competition need not lead to enhanced coverage of campaign issues, although quality competition among Dallas newspapers has resulted in extensive political coverage.

Two successful campaigns during the 1982 election demonstrate that a traditional effort to reach voters through media news coverage remains a lively possibility. Jim Hightower's race for agriculture commissioner capitalized on his colorful rhetoric and on the promotion of fresh issues, while Ann Richards' campaign for treasurer successfully addressed personal attacks against her while further proposing reforms to modernize a rather somnambulent state bureaucracy.

While the rise of political marketing and expensive new techniques have increased the cost of elections, Table 3–5 does suggest that commentators may be exaggerating the degree to which campaign expenditures in Texas are appreciably higher than campaigns in comparable states. Higher expenditures in Texas and California may result from high rates of mobility and the influx of new voters, and from the relative lack of public places (such as main streets) where candidates can appeal directly to voters.

To summarize: More Texans are voting, especially in general elections. Turnout began rising well before statewide restrictions on voting were eliminated and compensatory registration campaigns were undertaken. A substantial number of voters vote the party ticket. Substantial differences in pluralities in any election encourage vigorous campaigning. This incentive is unusually strong in competitive elections. Campaign expenditures in Texas are high and are at least partially effective in mobilizing citizens to vote.

The Urban Presence in Texas Politics

Important developments in Texas politics have accompanied the dramatic transformations of the state's major cities into sprawling, economically dynamic, self-sustaining conurbations. What were once regional commercial centers dependent on the economy of the rural hinterland are today international centers of high technology, fashion, services, and culture. The accompanying sophistication of residents has generated in turn new expectations and demands which the state's home-style politics may be ill-equipped to satisfy.

Approximately 40% of all citizens live in the Houston and Dallas-Fort Worth metropolitan areas. Add San Antonio and Austin and, as is illustrated in Table 3–6, a near majority of Texans are concentrated in 11 of the state's 254 counties. Commonly, urban residents are less inclined to vote, but as the table indicates, urban turnouts are occasionally higher than an area's share of the state population.

Table 3–6. The Urban Presence in Texas Politics.

County	% of State Population	% of Votes 1980 Election	% of Votes 1982 Election
Harris (Houston)	16.93	15.85	14.90
Dallas	10.94	11.36	10.84
Tarrant (Fort Worth)	6.05	6.71	6.68
Bexar (San Antonio)	6.95	6.81	6.20
Travis (Austin)	2.95	3.51	3.87
Houston Metro counties: Brazoria, Fort Bend Galveston, Montgomery	3.86	4.15	4.28
Dallas Metro counties: Collin, Denton	2.02	2.27	2.29
Total	49.70	50.66	49.06

Source: See Appendix.

As was true nationally, Texas legislators resisted efforts to redistrict in order to balance a sharply increasing urban population, and they continue to gerrymander electoral districts to enhance what remains of the rural base. Urban legislators, in this view, promote state expenditures to relieve a host of urban problems: public housing, hospitals, traffic congestion, inadequate schools and universities, and so on.

By the same token, a tacit quid pro quo has emerged between state and municipal officials along the lines of "You don't bother us; we won't bother you." As a result, Texas municipalities have been granted remarkable autonomy, while state government has not been pressed to establish large-scale urban programs.

Where Northern cities served as beacons of liberalism, Texas cities have become centers of conservatism, which are as restrictive of government activities as their rural counterparts. Thus even before the emergence of the modern Republican party, the "shopkeeper mentality" of Texas cities favored conservative Democrats.[19]

Northern city politics continues to retain the basic Rooseveltian urban coalition which linked significant portions of a city's intellectual and "old wealth" establishments with well-organized ethnic minorities and blue-collar workers. This assured both the coherent articulation of problems and the presence of a bloc of voters who could be mobilized behind an issue.

Texas cities, by contrast, only began to grow when both Northern cities and urban coalitions were in decline. Where Northern cities such as New York, Philadelphia, and Chicago lost 9% to 15% of their population during the 1960s and '70s, Houston, Dallas, and San Antonio, respectively, grew 70.02%, 33.01%, and 33.74%. This growth came during eras when it was difficult to align heterogeneous groups in an issue-based coalition: minority groups sought to preserve their autonomy; single-issue groups discovered greater opportunities in promoting their causes independent of party; workers were either unaffiliated with unions or detached from the union movement.

Municipal and school board elections are nonpartisan and are scheduled not to coincide with statewide or national general elections. This reform measure, intended originally to remove local government from politics, has had the desired effect: party organizations suspend efforts, such that turnout in municipal elections is chronically low; 20% is considered a remarkable turnout. Major multiyear school district bond elections can often attract 6% or 7% of potential voters even in upper-middle-class jurisdictions.

Instead, chambers of commerce or self-selected citizens' committees have retained much of the power they first accumulated in the 1920s and '30s without significant concessions to neighborhood and ethnic groups. Yet one can readily exaggerate the vise imposed by business-dominated elites in Texas cities, especially on nonmunicipal issues. City governance is less a machine and more a philanthropy of business elites. Thus it has been relatively easy for both Republicans and progressive Democrats to attract voters in the major cities.

This leads to the vital implication of the urban presence in Texas politics, illustrated in Table 3–7. In each of the fifteen elections examined over the 1976–82 period, Republican candidates derived a majority of their votes from eleven urban counties in four metropolitan areas. Yet in these same elections, Democratic candidates also derived 40% to 50% of their votes from these counties.

The operative strategy for both parties is to concentrate resources in the major metropolitan counties. For Republicans, this strategy is crucial, as Table 3–7 attests. Of the three victories, Republicans in two contests, the 1978 gubernatorial and 1978 senatorial, required urban county majorities to offset Democratic majorities in

Table 3–7. Urban County Share of Statewide Vote in Selected Elections.

Year	Race	Party/Candidate	Harris County	Houston Metro Counties	Dallas County	D-FW Tarrant County	Metro Counties	Bexar County	Travis County	Total % 11 Urban Counties	Plurality in Urban Counties	Statewide Plurality
							% Share of Statewide Vote						
1984	President	D (Mondale)	17.1	4.4	10.4	6.1	1.6	7.0	2.3	48.9		
		R (Reagan)	15.6	4.6	11.8	7.2	3.3	5.9	3.6	52.0	R-833,560	R-1,484,152
	Senator	D (Doggett)	16.7	4.5	10.4	6.2	1.8	6.9	5.3	51.8		
		R (Gramm)	15.9	4.4	11.9	7.3	3.4	5.8	3.3	52.0	R-489,957	R-908,791
1982	Governor	D (White)	14.2	4.4	9.1	6.4	1.7	5.9	4.2	45.9		
		R (Clements)	15.8	4.1	12.8	7.1	2.9	6.6	3.4	52.7	D-7,792	D-231,993
	U.S. Senate	D (Bentsen)	14.9	4.2	8.3	6.3	1.7	6.2	4.5	46.1		
		R (Collins)	15.8	4.2	11.6	7.4	3.2	6.2	3.3	51.5	D-190,506	D-561,464
	Lt.Governor	D (Hobby)	13.4	3.8	9.5	6.5	1.9	6.0	4.4	45.3		
		R (Strake)	17.3	4.1	12.9	6.7	2.9	6.4	3.3	53.6	D-146,537	D-558,226
	Attorney-Gen.	D (Mattox)	13.7	4.0	8.9	5.7	1.7	5.9	4.2	48.1		
		R (Meier)	15.8	4.6	14.1	8.1	2.2	6.3	3.5	54.6	D-126,917	D-584,110
1980	President	D (Carter)	14.5	3.9	10.1	6.4	1.7	7.3	4.0	47.9		
		R (Reagan)	16.6	4.3	12.2	6.9	2.6	6.4	2.9	51.9	R-400,622	R-629,558
	Railroad Comm.	D (Temple)	13.5	3.9	8.7	6.3	1.7	7.1	4.2	45.4		
		R (Grover)	18.2	5.6	13.3	6.9	3.1	6.7	3.0	56.8	R-61,922	D-300,522
1978	Governor	D (Hill)	14.9	3.6	8.8	5.7	1.4	6.8	4.0	45.3		
		R (Clements)	16.9	5.1	12.3	5.8	2.3	7.0	3.9	53.8	R-66,369	R-16,908
1976	President	D (Carter)	15.5	4.1	9.4	5.9	1.6	7.0	3.6	47.1		
		R (Ford)	18.3	4.0	13.5	6.4	2.2	6.2	4.0	54.6	R-73,979	D-129,019

Source: See Appendix.

Note: Harris County includes Houston, Tarrant, includes Fort Worth and Arlington; Bexar includes San Antonio; Travis includes Austin. Houston Metro Counties are Brazoria, Fort Bend, Galveston and Montgomery. Dallas-Fort Worth Metro Counties are Collin and Denton.

the rest of the state. In 1980, almost two-thirds of Reagan's plurality derived from eleven urban counties. Because Republicans in the short term cannot develop either the organization or the voter support in the bulk of the state, metropolitan areas are vital.

Democrats possess equally strategic reasons for concentrating on metropolitan areas. The City of Dallas and Dallas County are cases in point. Both are regarded as Republican strongholds which only an exceptional candidate, such as Lyndon Johnson or Lloyd Bentsen (in 1982), can carry. Yet there are few areas of Texas where a Democratic candidate can acquire the massive Democratic majorities possible in southern Dallas County precincts. These precincts range demographically from black and Hispanic to working-class and lower-level management neighborhoods. Turnout here varies dramatically, and voting is not automatic. Yet for a modest expenditure on bait, the fishing is extraordinarily good. Table 3–8, part A, shows the distribution of precincts by Republican share of the vote for Dallas and Dallas County in 1982. The fifty-three precincts where Clements received less than 10% of the vote offset North Dallas County precincts with 75% or higher shares of the vote.

Democrats have been inclined to concentrate more resources on Houston and San Antonio and to anticipate a healthy showing in Austin. As Table 3–8, part B, illustrates, in 1982, Democrats were able to make sufficient inroads into the urban Republican strongholds to emerge in the close governor's race with a 7,800 vote plurality in urban counties responsible for 49.07% of the total state.

For both Republicans and Democrats a major prize remains to be caught. The urban areas have been catchments for persons from rural areas and small cities both in Texas and neighboring states. Far removed from the stereotype of the urban cowboy, they are modest homeowners, industrial or clerical workers, church members, and individuals with traditional views on the more controversial valence issues. Their turnout in elections has been disproportionately low, especially when compared with demographically similar neighborhoods in the North. Southern Democracy is their natural home, which suggests they could prove amenable to either party.

As success in Texas elections frequently means mobilizing targeted voters favorable to specific candidacies, Texas' urban counties offer high concentrations of potential voters. Resources can be profitably invested in urban areas to attract the marginal voters. And campaign issues will increasingly stress urban issues.

Paradoxically, the more intense urban campaigns become, the more likely elections will be won or lost in rural areas. For today's candidates, rural Texas is a forbidding swamp. Demographics, even

Table 3–8. The Gubernatorial Race in Urban Counties, 1982.

A. % Share of Votes for Clements, Dallas County Precincts

Precinct	% Share of Vote									
	0–10	10–20	20–30	30–40	40–50	50–60	60–70	70–80	80–90	90–100
City of Dallas	51	10	10	26	34	25	34	38	22	1
Other County Cities	2	0	2	7	26	48	39	19	11	2
Total	53	10	12	33	60	73	73	57	33	3

B. Urban County Breakdown

County	Votes Cast	% Share of Vote		Majority
		Rep.	Dem.	
Harris	471,324	49.02	50.98	D- 9,234
Dallas	342,993	54.71	45.29	R- 32,319
Tarrant	211,472	48.94	51.06	D- 4,470
Bexar	196,331	49.12	50.88	D- 3,449
Travis	122,559	41.13	58.87	D-23,739
Houston Metro	135,381	49.55	50.45	D-14,769
Dallas Metro	72,438	59.35	40.65	R- 13,550
Total	1,552,498	49.75	50.25	D- 7,792

Source: See Appendix.

voting trends, are elusive and defy generalization. Prosperity and poverty, economic booms and busts, may depend on highly particularistic conditions within county lines. Counties with very similar conditions can diverge sharply on partisan lines in statewide or national elections. Candidates are tempted to wrap up their campaigns early in rural areas to focus on the major cities, as both Lloyd Doggett and Phil Gramm did in the 1984 election campaign where personal appearances in rural areas virtually ceased after Labor Day. Yet Mark White in the 1982 governor's race picked up 96% of his plurality from East and Central Texas rural counties where turnouts were 25%, even 50% higher than in the 1978 election, a clear indication of rural counties' potential importance.

The Hispanic Challenge

The political situation of Texas Hispanics can be catalogued into three categories: (1) a group of twenty South Texas counties paralleling the

Rio Grande River with substantial Hispanic majorities;[20] (2) the numerically larger Hispanic concentrations in San Antonio, Houston, El Paso, and other Texas cities such as Corpus Christi, where a modicum of political power is possible; (3) a vast crescent-shaped band of counties extending from the High Plains southeastward to the coastal plains north of the Valley.

South Texas counties contain some of the highest proportions of Hispanics in the nation as well as some of the very lowest per capita incomes. At the time of the 1982 election, average weekly wages in the most populous of the counties, Hidalgo, were 51.1% of wages in Houston.[21] Poverty and discrimination should naturally favor the Democrats, who indeed win most elections in the region. Nonetheless, the Republicans routinely receive between 20% of the votes in the barren counties of the Upper Valley to 40% in the populated Lower Valley. Even absolute numbers of voting-age Anglos fall short of Republican returns, indicating that a substantial number of Mexican-Americans vote Republican.

A possible explanation is that Mexican-Americans when they achieve a modicum of economic security and comfort (what was signaled among Boston's Irish as putting up lace curtains in the window) are prepared to switch political allegiances. Values stressing the cohesiveness of the family, hard work and entrepreneurship, the stigma of welfare (values common among Mexican-Americans) are frequent themes of Republican domestic policy.

Alternatively, Hispanic Republicanism might be viewed as a protest vote against the entrenched patronal politics of South Texas machines. Their votes register disaffection with local bosses who have delivered few programmatic benefits to South Texas, allowing the region to stagnate into one of America's worst pockets of poverty. A reformed, open Democratic party might readily recapture these votes.

The strategic opportunity for Republicans is to cut Democratic majorities in South Texas and to force the Democrats to divert resources to campaign efforts in the Valley. A rather intensive Democratic effort was needed in the 1982 election to yield a 66–34 split in South Texas. Reagan in 1980 received 43.75% of the South Texas vote, losing by 21,000 votes to Carter. If El Paso with its Hispanic majority is added to South Texas, the Republicans virtually break even, losing by 8,100 votes out of 292,000 votes cast.

Yet few areas of the country have experienced such extreme economic crises in recent years. The swinging devaluation of the Mexican peso eliminated much of the transborder commerce between American retailers and Mexican customers. It similarly created dramatic wage differentials, making it suddenly attractive for workers in Matamoros to seek jobs in Brownsville, thus demoralizing labor markets with traditionally high rates of unemployment. A severe freeze during 1983–84 devastated citrus production, with full recovery taking several years.

South Texas also serves as a microcosm of the undocumented aliens issue and current efforts to restrict Mexican immigration. Ambivalence understates the wide emotional swings of opinion a Mexican-American is likely to feel. Proximity and free passage made it possible for generations to maintain extended families on both sides of the border, while discriminatory practices and harsh living conditions vitiated the desire to establish permanent residence and citizenship.[22] Thus an attempt arbitrarily to superimpose an international frontier cuts directly into family relations. Yet Mexican-Americans are most directly affected by an inexhaustible pool of Mexican workers competing for jobs and possible depressing wages. Ethnic pride and feelings of being part of a targeted group further heighten emotions.

The largest concentrations of Hispanics reside in the San Antonio, Houston, and El Paso areas, respectively. As Table 3–9 illustrates, half the Hispanic population resides in Texas cities where Anglo or Anglo-black influence will frequently prevail. As was true in South Texas, an emerging middle class of Mexican-Americans, still choosing to live in a *barrio*, may switch political allegiances.

Collective action by Hispanics has assumed the form of Saul Alinsky-style neighborhood organization, which were goal-oriented movements with specifically defined objectives. Thus it is possible that the long-term, open-ended commitment blacks made to the Democratic party may not be repeated among Hispanics. Individual politicians may arise and party organization may be established in Hispanic neighborhoods. But a well-oiled party machine is unlikely.

The moderate 20% to 30% concentrations of Hispanics in sixty lightly populated Plains counties from Amarillo to Corpus Christi add another dimension to the situation. Here, Hispanics work on farms and ranches, as rail and oil production workers, in jobs for which they have been specifically recruited over the past century.[23] Economic realities rather than community affiliations account for their continuing presence, a fact that is likely to encourage disinterest in politics.

The Partisan Dilemma

Political parties and public policymakers share a common imperative: to succeed each must propose and then promote an articulate phi-

Table 3–9. Distribution of Hispanic Population, 1980.

	% of Hispanic Population
Counties with Hispanic Majorities	
El Paso	10.0
Hidalgo (McAllen)	7.8
Cameron (Brownsville)	5.4
Webb (Laredo)	3.0
Other South Texas	7.0 (33.7)
Counties with Large Hispanic Concentrations	
Bexar (San Antonio)	15.5
Harris (Houston)	12.3
Dallas	5.2
Nueces (Corpus Christi)	4.4
Travis (Austin)	2.4
Tarrant (Fort Worth)	2.3
Rest of the State	24.2

Source: U.S. Bureau of the Census, *1980 Census of Population*, Volume 1, Chapter C, *General Social and Economic Characteristics*, Part 45, *Texas* (Washington: Government Printing Office, 1983):Table 59, 59–86.

losophy and plan for the long haul that is so attractive and compelling as to override temporary setbacks. Pragmatism and compromise may be the warp and woof of politics, but one will never laud parties of policymakers for blundering into dead ends or frequently executing U-turns. Where the two are allied, as with the New Deal coalition stretching from the 1930s to the 1960s, fundamental changes can be made deliberately in the American polity and society. Where the two simultaneously lack coherence, our collective sense of purpose evaporates.

So far, we have seen that Hispanics have not been mustered into a front-line division of the Democratic party. Concentration on urban issues and urban elections risks both parties' capacities to mobilize the rural vote where statewide elections are often won. The attractions of party competition, if now underscored by active competition, are lightly established, such that individual campaigns must prod the voter into voting.

The partisan dilemma is this: on the one hand, local Texas conditions provide significant incentives for opportunism by both candidates and parties (this is especially true for future Republican campaigns where further setbacks might undermine the resolve of supporters); on the other hand, for parties to prosper, there must be motives for supporters to back their respective parties through thick and thin. This is rarely accomplished without some, dare we say, ideological impetus. Some set of ideas, some vision, must be articulated to retain the faithful.

Can Texas parties overcome this dilemma? I believe they can.

Republicans

Maury Maverick, Jr., the Democratic sage of San Antonio, recently quipped: "One Republican Party in Texas is fine, but do we really need two Republican Parties?"[24] Indirectly, Maverick captured the fact that Texas Republicans have taken the initiative in Texas politics. In terms of physical strength and sheer numbers, such an assessment is unwarranted. But the Texas Republican party is a party of ideas and ideologies, and on these terms the success has been phenomenal.

Modern Republicanism in Texas began in the revulsion of Texas oil and business magnates with the postwar continuation of the New Deal, and in equal frustration with the guerrilla wars within the Texas Democratic party rendering it ineffective in opposing the slide into "socialism." They consequently diverted monies into toppling the patronage-based Republican machine. In turn, scores of people, many of them women, switched from counterproductive library watchdog committees and community decency campaigns to activities on behalf of a stern, doctrinaire Republican party.

As a spontaneous, ultraconservative movement, party activists of the 1950s and '60s placed some distance between their revolutionary sense of mission and the immediate political fortunes of candidates. Thus, John Tower's surprising election in 1961 did not result in Texas Republicans clutching to the slender reed of a a rare Republican officeholder, but whetted the appetite for larger gains. The party ranked before the individual candidate.

For the average Texas voter, far removed from the River Oaks or Highland Park sitting room where Republican strategy emerged, the 1952 actions of Governor Allan Shivers encouraging cross-voting for Eisenhower most likely broke the hammerlock of one-party politics. Eisenhower, a politically androgynous campaigner of rare appeal to everyone from Roosevelt's three sons to segregationists, encouraged in his campaigns and in his subsequent administrations a spirit of bipartisan cooperation which locally dissolved Democratic loyalties.

Hence, the antecedents of the Republican party of the 1980s invigorated the party with a sense of mission among the legions of true believers, while the mass of less doctrinaire voters found common cause when Democrats from Shivers to Lyndon Johnson celebrated the virtues of bipartisanship.

What, however, constituted Republican ideology and how did it differ from the Democrats? To begin, it reaffirmed unbridled capitalism, the general benefits of business enterprise, the work ethic and the denunciation of government interventions in the economy. Over the years, many Texas Democrats would concur. But the Republicans were able to escape the Democrats' unavoidable involvement in Austin's special-interest politics, which was a necessary price for holding power. Practical affairs forced Democrats to equivocate. In addition, the Republicans were able to embrace a concern for fundamental values, such as issues of family, religion, community morals, and the like. Strong stands on national defense and attacks on the welfare state rounded out the basic program.

Only in the mid-to-late 1970s did the party become an electoral organization. By this I mean nominating and working on behalf of a full slate of Republican candidates, especially for offices at the county level. In 1980, it achieved an exemplary breakthrough in Dallas County where, heavily assisted by straight-ticket voting, it won twelve of fourteen judgeships. Winning elections motivates many citizens who regard politics as a recreational sport, who nevertheless are indispensable workers in partisan campaigns.

Statewide, the party's electoral organization remains embryonic. In West Texas cities like Midland, Odessa, and Amarillo, Republicans are in a position to control county politics. The German Hill Country counties have remained Republican since the Civil War, and Republicanism is creeping back into the North Side neighborhoods of San Antonio, which Harry Wurzbach had represented as a Republican in the 1920s.[25] Dallas County and its suburban neighbor, Collin County, are solidly Republican.

The belated organizational efforts may have been advantageous in the long run. Texans when they do vote Republican may have a clearer sense of the political values they are supporting. The party has etched a distinctive appeal (which undoubtedly accounts for why some candidates during the seventies discreetly left the Republican tag off their advertising).

But to make a significant difference in Texas politics, the party requires an extensive organizational base capable of regularly electing legislators and county officials. Without it, it is unlikely that the Republicans can play more than a nominal role in the state legislature or stand a reasonable chance of seizing the statewide offices which exercise a policy role in the state.

Progressive Democrats

Texas politics has long flourished with two Democratic parties. During the 1940s and '50s, the need for a Democratic State Convention to nominate delegates to the quadrennial national convention provoked major controversies on the issue of the state party's support or nonsupport of the Democratic presidential nominee. As respective positions hardened in the step-up to the convention, ill will and hard feelings accentuated the factionalism. Changes in national party rules have eliminated this bitter confrontation. And with prominent Democrats and loyal financial backers willing to work unstintingly for candidates from either wing of the party, each wing is able to thrive independently.

In virtually all respects (number of congressmen, state senators, and legislators, primary voters, and so on) each wing is larger than the Republican party. Thus even with highly spirited primary campaigns, either wing appears to have the wherewithal to mount an effective challenge to the Republicans. By the same token, a precipitate fusion of the two wings into a unified party might provide defections to the Republicans of graver consequence to the party as a whole.

The term *progressive* is at best a choice among equally misleading labels, and I use it because it appears to be taking hold in recent years. The wing's long-standing affiliations with Liberal Democrats at the national level remain, but it has broadened and adjusted its focus to reflect Texas realities.

Politically, to champion the underdog in Texas means being a friend of family farms, small businesses, and ordinary workers. It means to be opposed to powerful corporations, public utilities, and public officials who cater to powerful special interests. This focus, which is more congenial to Louis Brandeis or Sam Rayburn of the era before World War I, appears anachronistic to non-Texans. Yet it has been continually articulated as the "liberal" view in Texas throughout the century, as if there had never been a Franklin D. Roosevelt.

Progressivism does not prevent embracing contemporary liberal causes, reflected in the wide variety of movements championing the poor, minorities, victims of the moralistic crusades which force puritanical values on the general public, etc. But it is an arms-length commitment, and it is especially qualified in accepting the long-term implications of implementing liberal programs. Thus, one can champion workers protesting practices at a nuclear reactor site without demanding a halt to all reactors. One can fight slum-lords without proposing public housing. Especially can one champion measures that will improve regulation or reform government, while drawing the line at reforming society.

The Progressive appeal is economic and class-based. It targets its appeal to people of modest, but comfortable, means, people who are both consumers and taxpayers. An illustrative proposal is Jim Hightower's idea to promote farm marketing cooperatives to link family farmers and consumers, thereby eliminating the high-cost "middle man." Modest state expenditures are envisioned, and the state's role is restricted to advocacy.

Liberal critics may complain that the state's problems are far more fundamental and involve the need for massive financial infusions into public services. Yet one might argue that Texas liberals have always turned to the federal government and the federal courts to promote their causes. Neither was New Deal liberalism imported for statewide consumption, nor have liberals taken the offensive to demand public programs found in other states.

Liberal Democrats during the factionalist era embraced New Deal rhetoric and forged ties with unions and minorities. What has changed is that the rhetoric has been quietly discarded, while the various constituent groups have seen it to their own advantage to promote goals independently.

Without the rhetoric, Progressives may have chanced upon a formidable coalition. Texas contains a large urban working class that is neither receptive nor hostile to trade unions or poverty programs, but which shares a lively concern about utility bills, traffic congestion, neighborhood preservation, and taxes. It includes large numbers of blacks and minorities, middle-class homeowners, well-educated professionals, and so on. The focus on very concrete issues, such as utility rate increases or property taxes, may have greater appeal than grander speculations about how to eradicate racism or sexism from American society.

Lloyd Doggett's campaign for senator in 1984 is instructive. He is sympathetic towards and received support from all components of the liberal coalition. His State Senate record is more moderate than liberal. Doggett's primary campaigns were fought almost exclusively in the urban areas. In the first primary, he had a majority in only seven counties (versus Hance's ninety-one counties and Krueger's sixteen counties) but had significant pluralities in Harris, Dallas, Tarrant, Galveston, Jefferson, and El Paso counties. In the second primary, he received between 63.4% and 75.1% of the vote in the five principal urban counties, a ninety-nine thousand vote majority, to which he added South Texas victories with a twenty-seven thousand vote majority.

If viewed cautiously, Table 3–10 offers some useful insight. The table merely reflects the winning of elections. Doggett's share of the total vote compares favorably with liberal contenders in classic liberal/conservative elections. With exceptions in Nueces and El Paso counties, Doggett fared remarkably well in urban areas. This contrasts with Yarborough's campaigns of the 1950s in which the liberal strength consisted of an assortment of rural counties, many of which were Populist strongholds in the 1890s.

When we turn to the cities, a more complicated picture emerges. First, Democratic turnout has declined dramatically in urban counties. Despite the 1984 presidential precinct conventions where participation was contingent on voting in the Democratic Primary, turnouts in Dallas and Houston were only 52.4% and 59.1% of the 1978 primary. Second, the growth of the Republican Primary, especially in urban areas where many local races on the Republican side now attract some interest, has discouraged the practice of Republican cross-voting. To some degree, party competition may allow liberal candidates to contest and win Democratic primaries. Up till now, statewide conditions have yet to crystallize, such that Doggett's primary victories appear to reflect a shrewd and successful appeal to "progressives."

Conservative Democrats

It is tempting to suggest that bipartisan politics is beginning to polarize and reconfigure Texas politics along Conservative Republican/Progressive Democrat lines, and that Conservative Democrats, surely the largest bloc, will ultimately be cannibalized. I don't think this is likely to happen.

For most of this century Conservative Democrats have been the state's power brokers. They have voted significant increases in taxes and expenditures, yet their tenure has ensured that the scope of Texas government was restricted to highways and public education. Neither Republicans nor Progressive Democrats have controlled the hundreds of levers of power one must orchestrate to make a difference in Texas government.

The special interest vote and the rural vote will prolong, even enhance, the role of Conservative Democrats. The special interest vote

Table 3–10. Progressive Liberal Pluralities in Selected Democratic Primaries.

	1984 Senatorial		1978 Gubernatorial	1972 Gubernatorial		1958 Senatorial	1954 Gubernatorial
	1st Primary Doggett[a] Hance Krueger %	2nd Primary Hance[a] Doggett %	Hill[a] Brisco %	1st Primary Farenthold[a] Barnes Briscoe Smith %	2nd Primary Farenthold[a] Briscoe %	Yarborough[a] Blakley %	2nd Primary Yarborough[a] Shivers %
Statewide plurality for liberal candidate	31.1	50.1	52.4	27.9	44.7	59.1	46.6
Major urban counties							
Harris (Houston)	46.5	65.3	51.0	43.5	61.2	57.6	46.9
Dallas	44.1	69.4	51.0	30.5	47.0	51.3	40.2
Tarrant (Fort Worth)	42.0	63.4	53.9	30.4	44.6	57.3	45.8
Bexar (San Antonio)	36.1	65.8	59.7	27.0	44.2	58.0	45.0
Travis (Austin)	72.5	75.1	65.0	44.8	48.6	58.5	42.7
El Paso	38.9	54.7	62.5	39.1	61.2	63.5	62.5
Jefferson (Beaumont)[b]	40.9	61.8	53.7	37.8	54.2	61.6	53.7
McLennan (Waco)[c]	37.9	57.9	43.7	24.8	39.4	66.1	53.5
Nueces (Corp.Christi)[c]	35.1	55.1	57.1	45.1	53.2	66.6	50.1
South Texas							
Cameron (Brownsville)	35.3	64.3	57.2	20.1	48.3	48.6	37.6
Hidalgo (McAllen)	48.5	70.6	50.6	26.2	47.0	50.6	35.1
Selected "liberal" rural counties ('57-'62)[d]							
Castro (West Texas)	1.4	8.7	66.8	9.9	28.5	69.8	44.9
Fannin (North)	19.8	38.5	50.6	14.3	30.9	74.1	68.1
Henderson (East)	39.9	60.9	57.2	19.2	37.3	74.5	74.1
Limestone (Central)	29.7	47.7	42.6	10.5	27.2	63.7	59.1
Robertson (Central)	36.6	53.3	54.3	26.1	49.4	70.2	62.6
Trinity (East)	25.3	47.0	57.8	21.3	48.4	68.3	52.9

Source: See Appendix.

Notes: [a]The liberal candidate; [b]Jefferson County has had high levels of union participation and is often a bellwether of trade union support; [c]McLennan and Nueces were cited by Soukup, McCleskey, Holloway, Party and Factional Division in Texas (Austin, 1964) as "More Liberal" refers to the numerous businesses and industries which have come, over the years, to rely on restrictions and regulations to curb full-scale, "cut-throat" competition in the state. Regularly misperceived as powerful interests, most groups, if unregulated, would be both powerless and uncompetitive. The spectrum ranges from independent oil producers who, if unregulated, would succumb to the economics of unitization and controlled production under the aegis of the majors, to barbershop owners and liquor store owners for whom barriers to entry are essential to survival. Like French Conservatives seeking to reverse the inroads of supermarkets and Coca-Cola, Texas Conservative Democrats are charged to hold the line on allowing a free-market economy.

For many Texans engaged in business, the chance to be an entrepreneur depends on state regulation. Unit banking is a case in point. Through the slightly inefficient device of bank holding companies, major banks have, through regulatory interpretation and legislative assent, established the equivalent of branches. But two advantages accrue to the entrepreneur. First, holding companies cannot create new banks. This opens the market to persons prepared to capitalize a new bank. To sustain even modest profits, one must locate the bank at some distance from existing banks. To the degree one can exploit a local monopoly position and generate above-average profits, one's capital investment pays off through the capital gains realized from sale of the bank to a major holding company. In branch-banking states, a well-established oligopoly principle suggests location of branches adjacent to existing banks, initially to tap marginal customers, ultimately to compete for market share. To do so requires considerable financial resources during the initial stages. But absent such backing, established banks, many of which are owned by holding companies, gain added profits because they are spatial monopolies. In short, one has evolved a set of laws favorable to all sorts and conditions of bankers.

To decry economic inefficiencies of government overregulation, as Republicans are prone to do, or to decry corrosive concentrations of power, as Progressive Democrats are prone to do, misses the point: large numbers of Texans, operating what people broadly perceive as constructive businesses, are vitally dependent on state rules and regulations, without which they could barely survive.

Rural districts remain Conservative Democratic strongholds. They retain continuity with the governing Democratic party. Personal networks of friends, face-to-face campaigning, and detachment on issues create a formidable defense against Republican and Progressive inroads.

Table 3–11. Hance's Dominance in Rural Counties, 1984.

Percent share of vote for Hance	Counties	
	1st primary (3-way race)	2nd primary (2-way race)
90–96	16	25
80–90	11	37
70–80	19	36
60–70	22	39
50–60	24	39

Source: See Appendix.

Yet there is great instability within the Democratic majority. Turnout can vary significantly and this can frequently result in fluctuating margins. Thus, for example, in the 1982 gubernatorial election, turnout in thirty-nine counties was 50% higher than 1978, while in eighty-six counties it was 25% or more higher. While two counties swung into the Republican column, party share increases in the remaining counties ranged upward to 20%.

The strength of rural conservatives was reconfirmed in the 1984 Democratic senatorial primaries where Kent Hance, congressman for the West Texas 19th District, defeated the front-runner, Bob Krueger, and ran neck-and-neck in both primaries with Lloyd Doggett. Table 3–11 summarizes his strength. An 80% share, even in a two-way race is remarkable. Hance carried his congressional district with no county share below 80.5%. Hance's first primary majorities focused on West Texas, with only two majority counties, Rockwall and Fannin, east of the 98° meridian. Yet he ran first in much of East Texas in the first primary and carried the bulk of nonurban East Texas in the runoff against Doggett.

The 1984 Landslide

In 1984, Ronald Reagan carried Texas with 63.6% of the vote, a majority slightly larger than Johnson's in 1964 but lower than Nixon's in 1972. What happened to the rest of the ticket told a more important story. Republican Phil Gramm defeated Doggett in the senatorial race with a 58.6% majority. Republicans won ten of the twenty-seven congressional seats, a net gain of four. Substantial gains were made in the Texas House, while at the county level straight Republican tickets were elected. Even many Democratic survivors encountered unusually intense opposition for the first time.

As noted above, a realignment has been under way in Texas for some time, characterized by *both* a more organizationally effective Republican party and renewed vigor in the Democrats' liberal wing. This is a gradual process, and one should not expect a single election to alter decisively the political situation.

This being said, the 1984 election raises interesting speculations. Rarely has there been such a coherent contrast between parties at the top of the ticket: Ronald Reagan and Phil Gramm share a political affinity uncommon in Republican ranks while Lloyd Doggett endorsed a liberalism approaching Walter Mondale's own. This established a clear-cut polarity, reducing the ambivalences and cross-pressures common between national and state tickets. In many congressional districts, local congressional candidates, especially on the Republican side, reinforced the respective parties' positions. This created a "surge effect" where the combined appeal of major candidates reinforced the partisanship of the election.

A barometer of this surge effect was straight-ticket voting. In Dallas County, for example, 51% of all ballots cast were straight-ticket votes, in themselves giving Republican candidates a fifty-two thousand vote lead. This understates the possible partisanship of voters as excluded are those who vote individually for each candidate, but whose choices preponderantly favor one party. Conventional wisdom in Texas since the 1950s has emphasized ticket-splitting in the belief that conservatives don't hew to the party line, but favor individual candidacies. Straight-ticket voters were pervasive: in only 19 of Dallas County's 411 precincts did the percentage of straight-ticket ballots drop below 40%, thus suggesting a phenomenon that crossed socioeconomic lines.

The immediate beneficiaries of the landslide are Conservative Democrats who claim that they represent the crucial swing between success and failure. They argue that when leadership positions are filled with more conservative candidates, the Democratic party can break the contagion of Republicanism. The Republican party, by contrast, perceives itself as organizationally overextended, lacking the grass-roots organization in nonmetropolitan counties and the financial wherewithal to underwrite only a limited number of strategically significant races. Given the state of partisan flux, even the Progressive Democrats can claim certain gains. Liberal Democrats have always required modest sufferance by Conservative Democrats; but as 1982 proved, they are electable and do add leavening and untapped resources to the Democratic fold. In addition, when conservative Democrats were pitted against Republican challengers in 1984, the results were rather unpromising for the long run: their majorities were eroded, while in many instances they suffered embarrassing defeats.

As a result of 1984, the Republican party is no longer a Texas aberration where a handful of candidates win because of their individual appeal and finances or the tactical mistakes of their opponents. In much of the state, the Republican party is a viable alternative whereby ambitious women and men can rise to judgeships, commissionerships, and beyond. In some counties, such as Dallas County, it is possibly the only route to success. Thus a more talented pool of potential Republican candidates is likely to emerge in the years ahead. By the same token, the Democrats still hold a strong majority of supporters capable of reversing present trends in 1988 and 1990. The landslide heightened the electoral stakes for the Democrats who must re-establish bases in natural constituencies, notably blue-collar and rural districts which have now proven vulnerable to Republican inroads.

This sets the stage for a more fundamental challenge. While the 1984 election was an impressive Republican victory, it hardly altered the challenges posed by a more "democratic" Texas, ready to promote individual issues and candidates. It has been a century since Texas experienced similar flux in its electorate and partisan programs, equally as long since its citizens were as efficacious and participatory in electoral politics. Where does this lead?

The New Populism and Public Policy

The contemporary party system in Texas seems to offer a rich menu of choices to voters. Individual candidates can further modulate their campaigns to targeted groups of voters, thereby enhancing the prospects that key issues will be decided through elections. Citizens unintendedly benefit from an anachronistic, hyperspecific state constitution which virtually assures that a significant change in any area of public policy requires voter approval of a constitutional amendment.

This sanguine view presumes that public initiatives extend "from the top down," that is, that policymakers and elected officials continue to control the policy agenda. Voters have gained wider choice among candidates, more sharply focused choices as a result of more partisan elections, and more frequent choices on specific issues because of the obligatory bond and constitutional elections. These added opportunities help to legitimize public policy, and this in itself is an important democratic objective.

But a "bottom-up" perspective is equally consistent with the trends cited in this chapter. This perspective emphasizes the romantic revolt of the 1960s and '70s in which widespread disaffection with governance caused people to repudiate their leaders' programs and to seize the policymaking initiative. The success of that revolt was hardly a systematic overhaul of the American polity, but due rather to the ability of single-issue organizations to change, often very dramatically, the direction of specific public policy initiatives. What's most material, perhaps, is the ability to hold elected officials accountable for their actions on highly sensitive policy concerns.

Texas' elected officials and policymakers have been curiously reticent in trying to defuse single-policy initiatives. For example, confronted with strong protests to the inclusion of evolutionary biology and sex education in state-approved and -financed high school textbooks, protests sharply corroborated by opinion polls, it is somewhat surprising that officials failed to embrace local community adoption procedures whereby local school boards freely chose textbooks. Such a position is, respectively, conservative, consonant with Reagan administration policies, and politically serendipitous in removing a volatile issue from the statewide agenda. One must reckon that many politicians found it more attractive to force the liberal/conservative dichotomy to mobilize extreme voters to the respective partisan causes. But this strategy enhances the chances for single-issue organizations to emerge as "veto groups," that is, groups able to veto specific policy initiatives while failing to provide feasible alternatives.

At a deeper level, the rise of the single-issue organization registers the increasing importance of valence issues, issues of fundamental moral and ethical value. These issues cannot be dismissed as anachronistic, traditional residues, for they especially appear to surface among people and groups whose fundamentalism specifically denies traditional organizational ties. At the same time, they effectively challenge scientific rationalism, the conformity of expert opinion unaccustomed to having its findings challenged.

Perhaps the most consequential challenge consists of an electorate's ability to change its mind. As the authors of this volume demonstrate, substantive public policy initiatives increasingly oblige a long-term, systematic commitment to specific programs. First initiatives must be reinforced, resources must be concentrated and sustained for the long haul. But people can change their minds, indeed are likely to change their minds when initial soundings suggest a program is less desirable than the program originally promoted. Texas' more competitive political environment can readily exploit these changes of mind to electoral advantage. In doing so, they may correctly register democratic wishes, for people are quite voluble and emotional about their concerns, thereby defying the rational self-interest assumed as fundamental by policymakers.

It is vital to emphasize that this New Populism is quite rational. Appeals to rhetoric to change minds, after all, are part and parcel of most policy campaigns to "educate" the public. The virtue of "veto groups" reflects a longstanding American preoccupation with the problems of majority tyranny. Support of basic values is both compatible with a need to satisfy human wants and consonant with efforts to create a better civic community. Where one can correctly challenge the New Populism is on issues of contemporary materiality and significance, to wit: "Is what you value today likely to matter or to make any difference over the next ten or twenty years?" Yet this is a challenge few policymakers are equipped to undertake.

Thus the problem: Texas' public agenda consists of broad economic and social programs where the role of government is clearly established and where extensive initiatives are required to meet economic and social needs. This agenda may not be the same as the democratic polity's. The latter may be more individualistic, program-specific, value-oriented, and volatile. At the very least, it can restrict the maneuverability of policymakers to shape effective public policies. More seriously, through its political ability to veto initiatives and by its readiness to change its mind, a democratic polity can reduce policymaking to a pattern of drift.

These mixed blessings of democracy must be countered by some positive outcomes. Electoral choices for Texans have expanded dramatically. It appears that Texans in their voting behavior are increasingly willing to make those choices. Partisanship has increased, and with it, more sharply delineated issues. And through these developments, a most important consequence: Texans who previously regarded their politics as an important though immaterial game, like Friday night football, are discovering that it both behooves and benefits them to take their politics more seriously.

Appendix: Data Sources

The election data analyzed in all non-documented tables were drawn from results published biennially in the *Texas Almanac* (Dallas: A.H. Belo Corporation, 1922 to present). Data for the 1982 and 1984 elections were drawn from tallies printed in the *Dallas Morning News* and the *Austin American-Statesman* one or two days after each primary or general election. The results will differ slightly from official results available from the Office of the Secretary of the State, primarily because of the exclusion of minor candidates with less than 1% of the vote. The results will also differ from Numan V. Bartley and Hugh D. Graham, *Southern Elections: County and Precinct Data, 1950–1972* (Baton Rouge: Louisiana State University Press, 1978), and from Alexander Heard and Donald S. Strong, *Southern Primaries and Elections, 1920–1948* (University: University of Alabama Press, 1950). Both of these studies exclude candidates which have been included in this study's data set. The differences between the various data sets are modest.

Editions of the *Texas Almanac* before 1966 reported statistics of the "Estimated Qualified Electorate" based on poll tax payments and exemptions. These were used in compiling Figure 3–1. Population estimates for this figure were drawn from U.S. Bureau of the Census, *Historical Statistics of the United States* (Washington, D.C.: 1975), p. 35 with a straightline extrapolation for non-census years. Population data for 1980 were drawn from U.S. Bureau of the Census, *1980 Census of Population*, Volume 1, *Characteristics of the Population*, Part 45. *Texas* (Washington, D.C., 1983), Tables 56, 57, 59 and 62.

Notes

1. A phrase first applied to the Jeffersonian Era. See James Sterling Young, *The Washington Community, 1800–28* (New York: Columbia University Press, 1966), 13.

2. T. R. Fehrenbach, *Seven Keys to Texas* (El Paso: Texas Western Press, 1983), 92–93.

3. This point was suggested in an important paper, John Kincaid, James L. Danielson, and John R. Todd, "The Politics of Acquiring Citizen Control of a New Residential Development: The Colony, Texas," Department of Political Science, North Texas State University (1983).

4. Specific sections of the Texas Constitution pertaining to elections include Art. 3, secs. 3, 4, 27, 48d, 52d, 52e, 63, 64; Art. 4, secs. 2, 3, 16, 22, 23; Art. 5, secs. 2, 4, 6, 7, 9, 15, 18, 20, 21, 23, 49b, 49c, 49d, 49d-1, 50a, 50b, 50c, 51a, 51d; Art. 6, secs. 1, 2, 3, 4; Art. 7, secs. 3, 8; Art. 8, secs. 9, 14, 16, 16a; Art. 9, secs. 2, 4, 9, 12; Art. 11, secs. 5, 7, 11; Art. 12, secs. 6a, 20, 20b, 20c, 23, 30, 44; Art. 17, sec. 1.

5. Texas *Constitution*, Art. 3, sec. 51: "The Legislature shall have no power to make any grant or authorize the making of any grant of public moneys to any individual, association of individuals, municipal or other corporations whatsoever."

6. Fehrenbach, 75–77.

7. To illustrate: Plano is a suburban city with a population of 72,331. To allow 1% of residents ten minutes a year to express their views would require a weekly meeting of slightly over 2 hours. To allow 5% of residents equivalent voice would each week consume over 11.5 hours of council time.

8. A short biographical sketch of Orrville Bullington, the Republican candidate, is provided in Eldon Stephen Brands, ed., *The Handbook of Texas: A Supplement, Volume III* (Austin: Texas State Historical Association, 1976), 123.

9. A good survey is Everett Carl Ladd, *Where Have the Voters Gone?* (New York: W. W. Norton & Company, 1982).

10. See *Statistical Abstract of the United States, 1976, 1979, and 1983* (Washington, D. C.: Government Printing Office), 369, 513, and 491 respectively.

11. See the annotation for Art. 6, sec. 1 in the copy of the Texas Constitution printed in *The Texas Almanac, 1984–85* (Dallas: A. H. Belo Corporation, 1983), 504.

12. Wilbourn E. Benton, *Texas: Its Government and Politics*, 4th ed., (Englewood Cliffs, N. J.: Prentice-Hall, 1977), 56–57.

13. See Lawrence D. Rice, *The Negro in Texas, 1874–1900* (Baton Rouge: Louisiana State University Press, 1971):34–52.

14. V. O. Key, *A Primer of Statistics for Political Scientists* (New York: Thomas Y. Crowell, 1956), 40.

15. David F. Prindle, *Petroleum Politics and the Texas Railroad Commission* (Austin: University of Texas Press, 1981), ch. 8.

16. See V. O. Key, *Southern Politics in the State and Nation* (New York: Alfred A. Knopf, 1949), 254.

17. Anthony Champagne, *Congressman Sam Rayburn* (New Brunswick, N. J.: Rutgers University Press, 1984), 162–63, and ch. 3.

18. A good description of this style of campaigning is presented in Robert A. Caro, *The Years of Lyndon Johnson: The Path to Power* (New York: Alfred A. Knopf, 1982), 389–436.

19. See James R. Soukup, Clifton McCleskey, and Harry Holloway, *Party and Factional Divisions in Texas* (Austin: University of Texas Press, 1964), 100–108.

20. The counties moving southeast to northwest up the Valley are Cameron (Brownsville), Hidalgo (McAllen), Willacy, Kenedy, Kleburg, Brooks, Jim Wells, Duval, Jim Hogg, Starr, Zapata, Webb (Laredo), LaSalle, Dimmit, Frio, Zavala, Maverick, Uvalde, Kinney, and Val Verde. Note that four West Texas counties including El Paso also had Hispanic majorities in 1980.

21. Texas Employment Commission, *Covered Employment and Wages by Industry and County*, 4th quarter, 1982 (Austin: 1983), 20.

22. A most useful discussion of the historical background is Mario T. Garcia, *Desert Immigrants: The Mexicans of El Paso, 1880–1920* (New Haven: Yale University Press, 1981).

23. See Carey McWilliams, *North from Mexico: The Spanish Speaking People of the United States* (New York: Greenwood Press, 1968), ch. 9.

24. Quoted in Geoffrey Rips, "The Special Interests of Kent Hance," *The Texas Observer* (May 18, 1984), 4.

25. See Roger M. Olien, *From Token to Triumph: The Texas Republicans Since 1920* (Dallas: S.M.U. Press, 1982), 30–54.

PART TWO

THE ISSUES

Chapter Four

WATER FOR TEXAS

Joe G. Moore, Jr.

Texas citizens have repeatedly reacted to floods and droughts by calling upon various levels of government to moderate the consequences of extremes in the volume of rainfall and runoff. They have come to expect policymakers to adjudicate the various conflicting demands for water and to determine the distribution of the costs for any action taken to redistribute available supply. Constitutional amendments have been proposed and sometimes passed empowering state and local governmental officials to grapple with Texas' various water problems. In addition, a variety of interstate and federal efforts have been initiated over the years to cope with floods and droughts.

Water policymaking has not all been smooth sailing. A variety of factors have complicated intrastate and interstate efforts to develop a rational water policy for Texas. There is a wide range in the rainfall pattern found in Texas, from an annual average of fifty-six inches in Southeast Texas to eight inches in far West Texas to fourteen inches in the northwest. Moreover, neither population nor economic growth has always taken place where there is a readily available supply of usable water. Additionally, continued growth will likely exacerbate the problem in various parts of the state by increasing the demand for a relatively scarce commodity. As Table 4–1 notes, by 2030 it is possible that water use in Texas will more than double.

Added to these problems have been some purely political ones. Governmental attempts to cope with the water problems of Texas have spawned a number of significant regional tensions within the state as well as intergovernmental conflicts between the state and the federal government. In addition, demands have been made by a variety of groups to take into account the environmental impact of water policies. Water storage facilities and massive conveyance systems have often been opposed in recent years on environmental grounds. Such political problems have played a major role in shaping the issues defining water policy in Texas and in constraining the solutions to Texas' water problems.

Table 4–1. Reported and Estimated Population and Water Use, 1980, 2000, 2030, Low and High Series.

Year	Type of Use	Acre Feet of Water Used	
		Low Series	High Series
1980	Municipal	2,813,182	
	Manufacturing	1,519,992	
	Mining	239,438	
	Steam-electric	330,057	
	Agriculture (Irrig. & Livestock)	12,950,357	
	Total*	17,853,026	
	Population	14,229,191	
2000	Municipal	3,512,065	5,080,510
	Manufacturing	2,407,092	2,717,673
	Mining	267,967	267,967
	Steam-electric	717,440	816,940
	Agriculture (Irrig. & Livestock)	10,426,522	17,473,266
	Total*	17,331,086	26,356,356
	Population	19,567,335	21,239,279
2030	Municipal	5,058,994	8,177,532
	Manufacturing	4,230,531	5,013,989
	Mining	389,350	389,350
	Steam-electric	1,118,619	1,417,449
	Agriculture (Irrig. & Livestock)	11,385,821	21,111,305
	Total*	22,183,315	36,109,625
	Population	28,254,495	34,276,928

Source: Texas Department of Water Resources.
* In addition, Texas bay and estuary requirements range from a low (survival limit) of 4.7 million acre-feet annually to a high of 13.6 million acre-feet annually.

This chapter seeks to understand the problems surrounding water policy in Texas. After considering some of the legal and technological issues that have come to define water policymaking, it will consider the various governmental responses that have taken place over the years to grapple with the water problems in Texas. The chapter concludes with an assessment of the problems that will confront policymakers concerned with the water problem in Texas for the next twenty years.

The Legal Issues

The legal status of rights to use water affects the quantity of water available. Fortunately, Texas has not been plagued by two issues that have had an impact on water development in other western states. Since no federal lands existed at the time of annexation, the reservation of adequate water to develop federal public land is of no concern. Similarly, there are no Indian reservations in Texas except those established by state law and administered by the state through the Texas Indian Commission. Hence there are no Indian water rights protected by the federal government to further complicate the allocation of water.

In Texas, surface- and groundwater are governed by different legal concepts. "Surface water flowing in public watercourses is public property, the use of which is subject to administration by the state" with recognition accorded claims granted under Spanish, English, Republic of Texas, United States, and State of Texas laws.[1] On the other hand, groundwater or percolating water is owned by the surface landowner, who has "the right to take for use or sale all the water he can capture from beneath his land."[2] Even if a landowner captures so much groundwater from beneath his land that a neighbor's well dries up, the neighbor cannot secure damages unless the groundwater from an artesian well is wasted. Similarly, damages can be recovered for trespass, wanton or malicious conduct intended to harm a neighbor, or contamination, for example, in oil well drilling operations.

Surface landowners may voluntarily accept groundwater regulation through formation of underground water conservation districts, of which nine are currently active, and there is one district in Texas (the Harris-Galveston Coastal Subsidence District) created to reduce land subsidence by regulating the taking of groundwater. Various governmental subdivisions may, by vote, elect to join or be excluded from the underground water districts; thus surface coverage does not necessarily extend over an entire aquifer.

Two basic doctrines of surface water rights law affect determination of available supply: the Prior Appropriation Doctrine, and the Riparian Doctrine. Because Texas in 1840 adopted the common law of England as the rule for decisions in court cases, the riparian concept was first applied. Under this concept, a landowner whose land abuts a stream or watercourse is entitled to that quantity of water from the stream needed for the use of his household and domesticated animals. Conflicting rulings arose when riparian owners started using water for irrigation, which raised the issue whether this was a "natural" or "artificial" use. In a 1962 case the Texas Supreme Court reversed a 1926 ruling and concluded that Spanish and Mexican grants did not grant riparian owners the right to irrigate unless specifically stated.[3]

The prior appropriation doctrine for Texas borrowed from the laws of Nevada, Colorado, and Texas. The Irrigation Act of 1889 established the concept "within the arid portions" of Texas and an 1895 rewrite extended it to areas where "irrigation is beneficial for agricultural purposes." The doctrine developed in the arid and semi-arid western states as a means of protecting the water distribution systems of early settlers, particularly diversions initially constructed to provide water for gold mining, from latecomers. There are several component concepts. The doctrine of priority ("first in time is first in right") protected the chronological sequence of diversion or users. The doctrine of relation assumed careful construction of diversion facilities, relating the right back to the time work began rather than when the use started. The concept of due diligence was introduced to assure that, once started, construction would proceed in an orderly fashion until diversion was possible. Some sort of notice was required so that subsequent settlers or users could be made aware of prior appropriations. Initially, notice was merely a posting at the point of diversion. Later some more formal system became necessary. In Texas, the system of notice became known as "certified filings" because the 1913 Irrigation Act required all prior claimants of water rights to file sworn statements with the county clerk in the county where the diversion occurred and with the Board of Water Engineers. While the appropriation system is intended to allocate the state's surface water fairly, it has resulted in the surface water in every Texas river being overappropriated.

Planning Problems

The scarcity of water in much of the state and the unregulated use of much of the state's groundwater has long created a need for water resources planning. However, water planning for the state has been characterized by a multiplicity of governmental agencies and a lack of interagency cooperation.

At the federal level, the Corps of Engineers has concerned itself with navigation and flood control throughout the nation and municipal and industrial water supply in the eastern United States, whereas the Bureau of Reclamation has operated in the twelve contiguous western states to provide irrigation water where there is federal ownership of extensive public lands. Texas did not initially fit within the jurisdiction of the Bureau since it retained its public lands to pay off the national debt it accumulated as a republic in a compromise connected with its annexation by the U.S. The Bureau's authority was extended to Texas in acts of Congress in 1905 and 1906, but its activity is generally restricted to the area west of the 100th meridian.

Relationships among the Corps of Engineers, the State of Texas, and regional and local water officials are complicated by the Corps' divided geographic jurisdiction within Texas. Five district offices headquartered in Fort Worth and Galveston, Texas; Albuquerque, New Mexico; Tulsa, Oklahoma; and New Orleans, Louisiana, oversee the agency's activities in the state. All of these except the one in Louisiana are under the jurisdiction of the Corps Division office in Dallas, Texas. Two of Texas' most prolific drainage areas with substantial projected developable water excess to projected needs, the Sulphur River and Cypress Creek in Northeast Texas, lie within the New Orleans district's jurisdiction and this office reports to the Corps division office in Vicksburg, Mississippi. Thus Louisiana and Mississippi political leaders concerned with main stem Red River and Mississippi River water resources have exerted more influence in this significant geographical area than have their Texas counterparts. Chairmen of congressional committees with control over planning, taxation, and appropriations for water projects have come from these states as well as Oklahoma, through which flows rivers tributary to the Red and Arkansas rivers and ultimately the Mississippi. In addition, a supporting private organization, the Red River Valley Association, headquartered in Shreveport, Louisiana, has always exerted powerful influence over developments in the main stem Red River and its tributaries, often favoring Louisiana water interests.

The Soil Conservation Service of the Department of Agriculture constructs, with local support, sediment-storage and flood-retardation structures with limited quantities of water supply for small cities and rural water districts. These three federal agencies are not always in agreement about the Texas water development projects each is undertaking. The three departments report to different committees of the Congress both for project authorization and for actual appropriations.

At the local level, in addition to fifteen river authorities, multicity water districts, and city districts, Texas laws allow for the formation of eleven other types of water districts. All of these entities have been accustomed to communicating directly with federal agencies and with the Congress. In the case of the Texas Colorado River basin, the large number of agencies has led to multiple agencies having jurisdiction over separate portions of the basin's geography and there have been upstream-downstream conflicts in water supply predictions and rights allocations.

Summarizing the status of federal, state, and local interrelationships, the Texas Research League reported:

> Texas already has nearly a thousand miles of navigable waterways (over which the Federal Government has always exerted preeminent authority) developed by the Corps of Engineers, and a whole new network of barge canals is now under consideration. More than 80,000 acres of irrigated land in Texas are fed by waters produced from Bureau of Reclamation projects, and the Bureau has proposed the development of three-quarters of a million acres more. Some 725,000 acres of land have been protected or improved through 74 U.S. Soil Conservation Service upstream flood retardation developments, with more than 100 additional projects involving well over a million acres projected. The U.S. Boundary Commission's Falcon Reservoir on the Rio Grande will provide water supplies for most of the municipal and industrial needs of the Texas Valley and for several hundred thousand acres of irrigated farmland. The huge Amistad Reservoir farther up the Rio Grande will be of great additional value.
>
> When the importance and validity of the federal involvement in Texas water development have been acknowledged, however, the fact remains that the conditions of federal participation have not always been ideal from the standpoint of efficient and economical resource utilization. Some projects have been built to less than optimum size and the subsequent cost of necessary enlargement for water supply purposes has been many times higher than full-scale development at the outset would have been. Allocation of reservoir space to municipal and industrial use has sometimes been inadequate. Timing of land acquisition and construction has sometimes been scheduled in uneconomic sequence.
>
> These same criticisms apply (sometimes in greater degree) to projects constructed by local governments–and for the same reason: Only the State has broad enough jurisdiction to plan the most effective coordination of water project development, and up until now the State has dispatched its responsibility for such coordination very poorly. Fortunately, that fault is being remedied through the preparation of a comprehensive State Water Plan which will point the way to the most effective and economical means for developing Texas' water resources. But there remain a number of serious structural barriers to the implementation of State plans at both the federal and local levels.[4]

The Problems and Politics

Yet coordination among agencies is required in order to deal with the enormous problems associated with the depletion of the Ogallala underground aquifer and how to provide supplemental or replacement surface water for irrigation on the Texas High Plains. Distance (three hundred miles), elevation (three thousand feet above sea level), and available in-state excess surface water (2.5 million acre-feet according to the most generous estimates), combine to discourage even the most imaginative water planners. The preliminary 1966 water plan noted that "there is not enough surface water in the rest of Texas, excess to foreseeable requirements, to provide for the present level of water use in the West Texas areas. If excess water were available, under the concept that each user and those who benefit directly by such use should pay the cost of water delivery, west Texas irrigators could not pay the price, estimated to be at least $168 an acre-foot, to develop and transport east Texas water to the west."[5] Six "specific actions" were proposed to aid in meeting the water needs of this area (El Paso, the Trans-Pecos, and High Plains):

1. Active and vigorous leadership at the state level in proposals before the Congress for inclusion of West Texas in regional plans for the movement of water from northwestern United States, or from the Mississippi and Missouri Rivers, to the West Texas area, and participation by the Texas Water Development Board in development and financing of such plans.

2. State financial participation in carefully designed recharge projects to increase the storage in underground waterbearing formations which supply the West Texas area. State financial assistance for Playa Lake modifications to conserve and utilize these 36,000 shallow depressions as storage facilities.

3. Establishing an office of the Texas Water Development Board in West Texas, adequately staffed with able personnel to assist in the wide range of research, data-collection programs, improved water-application studies, and continuing technical and economical analyses, required to assure the optimum conservations and utilization of available water supplies.

4. State financial participation with local and federal agencies in a modern, large-volume inland desalination plant to provide additional municipal and industrial water supply.

5. Continued exploration of the economic feasibility of import of water from in-state sources for municipal and industrial purposes as specific unforeseen needs are projected.

6. Intensified efforts to improve surface water quality in the upper reaches of the Red, Brazos, and Colorado Rivers to permit multiple uses.[6]

The need for freshwater inflows to Texas' bays and estuaries had received special attention. An attempt was made to document the dollar value of these resources. Extrapolating from 1958 data for the Corpus Christi area developed by the Bureau of Business Research of The University of Texas at Austin and the Institute of Marine Sciences of The University of Texas System, the board's studies concluded, "The bays of the Texas Coast have a present value of $4.55 billion," utilizing U.S. Department of Commerce data, "the Texas salt-water sport fishing activity has a present value of $4.0 billion."[7] The board determined that available information suggested a total need of 2.45 million acre-feet from storage to provide adequate freshwater inflows to assure optimum productivity of Texas bays and estuaries.

The final Texas Water Plan, resulting from the four-year effort, carried a total cost estimate for meeting all Texas' needs of some $9 billion.[8] It contemplated the delivery of 7.6 million acre-feet to West Texas for irrigation, 1.2 million acre-feet for municipal and industrial use in North Central Texas, and 1.5 million acre-feet to eastern New Mexico, in addition to meeting all other needs for all uses in Texas to the year 2020.[9] To finance the state's share of the cost of this elaborate system to import water and redistribute the state's surplus surface water, a constitutional amendment was scheduled for a vote on August 5, 1969. The amendment failed by about 5,000 votes out of a total of 625,000 votes cast.

Meanwhile, a new federal agency, the National Water Commission, appeared on the scene. Created by Congress in 1968, the commission had five years to develop and propose a national water policy. Two Texans served on the five-member commission at different times: Myron A. Wright, chairman of the board and chief executive officer, Exxon Company, U.S.A. (1968–69); and Josiah Wheat, an attorney from Woodville who had been active in Texas water development (1969–83). Among the commission's conclusions and recommendations was one which raised the ire of West Texas irrigators: "There appears to be adequate productive capacity in the nation's agriculture to meet food and fiber demand under various alternative futures at least until the year 2000. In such case there would be no need in the next 30 years to continue federally subsidized water resource development programs to increase the agricultural land base of the country." The recommendation was that "legislation should be enacted to require full repayment of costs of Federal water resource development projects that result in increases in production of food and fiber."[10]

The handwriting had been placed on the wall for all to see. Despite efforts of a Texas member, Mr. Wheat, who prevailed upon his comembers to make a special trip to Lubbock to hear the West Texans' pleas, the commission still adopted its conclusions and recommendations.[11] The outcome had been signaled by a Bureau of Reclamation report earlier that same year on the importance of Mississippi River water to West Texas. While "physically possible," such importation was characterized as "not economically justified."[12]

Two attempts subsequent to the 1969 vote on a proposed constitutional amendment were also defeated. On November 21, 1973, Governor Dolph Briscoe created by executive order a Water Resource Conservation and Development Task Force and named to it thirty-one persons who had been associated with state water resource authorities.

Among its recommendations were a gubernatorial focus on importation of water which "must proceed concurrently with full development of Texas' own water resources" and a constitutional amendment doubling the Development Fund to $800 million. The recommended amendment was presented for voter action on November 2, 1976, and failed of adoption by a margin of three hundred thousand votes of two million cast.

The following year, 1977, the Texas Water Development Board published documents intended to update the 1968 Texas Water Plan.[13] The planning horizon was extended to 2030. Comments were invited from Texas citizens and a series of hearings scheduled throughout the state. The Lone Star Chapter of the Sierra Club, which had been very critical of the state's water policy proposals, published its own plan. A new hierarchy of water use was proposed:

> After meeting the needs of bays and estuaries ecosystems, we propose the following priorities for water use:
> (1) Agricultural production; when only irrigation is economically feasible and allows the efficient production of crops for direct human consumption. (Reduce irrigation of crops for animal feed.)
> (2) Other aspects of human life support, which is generally limited to 40 to 80 gallons per day per person.
> (3) Industrial needs. Analysis in dry areas should relate economics return to water consumed.
> (4) Municipal and discretionary domestic water needs.
> (5) Agricultural production of indirectly consumed crops (e.g., livestock forage crops).[14]

Arguing against large surface water reservoirs because of loss of agricultural lands, wildlife habitat, and scenic and recreational river environments, the Sierra Club also supported payment of full costs of water projects by the beneficiaries; limiting benefits in cost-benefit analyses to direct benefits only; use of actual realistic interest rates in calculating the long-term cost of capital; uniform, flat water rates for all water sales, regardless of intended use; and inclusion of "the cost effect on demand of using critical nonrenewable resources in the project (e.g., energy and land)."[15] A spokesperson for the club concluded a detailed critique of the 1977 planning effort before a legislative committee on October 28, 1977, with a prediction: "The 'bottom line' of all my comments is this: I don't think Texans will approve any more TWDB bonds unless a more balanced approach is pursued concerning our scarce water resources. My comments are made in order to help you do just that. To ignore some of the issues I have raised is to court disaster, i.e., drought with a drought, you can probably pass a bond issue, but such strategy is a game of brinksmanship, merely a game and not the exercise of leadership."[16]

In 1981 there was another proposal for amending the state constitution to fund water projects. Since 1941 Texas state government has functioned under a constitutional "pay-as-you-go" provision requiring balanced budgets for each biennial financing period. Historically, actual tax revenue to the General Fund has often exceeded predictions made two years and eight months before the biennium ends. Thus, the legislature has sometimes convened with a surplus available for new expenditures. Speaker Billy Clayton capitalized on this history when he proposed that one-half of this surplus be committed to a water project "trust fund." This proposal required a constitutional change and was on the ballot for an election on November 3, 1981. It, too, failed by more than 115,000 votes out of some 800,000 total.

The electorate has consistently made a choice between state funding for projects to provide water *quantity* and those for water *quality*. All amendments for bond issues to provide state low-interest loans for publicly owned wastewater treatment projects have passed while those for state-funded water supply projects failed in 1969, 1976, and 1981. In a recent study by Schoolmaster, it was noted that major reforms in water policies will be difficult. There is a sharp split between East and West Texas in support for water-quantity programs with strong opposition to those programs in populous East Texas.[17]

In the 1983 session of the 68th Texas Legislature a package of water bills passed the Senate. They ran aground in the House, confronted with upstream-downstream conflicts over water allocations to freshwater inflow for bays and estuaries and West Texas water interests. For irrigators, the package proposed state-funded low-interest loans for purchase of water-saving irrigation equipment. An additional $150 million would have been authorized for water-supply projects with an equal amount for water-quality projects. Under another amendment, the state would have been authorized to guarantee up to $250 million of water bonds issued by local or regional water governmental units. Freshwater inflows were assured under another bill.

Legislation passed in 1985 would for the first time establish a plan regulating groundwater use. Special groundwater control districts would be established and all cities requesting state aid for water projects would be required to develop water conservation programs. Water construction projects would receive $980 million, $200 million in loans to farmers who purchase water-saving irrigation equipment and a $250 million state insurance fund would be set up to guarantee water bonds issued by cities. Though the Senate approval of the legislation was unanimous and the water package received only seventeen negative votes in the House, the financing system had to be approved by a constitutional amendment.

The pattern of voter opposition to a comprehensive water plan was broken in November, 1985. Nearly 74% of the voters approved the amendment, which authorized $980 million in state bonds for water supply, water quality, and flood-control projects. The amendment providing $200 million for agricultural water conservation bonds was approved by nearly 70% of the voters.

The passage of the amendments was probably due to an increasing awareness of the state's water needs. Additionally, there were protections of bays and estuaries built into the legislation as well as limitations on transbasin transfers. In the past, concerns over inadequate bay and estuary protections and fears of transbasin transfers of water from east to west Texas had been important components of voter opposition to Texas water plans.

The financing scheme has been affected by the 1986 amendments to the Internal Revenue Code (federal income tax), but the bonds have not lost their federal tax-exempt status. The first sale of bonds was scheduled for March, 1987. For the first time, there is realistic recognition that the importation from out-of-state sources of massive quantities of surface water is probably not feasible within the foreseeable future. Although the plan has been criticized for being inadequate in preventing underground water depletion, conservation of the Ogallala rather than water importation is the watchword. This realism was undoubtedly fostered by the latest in a series of studies related to water importation.

In one of his last major contributions to Texas water planning, former congressman George H. Mahon of Lubbock secured federal appropriations for a study of a sustained water supply for the fifteen million acres irrigated on the High Plains in six states from the Ogallala Aquifer. As to augmenting existing supply, the secretary of commerce, through the Economic Development Administration, was directed, "If water transfer is found to be a part of a reasonable solution, the Secretary, as part of his study, shall include a recommended plan for allocating and distributing water in an equitable fashion, taking into account existing water rights and the needs for future growth of all affected areas." In its transmittal letter of results of the study, the High Plains Study Council, composed of the six states' governors, stated:

> The water importation parts of the study focused upon making importation cost estimates for four import routes from adjacent areas and for several different project sizes. It was not possible to conclude that major multi-state conveyance systems will be financially feasible in the foreseeable future; importation costs would be quite high in relation to ability of water users to pay for imported water. In addition, it was not possible to determine the quantities of water that might be surplus to the needs of adjacent areas, since, in some cases, future water plans have not been prepared for adjacent areas that could be studied under the terms of the authorizing legislation. The Council recommends that importation studies be continued in order to answer some of these questions, since it is clear that, even under the most frugal water use plans, large parts of the High Plains Region will ultimately be without sufficient quantities of water to continue irrigation and some areas may not have sufficient supplies of water for municipal and industrial purposes.[18]

The major thrust of the recommendations was water conservation through improved irrigation practices. Earlier studies had suggested more elaborate schemes. One, in 1966, extended as far as the Columbia River.[19]

Ten years later, the Texas Board was sufficiently presumptuous to employ an Arkansas consulting firm to identify waters in that state surplus to its needs which could be imported to Texas.[20] Yet the initial preliminary conclusions of the May, 1966 plan for Texas reiterated, "There is not enough surface water in the rest of Texas, excess to foreseeable requirements to provide for the present level of water use in the West Texas area. If excess water were available, under the concept that each user and those who benefit directly by such use should pay the cost of water delivery, west Texas irrigators could not pay the price to develop and transport east Texas water to the west."[21]

Nevertheless, the contribution of irrigated agriculture on the Texas High Plains utilizing Ogallala Aquifer groundwater is vital to the Texas economy.[22] The projected decline in that contribution with a return to dryland farming as the supply is exhausted should be of concern to all Texans. The livelihood of those who depend upon the irrigation-generated business, some three to five million of Texas' citizens, requires the attention of the state's political and economic leadership. Maintaining an economy that can support an equal number of Texas citizens into the future presents the most serious challenge the state has faced since its annexation by the United States. Solutions are grounded in the way the state as a whole, as a body politic, allocates and manages both the quantity and the quality of its water resources.

The Future of Water Policy

Water use is fundamentally a consequence of people's social mores and economic activity. Thus, population projections, per capita per day water use, maintenance of residential amenities such as shrubs, lawns, and flowers, as well as industrial and commercial activities and the level of irrigated agriculture determine future water needs. The last use, however, represents the most significant commitment of available supply, some 72% of 1980 water use. Thus relatively small quantities of additional water can meet the direct needs for increased human consumption and expanded industrial or commercial activity to provide jobs and amenities for larger populations. Herculean efforts are needed if irrigated agricultural use is to be sustained or expanded. Since the High Plains area irrigated by the Ogallala is the lion's share of irrigated acreage in Texas, water depletion there has significant impact on this use. Conversely, conservation of water can produce most dramatic results only if it is applied to the irrigation water use. Reductions in per capita per day municipal use have almost insignificant impact when paired with the results of irrigation conservation practices.

Total future water use obviously depends upon the proportionate mix of per capita per day municipal, industrial-commercial, and irrigated agricultural uses. Long-range predictions may tend to be self-fulfilling. Water allocations may gravitate toward the predicted division with the predictions utilized to justify the allocation.

Thus the matters of future quantity and quality of Texas water supply shape the issues that confront the state. The predominant issue in meeting future water supply for all of Texas, the declining water table underlying the Texas High Plains as water is mined from the Ogallala Aquifer, has not changed significantly since the mid-1960s when it was first identified. The only physical solution, importation from other states of substantial quantities of surface water through a surface water conveyance system, is neither financially nor politically feasible. This conclusion does not relieve the state of its responsibility to focus a legitimate portion of its attention and resources upon providing mitigation of the economic consequences of such depletion. The people who depend upon the economic base of the existing irrigation economy are entitled to whatever relief can be mustered, or should be mustered, for a major segment of the state's population. The proposal for state-provided low-interest loans for improved efficiency in irrigation equipment and practices is a beginning. Increased state support for research, development, and education in such equipment and practices is laudable. The state might also, for example, develop a deliberate state policy of encouraging low water use by locating industries and businesses with high economic return in the areas most directly affected by depletion of the aquifer. While importation of supplemental or replacement water for irrigation appears unlikely, attention to redistribution of East Texas surplus water for municipal and industrial use should be pursued.

Such redistribution raises issues on which West Texans must be prepared to accept some accommodation, such as adequate groundwater regulation, changing agricultural practices and crop patterns, and changes in the "basins of origin" protection now imbedded in the Texas Constitution.[23] While groundwater regulation can be local or regional (it need not be statewide and state-administered), it must be real in the sense that it is geographically comprehensive and administratively strong enough to prevent additional withdrawals by individual irrigators where such withdrawals adversely affect the well-being of the larger number of irrigators. As a practical matter and in fairness to West Texas, groundwater regulation there should be achieved in concert with groundwater regulation in other areas of the state, such as the land surface overlying the Edwards Underground Aquifer, where the problems are of the same or similar complexity. In the coastal areas, land subsidence and saltwater intrusion could receive equal regulatory attention. In the long run, the declining water supply of the Ogallala should be used to irrigate those crops which contribute most to the state's and the nation's agricultural interests. Cropping patterns should also change as new strains or species of crops are identified which will extend the economic life of the aquifer. While the condition that the reasonably foreseeable future water requirements of the basin of origin must be met before exportation of an excess of water can occur may seem onerous, residents of eastern Texas river basins will not easily forego the limitation. As a matter of political fact, the state's population is concentrated in those eastern basins or adjoining areas favorably affected by the reservation so that West Texans are not likely ever again to possess the political power to change it. Further, past water development has conclusively demonstrated that transbasin diversion, such as moving Sabine (Lake Tawakoni) and Neches (Lake Palestine) water to Dallas in the Trinity River basin, and Trinity (Lake Livingston) water to Houston in the San Jacinto River basin, does occur when the circumstances are right.

Probably the second most critical issue is assured freshwater inflow to Texas bays and estuaries at whatever level is required to sustain the state's economic benefit from the coastal sports and commercial fishing industries and the related support activities. There does not now exist in state law a clear definitive legal basis for commitment of any of the state's water to this purpose. The receiving areas should probably be protected from excesses as well as shortages. A broader understanding of the contribution of the fishing industry to the state's total economy is undoubtedly essential to acceptance of such a commitment. While studies have continued, the optimum needs of the estuaries should be quantified as accurately as possible and periodically evaluated.

Those who depend upon the coastal fishery for their livelihood are entitled the same degree of consideration from state policymakers as are West Texas irrigators even though neither now makes any direct payment for the value of the water essential to their well-being.

A related issue is maintenance of instream flows for fish and wildlife. Ironically, such flows often exist only because of upstream storage reservoirs, the cost of which has become an obligation of downstream water users. Instream flows might not occur during some dry years were it not for these releases from storage; thus, often those who enjoy the benefits from these flows and who fish, hunt, and participate in water recreation activities in fact get a "free ride." Now that they have come to rely on these flows, they are insisting that they be maintained even at the expense of the users of the stored waters who agree to bear the cost of storage. For example, in the Brazos River basin, where some costs of reservoirs have been borne by users of hydroelectric power or coastal irrigators, those who fish, hunt, or enjoy the river flows get the benefit of the passing flow for which others have paid. Now, these beneficiaries want their enjoyment assured by guaranteed minimum flows. A similar demand is made by lakeside landowners who object to lowering of lake levels by water releases to those users who have contracted to pay the costs of water supply storage.

Similar artificial hydrologic consequences follow use of a water supply and then its release downstream as treated wastewater. Rivers that under historical conditions flowed only intermittently now flow constantly because of treated wastewater; the upper reaches of the Trinity River flow during the dry summer months of low rainfall years only because of the volume of treated wastewater discharged by the Dallas-Fort Worth metropolitan area. To what extent should the "artificial" condition be maintained and the wastewater made "fishable-swimmable" under the mandate of the Federal Clean Water Act?

Thus water quality and multiple water use are integral elements of a future sustained water supply. As shortage becomes more widespread, quality to match uses will become critical. Each use also results in some consumption, thus the available volume decreases as it moves downstream through multiple uses. Texas has imposed higher treatment requirements for municipal wastewater than are applicable in other states, largely because of the reuse demands. In the future, even higher levels of treatment will be required if uses are to be maintained.

Finally, no solution to all of the Texas water supply problems is likely to be achieved without satisfying the concerns of environmentalists. While those in this group are not yet sufficiently numerous to assure their viewpoint will entirely prevail, they can prevent the prevalence of solutions totally contrary to their wishes. Thus an accommodation acceptable to them as well as the traditionalists of the Texas Water Conservation Association is essential if the existing stalemate is to be ended.

The diversity of the state's geography, topography, water supply, economic interests, and political focus presents real obstacles to a water supply solution. Intergovernmental relationships, both intrastate and interstate, as well as federal-state, are complex and worrisome. The fifty-year time span, almost mandatory because of the basins of origin issue, may pose continuing problems. Almost any alternative, even doing nothing, bodes worse for the state's future than continued searching for a water supply solution that serves the greatest number for the brightest future.

Notes

1. Texas Department of Water Resources, *Water for Texas: Planning for the Future*, (February, 1983), 1–13. (Draft.)

2. Ibid., 1–28.

3. *Motl* vs. *Boyd*, 116 Tex. 82, 286 S. W. 258 (1926); *Valmont Plantations* vs. *The State of Texas*, 163 Tex. 381, 355 S. W. 2d. 502 (1962).

4. This discussion is based upon Texas Research League, *A Pattern of Intergovernmental Relations for Water Resource Management in Texas* (Austin, Texas, February, 1966), 9–10.

5. See Texas Water Development Board, *Water for Texas: A Plan for the Future, Preliminary* (Austin, Texas, May, 1966), 18.

6. Ibid.

7. Mason G. Lockwood and H. P. Carothers, "Tidal Inlets for Preservation of Estuaries," in Texas Water Development Board, *Additional Technical Papers of Selected Aspects of the Texas Water Plan* (Austin, Texas, February, 1967), 68.

8. Texas Water Development Board, *The Texas Water Plan*, (Austin, Texas, November, 1968), 1–28.

9. Ibid.

10. U.S. National Water Commission, *Water Policies for the Future. Final Report to the President and to the Congress of the United States by the National Water Commission* (Washington, D.C.: Government Printing Office, June, 1973), 141–42.

11. See "$15 Billion Price Tag Eyed at Meeting," *Lubbock Avalanche Journal* (October 7, 1971).

12. See "Water Plan 'Not Feasible'," *Lubbock Avalanche Journal* (April 13, 1973).

13. Texas Water Development Board, *Continuing Water Resources Planning and Development for Texas*, 2 vols. (Austin, Texas, May, 1977).

14. See Lone Star Chapter of the Sierra Club, "Water for Texas, Alternatives for the Future," position paper (undated), 10.

15. Stuart H. Henry, Testimony before the Subcommittee on Texas Water Plan, House Committee on Natural Resources (October 28, 1977).

16. Ibid., 25.

17. F. Andrew Schoolmaster, "Water Development Referenda and Planning in Texas," *Social Science Quarterly* 65 (December, 1984):1147–56.

18. High Plains Study Council, "Letter of Transmittal," *A Summary of Results of the Ogallala Aquifer Regional Study with Recommendations to the Secretary of Commerce and Congress* (Austin, Texas, December 13, 1982).

19. See Leeds, Hill and Jewett, Inc., *Report on Importation of Water for West Texas*, prepared for Texas Water Development Board (Austin, Texas, May, 1966).

20. Stephens Consultant Services, Inc., *An Assessment of Surface Water Supplies of Arkansas, with Computations of Surplus Supplies and a Conceptual Plan for Import to Texas*, prepared for Texas Water Development Board (Austin, Texas, December, 1976).

21. Herbert W. Grubb, *Importance of Irrigation Water to the Economy of the High Plains*, Prepared for Texas Water Development Board (Austin, Texas, January, 1966).

22. The "basins of origin" provision requires that there can be no exportation of an excess of water until the reasonable foreseeable future water requirements of the water basin are met.

Chapter Five

ENERGY POLICY

Martin T. Katzman and
Patricia J. Osborn

If one word could capture the essence of Texas, it would be *petroleum*, and rightly so. For most of this century, Texas was responsible for close to half of the oil and gas production in the United States. Historians trace the divergent development between Texas and the rest of the South to its petroleum wealth.[1] In the decades between 1930 and 1950, Texas was a major international oil producer and exporter, and policies established in Austin rippled throughout the world. Texas' petroleum production has been in decline since the mid-1960s, but still accounts for one-third of the national total. In the past decade, the state's lignite resources have been undergoing rapid development. Virtually all of this fuel is devoted to electricity generation, in which Texas leads the nation. As utilities shift from petroleum to coal as the major fuel, the issues of electric rates and environmental impacts have become the focus of energy policy.

After a brief overview of the historical role of energy in the state's economic development, this chapter focuses on (1) contributions of the petroleum sector to the state's fiscal capacity, (2) state regulation of the petroleum industry, (3) public policy toward electric utility rate making, and (4) emerging issues of environmental impacts of lignite development.

While all of these issues concern energy in some way, they have not been dealt with as part of a coherent state energy policy. Rather, they can be viewed as discrete arenas occupied by different interest groups and regulated by different state and federal agencies. The disjuncture of energy politics and policy is not unique to Texas, but characteristic of national energy policy as well.[2] The action in these arenas follows an overlapping sequence:

1. The economic and fiscal impacts of energy on Texas span the entire twentieth century, but many of the important institutions, such as the Permanent Fund, date from the Republic. As recipients of royalties from public lands and severance taxes, all Texas citizens have a stake in the welfare of the petroleum industry. The Railroad Commission's vigilance against the waste of oil and gas resources,

often against the immediate interests of producers, reflects its role as steward of the public's interest.

2. The Texas Railroad Commission began formulating state oil policy around 1915. Fully developed in the 1946–73 period, state oil policy owed its success to a great extent to federal enforcement of state and interstate agreements limiting oil production. The major players in state oil politics have been the "majors" and the independents. The majors are large international companies which integrate production, refining, and distribution. The independents are mainly Texas-based producers and royalty owners. The conflicting interests of the producers and those of the public have been reconciled by the Railroad Commission.[3]

3. The natural gas industry has been shaped largely by federal price controls since 1954, and state policy has had relatively little leverage in this sphere.

4. There was virtually no state policy toward electric utilities until the 1970s, when rate shocks became a national issue. The establishment of the Public Utility Commission of Texas in 1976 created a new arena, in which the interests of consumers and investors are pitted. The rules of the game, such as the mode of selecting commissioners, are still controversial. How the commission responds to a new consumer activism and to federal mandates remains to be seen.

5. The environmental impacts of energy have always been of concern in Texas, because of the risks that petroleum exploration and extraction pose to the groundwater supply of municipalities, ranchers, and farmers. The conversion of the state's electric utilities to lignite may raise air pollution to a major issue in the late 1980s. The resulting acid precipitation may cause significant economic losses in East Texas. New coalitions of urban environmentalists and rural property owners may emerge.

Effect of Energy on the Texas Economy

At the turn of the century, the petroleum industry centered on Pennsylvania and Ohio, illumination was the major use of petroleum, and the automobile was a novelty. While commercial oil development in Texas began near Corsicana in 1894, the cornerstone for the state's role as an energy giant was laid in the Spindletop field, near Beaumont, in 1901.

In contrast to the two thousand barrels per day yielded by the Corsicana field, Spindletop yielded as much as one hundred thousand barrels a day, about fifteen times more than the largest field in the nation. The second largest field in the world, Spindletop had a revolutionary effect on Texas and the oil industry. Because the demand for petroleum was initially limited, Spindletop pushed the price of oil to an all-time low of three cents a barrel. In the long run, the cheapness and abundance of oil resulted in an epochal conversion of industrial societies of the world from a coal base to a petroleum base. Almost immediately, the Beaumont area became the hub of refining, a pipeline network, and oil ports. Texas' role as the premier oil-producing state was magnified by the discovery of many other fields, such as the Permian Basin in the 1920s. The discovery of the massive East Texas field in the 1930s became crucial in the development of state oil policy.

Politics and policy must be placed in the context of petroleum's characteristic as a depletable resource. *Resources* are minerals that are conceivably recoverable with foreseeable technology. *Reserves* are that portion of resources that can be recovered with existing technology at current prices. Rising prices and technological improvements transform submarginal resources into reserves. Furthermore, rising prices induce the development of new technologies, discovery efforts, and the application of existing enhanced recovery techniques.

Because Texas has been well explored, there have been few significant discoveries since the 1950s. Despite improvements in petroleum technology, both reserves and resources have been declining since the mid-1960s. Although production has been declining as well, the changes in petroleum prices in the past decade have had the greatest impact on the economy and public policy. The boom in oil prices in the 1973–81 period provided the fiscal basis for major public expenditures. The collapse after 1981 caused great fiscal strains.

Employment Effects   In 1970 over 150,000 Texans were employed in the petroleum industry, which includes the extraction of oil and gas, oil refining, gas transmission and distribution, and oil field machinery. By 1980, the industry employed over 330,000 Texans, or 5% of the civilian labor force. The state's share of employment in the petroleum sector as a whole is about five times the national average. In specialized sectors like oil field machinery, the state's share is ten times the national average.[4]

Employment in the petroleum sector reflects only a portion of its impact on the state's economy. For example, oil extraction in Texas requires inputs such as seismic services, financing, machinery, and labor. While all of these inputs can be imported, most of them are furnished locally, thus generating jobs and income in Texas. Extraction in less-developed areas abroad may require the importation of specialized services, equipment, and labor from Texas. In turn, the extracted oil and gas becomes an input into the petrochemical industry, which provides inputs into consumer goods industries. Incomes earned by workers in Texas are spent on locally produced services and many goods which are produced in-state.

The complex interindustry connections between petroleum and other sectors can be examined by a technique called "input-output analysis." An important summary measure that emerges from this analysis is the "multiplier." This represents the total jobs or income generated directly and indirectly by the oil extraction industry.[5]

Each million dollars of increased sales by the petroleum extraction industry generates an additional 2.3 jobs in that industry. Since this industry has a multiplier of about 12, about 27 new jobs are created by the additional sales. Oil and gas field services have a much lower employment multiplier, about 3, while petroleum refining has a much higher multiplier, about 16. The multiplier, thus, amplifies the effect of changes in oil prices or sales on employment.

The state's growth in the 1973–81 period reflects the multiplier effect of the international oil boom.[6] Domestic expenditures on exploration and enhanced recovery equipment increased dramatically. Furthermore, Texas exported oil field services and equipment through the world. The spectacular growth of Houston in the 1970s was due to its role as a world oil-service center.

The input-output multiplier works in both directions. When petroleum prices fall, so do sales. The depth of the recession in oil centers on the Gulf Coast and Permian Basin after 1981 can be traced to the collapse of oil prices. The pressure on banks in Texas that lent heavily to oil developers rippled throughout the nation. Less oil-dependent regions, like Dallas-Fort Worth, neither enjoyed the boom nor suffered the crash of these oil regions.

Fiscal Effects   The location of rich petroleum resources in Texas has had a dual influence on the state's fiscal strength. First, the state receives royalties from petroleum production on its public lands. Second, the state receives revenues from energy production, transmission, and distribution. In addition, local governments derive substantial revenue from taxing petroleum properties.

The state's ownership of oil-rich public lands is a lucky accident. When Texas negotiated joining the Union in the 1840s, a treaty stipulated that the federal government would assume $10 million of the Republic's debt and acquire 175 million acres of public land. Congressional opponents of annexation doubted the value of these lands, so the state retained both its public lands and its debts. Much of this domain was eventually sold or granted, but 50 million acres were earmarked as an endowment fund for public schools and colleges. In 1900 the legislature transferred the remaining public domain to the Permanent School and Permanent University funds. In 1939, the state's submerged lands onshore and offshore were transferred to the funds. These lands provided little revenue until oil was discovered on university lands in the 1920s and school lands in the 1930s.[7]

Following Spanish tradition, the Republic of Texas laid claim to submerged "tidelands" extending for three leagues (about ten miles) from the shore. The federal government disputed all state claims to submerged lands and recognized only a three-mile limit of national sovereignty. The dispute lay dormant until post-war technology made the exploitation of offshore oil resources feasible. In 1953, congressional passage of the Submerged Lands Act recognized the claims of coastal states, including Texas' unique jurisdiction over three leagues. The Outer Continental Shelf Act of 1953 legitimized federal ownership of lands beyond these state claims. These tidelands have proven to be a most lucrative portion of Texas' public domain.

As royalties are earned from lands belonging to the Permanent Fund, they are transferred to the respective Available Fund. In most years before the 1970s, the royalties and rentals earned by the two funds remained below $100 million. In the boom years of 1973–81, revenues increased ten times, or at an average annual rate of 35%. By 1981, the petroleum industry paid nearly $750 million in royalties to the two funds. Nearly three-quarters of this sum was received by the School Fund. These revenues supported as much as one-third of state aid to elementary and secondary schools in the 1970s. Moreover, they financed nearly all of the growth in state aid during this period (Table 5–1).

Initiated in 1905, the tax on oil production is now levied at 4.6% of the market value of crude oil at the wellhead. An additional tax of 3/16 of a cent is levied on each barrel produced. In the 1980s, the oil production and regulation tax generated over $1.1 billion, more than any other source of state revenue.

Second in revenue generation is the natural and casinghead gas tax. In 1931, the legislature passed a production tax on natural gas similar to that on oil. This tax is now levied at 7.5% of the market value of gas transmitted through both intrastate and interstate transmission pipelines.[8] This tax generated about $1 billion in the 1980s.

Historically, taxes on petroleum production (severance taxes) have provided a substantial share of state tax revenues. In the 1960s, the share was about 20%. In the 1970s, the share rose from about 15.1% to 23.9% (Table 5–2).

Table 5–1. Petroleum Royalties and Rentals Earned from Texas Public Lands, 1935–84 (current millions of dollars).

Year	Revenues Dedicated to University Fund	School Fund	State Aid to Public Schools	School Fund Revenues as % of State Aid
1935	1	2	29	7.2
1940	1	4	35	10.3
1945	4	5	54	8.8
1950	9	10	94	10.9
1955	24	30	135	22.4
1960	19	26	164	15.8
1965	27	86	212	40.5
1970	19	43	287	14.9
1971	21	43	316	13.5
1972	25	38	333	11.4
1973	26	48	353	13.2
1974	44	99	469	21.0
1975	67	96	481	20.0
1976	86	130	556	23.5
1977	89	218	607	35.8
1978	97	268	729	36.7
1979	89	245	798	30.7
1980	118	390	3,042	12.8
1981	254	491	3,090	15.8
1982	197	488	3,568	13.7
1983	157	378	5,428	7.0
1984	155	378	5,806	6.5

Sources: *Texas Almanac*, 1984, 435, 567; personal communications with General Land Office and Texas Education Agency.
Note: Revenues of funds calculated at year ending August 31; apportionments based on school year beginning in August of the same year.

State tax revenues are highly sensitive to changes in energy prices. Each $1 drop in crude oil prices translates into a $40 million loss of severance taxes. The same price drop translates into about a $3 million drop in taxes on sales of petroleum products, a $6 million drop in sales taxes from goods and services purchased by the petroleum sector, and about a $21 million drop in sales taxes paid by employees who earn their incomes directly and indirectly through the petroleum sector.[9]

Both severance taxes and petroleum royalties enabled the state to avoid enacting an income tax or increasing sales or excise taxes

Table 5–2. Contribution of Petroleum Taxes to State Revenues, 1957–84 (current millions of dollars).

Fiscal Year Ending	Oil Production Tax	Gas Production Tax	Total Tax Revenues	Petroleum Taxes as a % of Total Tax
1957	150	41	611	31.3
1962	121	60	964	18.8
1966	133	74	1,124	18.4
1970	173	96	1,782	15.1
1971	195	109	1,994	15.2
1972	193	114	2,344	13.1
1973	210	125	2,583	13.0
1974	347	173	3,026	17.1
1975	405	260	3,375	19.7
1976	431	365	3,922	20.2
1977	429	474	4,429	20.3
1978	437	518	5,032	18.9
1979	467	554	5,390	18.9
1980	785	734	6,343	23.9
1981	1,291	902	7,742	28.3
1982	1,317	1,057	8,650	27.4
1983	1,190	1,061	8,498	26.4
1984	1,120	1,095	9,306	23.8

Sources: *Texas Almanac*, various years; Comptroller of Public Accounts, State of Texas, 1978 Annual Financial Report and 1983 Annual Financial Report, Table 5.

until the mid-1980s. The subsequent drop in petroleum prices has placed a significant strain on the state's fiscal structure.

Regulation of Energy Production

Unlike solid mineral resources, which remain in place, petroleum flows like water. The fugitive nature of petroleum makes it a potential common property resource, that is, a resource whose rights are held jointly by many individual land owners.

Rights to extract petroleum in Texas have traditionally been defined by the "rule of capture," which was developed for groundwater use.[10] Under this rule, one can extract and use whatever can be captured on one's own property. In the arena of oil extraction, this rule effectively means "Do unto others before others do unto you." Unrestricted, individuals have an incentive to extract oil under their property as quickly as possible, lest it be withdrawn by an adjacent property owner who pumps even faster. These practices have two detrimental effects: (1) they reduce the proportion of a reservoir that can ultimately be recovered; and (2) the excessively rapid rate of production depresses petroleum prices.

Oil Regulation   The 1930 discovery of the East Texas field, then the largest in the world, resulted in events that altered the structure of the oil industry and created an atmosphere conducive to the development of an effective state oil policy. Mineral rights in this field were widely dispersed among small royalty owners and independents. Because of the disjointed management of the fields, the frantic pumping flooded the market and depressed prices from over $1 per barrel to 10 cents. Rivals threatened to blow up each other's pipelines. In 1931, the governor had to call out the National Guard to end the chaos.

It was clear that a laissez faire market in petroleum was disastrous, and that the rule of capture had to be modified. The Constitution of 1890 created the three-member Railroad Commission of Texas (RRC) to regulate railroad rates. In 1917, the legislature authorized the RRC to regulate pipelines as common carriers and to institute production controls. The commission issued its first production limitation order in 1919, but Texas oilmen had successfully ignored or fought these limits in court. Lacking legal authority, the commission's policies were ineffective before 1930.

The chaos in the East Texas oil fields induced the U.S. Supreme Court to uphold the state's right to restrict oil production. Again the Texas legislature increased the powers of the RRC. After 1930, the commission developed three major instruments for controlling oil production: (1) "prorationing"; (2) restrictions on well spacing; and (3) restrictions on slant drilling.

As it eventually evolved, prorationing comprised three steps. First, geologists and petroleum engineers determined the "maximum efficient rate" (MER) of production capacity of a reservoir.[11] Second, purchasers of crude indicated the amount they wished to acquire each month. The sum of these "nominations" provided an estimate of market demand. Finally, since the maximum efficient production capability generally exceeded monthly demand by some proportion, each producer was allowed to produce a prorated share of his capacity.

Because of their scale of operations, changes in output of major producers had significant impact on prices, while changes in output from small independents did not. For this reason, the majors were more favorable to production controls than the independents. The principle of prorationing was reluctantly accepted by most independents during the 1931–32 East Texas boom. Nevertheless, evasion of RRC prorationing orders was rampant until the mid-1940s. Court battles over which wells could produce, equitable adjustments for marginal wells, and spacing of new discoveries continued. The commission ultimately exempted from prorationing "strippers," which are marginal wells producing less than twenty barrels/day.

The prorationing system functioned effectively from 1946 to 1973. Because Texas produced about 45% of the domestic oil supply, it was able to affect domestic prices significantly. By adjusting the "allowable" percent of the maximum efficient rate of production, Texas served as the "balance wheel" of the national oil market, much like Saudi Arabia serves in OPEC.

Federal support was essential to the success of Texas' prorationing system. Key elements of this support were the 1935 Connally Hot Oil Act, which prohibited the interstate shipment of oil produced in violation of state prorationing limits, and the Interstate Oil Compact, which set production guidelines for producing states. Discoveries of new fields always strained interstate prorationing schemes, which gradually eroded after World War II.

The expansion of the Middle Eastern oil fields after the 1950s threatened to flood the domestic market with cheap imports, thus destroying the commission's ability to control prices. The establishment of national oil import quotas in 1959, therefore, was essential in enabling the RRC to maintain the protective prorationing system for Texas independents. In the period prior to the 1970s, "allowables" were generally set at about 50% of the MER, but occasionally they fell as low as 30%. The 1973 embargo completely changed the rules of the game: foreign oil was now expensive, and domestic oil cheap. The rapid ascension of prices combined with the gradual decline of domestic production capacity resulted in the virtual abandonment of oil prorationing in Texas. Now the commission sets the allowable at 100% of the MER.

Well-spacing restrictions are the commission's second instrument in controlling oil production. Created in the 1920s, this instrument was relatively ineffective. On the one hand, the majors who operated large tracts practiced optimum spacing on a voluntary basis. On the other hand, exceptions were readily granted to owners of acreages that were too small to meet the formal spacing rule. In fields where large and small tracts were interspersed, owners of the latter appropriated a disproportionate share of the resources under the rule of capture. In 1962 the U.S. Supreme Court required a uniform application of the commission's spacing rules, rendering them more effective.

One instrument which the legislature has chosen not to give the commission is the power to compel "unitization." Under unitization, the extent of a reservoir is defined by exploratory drilling. Next, owners of a majority interest in a reservoir can compel the minority to join on unified management. Finally, royalties are apportioned according to the estimated share of oil derived from each tract. Although bills are continually introduced into the legislature to compel unitization, Texas remains the only major oil-producing state without a compulsory unitization law. The opposition from independents stems from their doubts about the fairness of any schemes for apportioning royalties. However, voluntary unitization has been implemented in many large fields shared by few royalty owners.[12]

The absence of compulsory unitization gave rise to a serious abuse. By drilling at a slant, a royalty owner can exploit the reservoir lying below a neighbor's property. In the 1930s, many small independents in the East Texas field were engaged in exploiting the pools of the majors. While illegal, slant drilling was difficult to detect. Moreover, many Texans tacitly approved of independents' draining the majors' fields. As the detection technology improved the commission attempted to control this abuse. A scandal in which surveyors falsified measurements of drilling angles shook the commission in the 1950s. Now slant drilling is under control.[13]

The consequences of the RRC's policies can be evaluated in terms of both efficiency and equity. An efficient production-control policy is one that results in producing a given quantity of crude oil at the least cost. Allocating the allowables as some proportion of geological production capacity does not necessarily allocate allowables in the most efficient manner.[14] Production controls raised the prices for all wells. So long as this price was above the costs of discovering and producing from new wells, exploration was encouraged. Finally, the production controls have conserved the depletable stock of oil for a longer period than would have been the case in their absence. This stock proved to be useful during embargoes in the Middle East in 1956 and 1973.

Production controls altered the distribution of income between national consumers and Texas producers. All consumers, including Texans, paid more for oil during the 1950s and 1960s than would have been the case otherwise. On the other hand, the availability of additional reserves in the 1970s created a downward pressure on prices.

Natural Gas Regulation   Natural gas was originally produced as a by-product of oil extraction and called casinghead gas. Until the 1940s, this by-product was treated mainly as a dangerous nuisance. Because of its bulk, gas was difficult to store or to deliver to customers. Most casinghead gas was simply burned off, or "flared." In unassociated gas reservoirs, wastes from "stripping" natural gas of a condensate (similar to refined gasoline) were also flared. Where markets existed, gas prices were only one-tenth that of oil with comparable heating value.[15] Because technologies for using natural gas as a chemical feedstock or as a medium for rebuilding pressure in oil fields were undeveloped, flaring was clearly economical.

In the 1930s and 1940s, as much as 2.5 billion cubic feet per day were flared. (At 1980 prices of $2 per thousand cubic feet, this was a waste of $5 million a day or $2 billion a year). Throughout the 1930s, the RRC addressed the issue of gas wastage with little success. While the legislature banned this practice in 1935, the commission had insufficient staff to enforce the law.

By the early 1940s, profitable methods for repressurizing oil fields by injecting natural gas were developed. Many oil well operators found it in their self-interest to recycle casinghead gas by injection, but as much as half of this gas was still flared by the end of the 1940s. By 1947, threats of federal intervention spurred the RRC's efforts to restrict flaring. Between 1947 and 1949 the commission successfully shut down flaring in several fields and was upheld by court rulings throughout. The problem of eliminating the wastage of natural gas was solved more by technology than by policy.

Because of its bulk, natural gas is best delivered to customers through a network of pipelines. The creation of an interregional pipeline network after World War II opened up a vast national market for natural gas as a home-heating and industrial-boiler fuel. The invention of new petrochemical technologies, which used gas as a chemical feedstock, further augmented demand. With these developments, the flaring issue virtually withered away.

The regulation of natural gas extraction has been more complicated than that of oil extraction.[16] While the Federal Power Commission (FPC) was authorized to regulate transportation charges of the pipelines, the price of wellhead gas was originally set by market forces. A 1954 landmark decision of the Supreme Court, *Phillips Petroleum* vs. *Wisconsin*, allowed the FPC (now the Federal Energy Regulatory Commission) to regulate the wellhead price of natural gas sold through interstate commerce. Because this gas was perceived as a mere by-product, obtainable in fixed supply from oil operations, the FPC was persuaded to set the price of gas extremely low. (In fact, about 75% of the state's gas resources have been unassociated with petroleum.) This price was set on a reservoir-by-reservoir basis, with some reference to the price on intrastate markets, which remained unregulated.

Texas produced about half of the nation's natural gas, so the RRC might have been in a position to play a major role in natural gas markets by controlling supply. Although the supply of casinghead gas was determined by oil production, the prorationing of unassociated gas was conceivable. For several decades the RRC struggled with the technical problem of instituting prorationing with only modest effectiveness. The overriding federal control of interstate gas prices, however, preempted state attempts to influence prices through prorationing.

The Natural Gas Policy Act of 1978 completely revised the rules of the game. Congress eliminated the intrastate vs. interstate pricing distinction and created several new pricing categories. "New gas" discovered after 1978 was totally deregulated. Gas discovered in the period 1973–78 was to be deregulated in stages by 1985–87. Old gas discovered before 1973 was to remain under controls at contractual prices until the wells ran dry.

Like their counterparts elsewhere, Texas producers have mixed feelings about the partial deregulation of natural gas. On the one hand, owners of old reservoirs would like to see controls lifted completely. On the other hand, they are aware that when price controls were lifted from oil production, a windfall-profits tax was imposed. Rather than risking new taxation, producer associations are not anxious to have Congress pay much additional attention to gas pricing. With the falling of prices in the gas market in the early 1980s and the rapid exhaustion of price-controlled reservoirs, the issue of complete deregulation appears to be withering away.

Regulation of Electric Utilities

Electrification is one of the least-heralded achievements of modern life. Until recently electricity was so ubiquitous, reliable, and cheap, that it was taken for granted, like an unspoken natural right. But it was not always so. The hardships of farmers and housewives of the cotton country of East Texas made a searing impression on a congressman who was later to become speaker of the House. The knowledge that electricity could literally liberate people from drudgery fueled Congressman Sam Rayburn's drive to pass Rural Electrification by 1935.[17]

Advances in generating efficiency, expansion of transmission networks, and increasing availability of cheap oil resulted in impressive cost reductions. In 1906, a kilowatt-hour (kwh) of electricity cost a residential user 11 cents in current dollars. Over the next sixty years costs dropped continuously: from 8 cents per kwh around World War I, to 3.5 cents in World War II, to slightly over 2 cents in 1970. In the period 1914–70, the cost of residential electricity fell by 75% while consumer prices rose 300%, so the real cost fell by a factor of 15.[18]

Associated with this drastic price reduction was an extraordinary expansion in annual residential electricity use per household, from 450 kwh in 1925 to 8,850 kwh in 1978.[19] Since World War II, total electricity generation in Texas has increased an astounding twenty-five times compared to ten times nationwide. Texas generates more electricity than any other state and has two of the nation's top ten utilities in term of electricity sales and revenues.[20]

Before the Golden Age ended around 1970, utilities enjoyed a privileged position in capital markets. As regulated monopolies they were generally allowed to earn a return slightly above their actual cost of raising capital to build plants. Well rated by the credit agencies, they could issue bonds at interest rates slightly below those paid by blue chip industrial corporations.[21] Capital was so cheap that many economists hypothesized that utilities had an incentive to overbuild.[22]

The Crisis of the Utility Industry In the early 1970s, electric utilities were buffeted by twin crises. First was the epoch-shattering fuel price increases. Nationally, in the 1973–80 period, the prices paid by utilities for oil rose 430%, for coal 233%, and for gas 526% (Table 5–3). These far exceeded the 94% rise in consumer prices.[23]

These fuel price increases have been particularly damaging to utilities in Texas and the Southwest. In 1970, there was virtually no coal-burning capacity and no nuclear capacity in the state. The price of natural gas, the main utility fuel in Texas, increased faster than any other fuel. Despite the massive shift of generating fuels from expensive natural gas to cheaper coal, composite fuel costs in Texas rose from about 70% of the national average before 1973 to over 90% of the average in the 1980s.

Second, utilities came under scrutiny because of the environmental costs they inflict upon society. There are significant unpaid costs of electric energy inherent in the entire fuel cycle. These include injuries to coal and uranium miners, pollution of air and water by power plant emissions, and the prodigious disruption of land for mining and the disposal of solid waste.[24] The environmental legislation of the 1970s aimed at "internalizing" these costs on the balance sheets and income statements of all industries. This legislation had a major impact on the cost structure of the electric utility industry.

Table 5-3. Cost of Utility Fuels, 1961–1985, (current dollars per millions of British thermal units).

	Texas				West S. Central				U.S.			
	Coal	Oil	Gas	Total	Coal	Oil	Gas	Total	Coal	Oil	Gas	Total
1961	n.a.	0.52	0.17	0.17	0.18	0.48	0.19	0.19	0.26	0.35	0.26	0.27
1965	n.a.	0.45	0.19	0.19	0.18	0.45	0.20	0.20	0.24	0.33	0.25	0.25
1969	n.a.	0.43	0.20	0.20	0.31	0.38	0.20	0.20	0.27	0.40	0.26	0.27
1970	n.a.	0.51	0.21	0.21	0.40	0.50	0.21	0.21	0.31	0.49	0.28	0.31
1971	0.21	0.54	0.22	0.22	0.21	0.60	0.22	0.22	0.36	0.56	0.29	0.37
1972	0.22	0.75	0.24	0.25	0.22	0.69	0.24	0.25	0.38	0.62	0.31	0.41
1973	0.14	0.92	0.28	0.29	0.14	0.89	0.29	0.32	0.42	0.78	0.35	0.48
1974	0.18	1.51	0.49	0.46	0.18	1.81	0.44	0.51	0.68	1.83	0.50	0.89
1975	0.24	1.71	0.75	0.72	0.24	1.90	0.71	0.89	0.86	2.00	0.75	1.08
1976	0.31	2.00	1.00	0.94	0.31	1.88	0.96	0.97	0.89	2.01	1.02	1.15
1977	0.52	2.02	1.21	1.13	0.54	2.00	1.36	1.12	0.98	2.24	1.28	1.32
1978	0.69	2.05	1.34	1.23	0.73	1.97	1.14	1.29	1.16	2.23	1.41	1.45
1979	0.97	2.10	1.54	1.40	0.97	2.10	1.54	1.40	1.27	2.93	1.74	1.55
1980	1.17	3.12	1.82	1.62	1.19	3.71	1.85	1.73	1.40	4.18	2.20	1.97
1981	1.38	3.46	2.44	2.08	1.40	4.89	2.43	2.15	1.58	5.36	2.81	2.30
1982	1.51	3.84	3.12	2.51	1.56	4.79	2.97	2.49	1.69	5.07	3.40	2.34
1983	1.53	4.68	3.19	n.a.	1.72	5.16	3.07	n.a.	1.66	4.64	3.47	n.a.
1984	1.69	5.38	3.22	n.a.	1.77	5.50	3.14	n.a.	1.66	4.89	3.57	n.a.
1985	1.50	4.86	3.12	n.a.	1.59	5.00	3.05	n.a.	1.66	4.36	3.50	n.a.

Sources: Edison Electric Institute (EEI), *Historical Statistics of the Electric Utility Industry through 1970* (1974), Table 42S; idem, *Statistical Yearbook of the Electric Utility Industry*, annual volumes, Tables 42 and 43; Energy Information Agency, *Electric Power Monthly* (Sept., 1985), Tables 1, 20–22.

This industry bore about half of the capital costs of pollution control equipment from the act.[25] Tighter emission controls have raised the cost of coal-fired power plants by about 25%.[26] The financial burden of this act has been particularly heavy because electric utilities are the most capital-intensive industry in the economy. Moreover, the capital crisis was heightened by the shift of utilities from oil and gas plants (which are relatively cheap to build, but which use expensive fuel) to coal and nuclear (which are very expensive to build, but which use relatively cheap fuel).

As competitors with other industries for capital, the electric utility industry had to pass the cost of these twin shocks on to the consumers. While previously such requests had been relatively rare, utilities had to turn repeatedly to regulatory commissions for rate increases. Unaccustomed to inflation, consumers put considerable pressure on commissions to resist these requests. Unlike the price of oil, which appeared to be set by OPEC, electricity prices appeared to frustrated consumers to be subject to easy political control.

In the 1970s regulatory commissions were faced with conflicting pressures from consumers, who wanted to control their rising electric bills, and from utilities, which wanted to pass the rising costs of generating capacity and fuel onto the consumer. In response to the realities of rising cost, the monthly residential bill for 1,000 kwh more than tripled nationally in the 1973–85 period (Table 5–4). The average bill in Texas rose slightly faster than the national pace during this period, and much faster in selected Texas cities, like Houston, Fort Worth, and Dallas.[27]

In response to public pressure, regulatory commissions in the 1970s were generally reluctant to raise electric rates much faster than inflation. Since their own costs were rising faster than the rates they could charge, electric utilities were placed in an increasingly precarious financial position. By the end of the decade, few utilities received the highest credit ratings. The interest rates they have to pay in order to sell their bonds now exceed those of industrial borrowers. Once one of the safest financial investments, utilities nationwide have become one of the riskiest.

The Public Utility Commission of Texas   Texas was the last state to regulate electric utilities. Before 1975, municipalities regulated electric, telephone, water, and sewer rates. Rate shocks of the early 1970s induced the legislature to create the Public Utility Commission of Texas (PUC).[28] The commission has exclusive original jurisdiction over telephone, electric, water, and sewer utilities located in unincorporated areas. Municipalities retain jurisdiction over these utilities as

Table 5–4. Costs of Energy to Consumers in Texas and U.S., 1965–85 (current dollars).

	Texas			U.S.		
	Electric 1,000 kwh	Gasoline/ Gallon	Nat. Gas Thou. Cu. Ft.	Electric 1,000 kwh	Gasoline/ Gallon	Nat. Gas Thou. Cu. Ft.
1965	18.33	0.199	0.87	18.59	0.312	1.04
1970	17.40	0.319	0.97	18.31	0.357	1.09
1971	17.32	0.339	1.03	19.24	0.364	1.15
1972	17.51	0.339	1.04	20.70	0.361	1.21
1973	18.39	0.324	1.06	21.85	0.388	1.29
1974	19.82	0.379	1.19	24.85	0.532	1.43
1975	24.85	0.484	1.51	32.29	0.567	1.71
1976	29.27	0.530	2.09	34.85	0.590	1.98
1977	33.41	0.522	2.43	38.15	0.622	2.35
1978	35.03	0.538	2.68	40.98	0.626	2.56
1979	37.59	0.614	2.96	43.12	0.857	2.98
1980	43.87	1.000	3.39	48.79	1.191	3.68
1981	49.50	1.200	n.a.	58.16	1.311	4.29
1982	58.46	1.260	n.a.	66.39	1.222	5.17
1983	64.24	n.a.	n.a.	69.96	1.157	6.06
1984	69.48	n.a.	n.a.	72.77	1.129	6.12
1985	69.56	n.a.	n.a.	76.37	n.a.	6.54

Sources: General: Diane R. Burnett and James Chang, *Texas Energy History* (Austin: Texas Advisory Commission on Energy and Natural Resources, 1982). Electric: U.S. Department of Energy, Energy Information Agency, *Typical Electric Bills*, annual, 1978–85; Federal Power Commission, *Typical Electric Bills*, annual before 1978. Gasoline and natural gas: U.S. Department of Energy, Energy Information Agency, *Monthly Energy Review*, since 1974; Texas Railroad Commission, Gas Utilities Division, *Annual Statistical Report*. Recent data: Energy Information Agency, *Annual Energy Review*, 1984.

well as over gas, but may relinquish authority to the PUC. Few cities have chosen this option, and thus the PUC serves largely as a court of appeal. Appeals of gas rates remain with the RRC. Like commissions elsewhere, the Texas PUC is charged with balancing concerns of maintaining the "financial integrity" of the utilities with consumer interests, represented by the PUC's public counsel.

In contrast to the size and complexity of the business it regulates, the Public Utility Commission of Texas has one of the nation's smallest staffs. About 120 professionals regulate over 1,600 water utilities, 500 sewer utilities, over 70 telephone companies, and 174 electric utilities. In fiscal year 1982, the staff prepared reports and testimony for 229 electric utility cases, 125 telephone cases, and 227 water and sewer cases.[29] The four largest electric-generating states have staffs that are three to eight times larger. These comparisons raise the question of whether the legislature has appropriated resources comparable with the responsibilities assigned to the PUC.

Regulators grant a public utility "certificates of necessity and convenience within a given service area." In exchange for an obligation to provide adequate and continuous service to every customer, this certificate provides the utility with a monopoly as well as power of eminent domain for the construction of necessary transmission and distribution facilities. The utility must seek PUC approval for the construction of new generation and transmission facilities.

Because a utility must compete in national capital markets, regulators are required to allow a "fair" return on capital and to set "just and reasonable" rates for consumers. The rate-setting process aims to provide enough revenue for the utility to cover its taxes, operating costs (mostly fuel), and fixed costs (depreciation and return to investors).

Rate setting involves several steps. First, the utility estimates the total amount of electricity expected to be generated in the coming year, based upon anticipations of the weather and economic growth. The amount of fuel to meet this demand is estimated. Until 1983, the Texas PUC had allowed an automatic pass-through of fuel costs through the fuel adjustment clause. Now the fuel portion is estimated beforehand, and the utility must petition for a rate increase based upon fuel-cost escalation.

Second, the PUC determines the "rate base," which is the value of fixed capital invested in the provision of electricity. Because of the rampant inflation of the last decade, the cost of replacing existing facilities is far higher than the historical cost. In Texas, the PUC is directed to compute the rate base by attributing a weight of 60% to 75% to original cost and the remainder to replacement cost.

A controversial issue in the determination of the rate base is the treatment of construction works in progress (CWIP), which are not yet providing any service. The industry has generally argued that CWIP should be included in the rate base, because the utility has to provide a return to investors, whether or not the facility is producing. Consumer advocates generally argue that it is unfair to consumers to pay for investments before they receive a service. In most states, public utility commissions have granted only a fraction of CWIP in the rate base. The remainder of the capital expenditure is classified as "allowance for funds used during construction" (AFUDC), which is capital plus accumulated interest that is added to the rate base only upon completion of the facilities. Because many new coal and nuclear facilities become operative only after a five- to ten-year construction period, the accumulated interest can be as much as 40% higher than the outlay for construction. This accumulation opens the consumer to rate shock.

Third, the PUC must determine the allowable return on the rate base. Obligations to investors in existing facilities include (1) payments on debt (bonds) of different vintages, and (2) dividends on equity (stock). The interest on bonds is guaranteed, but the dividends on stock are not. Nevertheless, bondholders look at returns on equity as a cushion against unforeseen threats to their guaranteed earnings. Inflation in the last two decades has raised nominal interest rates in capital markets. Unless the PUC allows rate of return to rise with the market, investors suffer a loss on capital value. Indeed, this has occurred, as utilities' ratio of market to book value has fallen.

The rate-setting process determines an average rate per kwh of electricity. A related issue is the rate structure, that is, how the rate is allocated among different users, classified by residential vs. commercial, or large user vs. small user. The Public Utility Regulatory Policies Act of 1978 directs state utility commissions to (a) consider cost of service, time-of-day pricing, and lifeline rates (for low-income consumers) in its hearings; (b) encourage load or demand-side management instead of supply-side expansion; and (c) establish "just and reasonable" buy-back rates to encourage cogeneration and renewable energy. While commissions in such states as California and Wisconsin have aggressively encouraged demand management and cogeneration, until recently the Texas PUC has not.

The determination of just and reasonable rates and fair rates of return is not purely a technical matter, for they involve both judgments of fact and adjudication of competing interests. Throughout the nation, these matters have become increasingly politicized.

Investment bankers and credit-rating agencies generally measure the regulatory climate by actions of the state regulatory commission.[30] They rely heavily on such indicators as allowed return on equity, time lag in making decisions, timeliness of the fuel adjustment clause, and accounting procedures, such as percentage of CWIP allowed. The Texas Public Utility Commission has been perceived by the investment community as being quite sympathetic to concerns of utilities on all the important indicators, and as a consequence has received the highest rating in the nation.

Unlike the railroad commissioners, who are elected, the PUC commissioners are appointed by the governor. The performance of the appointees on the PUC was a salient issue in the 1982 gubernatorial campaign. Charges were hurled back and forth about the commission's role as a "watchdog" for consumers versus a "lapdog" for the industry, about the fuel adjustment clause, and about whether laymen, such as housewives, were as capable of understanding utility issues as were experts. Questions were even raised about whether Texans might not be better off electing their commissioners, as is the case in twelve other states.

Soon after the election of Governor Mark White in 1982, the legislature abolished the automatic pass-through of fuel costs, the "fuel adjustment clause." With resignations of his predecessor's appointees, White was able to appoint the entire PUC. In response, many of the brokerage houses put utilities in Texas on a "credit watch," pending a rate decision of the new commission. In early 1984, credit-rating agencies lowered the bond rating of Texas utilities, which formerly enjoyed the only AAA bond rating among the nation's electric companies. From the viewpoint of the utility industry and its investors, the regulatory climate in Texas has deteriorated.

How does the regulatory climate affect the cost of electricity? This question can be broken down into three components: What factors, such as elected vs. appointed commissioners determine this climate? And what is the relationship between the cost of capital and the cost of electricity?

The regulatory climate has been explained by the degree of political exposure of the commissioners (indicated by mode of selection and length of term) and the state fiscal support for the commission (indicated by commissioners' salary and expenditures on staff). Generally, the climate appears more favorable to utilities in states where commissioners are appointed by the governor directly. Longer terms result in less political exposure and a regulatory climate more favorable to utilities. Higher salaries and expenditures on staff also encourage a favorable climate.

An unfavorable regulatory climate generally results in lower bond ratings, lower market-to-book values of equity, and higher interest costs on debt.[31] The result is that investors demand a higher risk premium for securities of utilities faced with an unfavorable regulatory climate.

The linkages between regulatory climate or cost of capital and electric rates are not clear. In the short run, the conditions which result in an unfavorable regulatory climate (particularly elected commissioners) also result in lower electricity prices. Indeed, states with elected commissioners (a factor worsening the climate from utility viewpoint) enjoyed lower electricity rates in the inflationary 1970s.[32] In the long run, however, an unfavorable regulatory climate may take its toll. The cost of new issues of utility stocks and bonds, which reflects the market's evaluation of regulatory risks, may rise. These considerations may be particularly important for growing states like Texas, which must finance the construction of new, capital-intensive lignite plants.

A looming issue is the recovery of costs from two major nuclear power plants in the state. The cost of Comanche Peak in North Texas has escalated from $750 million when construction was authorized in 1974 to over $4 billion, when generation begins in the late 1980s. About half of the price increase is due to inflation, but the rest has resulted from a mix of regulatory delays and unanticipated safety problems. Delays and cost escalation have plagued nuclear utilities nationwide. In some states, public utility commissions have passed the full cost of nuclear overruns on to the consumers. The ensuing "rate shocks" have raised demands for tighter control on utility management. Increasingly, commissions around the nation have forced the utilities to bear most of the cost of the overruns, and similar pressures may build in Texas.

Energy-Environment Trade-Offs: An Emerging Issue

Nearly all of the national environmental acts passed since 1970 depend upon state implementation. For example, the Clean Air Act requires states to establish an implementation plan for meeting national ambient air quality standards. Texas has chosen to disperse the enforcement of environmental regulations among a wide range of agencies. The key agencies controlling pollution from the extraction of energy resources are the Texas Railroad Commission and the Texas Department of Water Resources (TDWR). The Texas Air Control Board (TACB) is the key agency dealing with air emissions from energy combustion.[33]

Historically, the RRC has played a major role in controlling the environmental impact of the petroleum industry. The RRC regulates (1) the deep-well injection of wastes from oil drilling; (2) the injection of saltwater into oil and gas formations for purposes of secondary recovery; and (3) the plugging of abandoned wells. Aimed at preventing groundwater contamination, these regulations have been far ahead of Federal efforts. Under the Federal Surface Mining and Reclamation Act of 1977, the RRC is responsible for issuing five-year permits for surface mining and supervising reclamation. The latter powers give the state considerable control of the emerging lignite mining industry.

The TDWR is empowered to grant permits for (1) wastewater effluents from lignite mines; and (2) siting of power plants. In collaboration with the RRC, the TDWR regulates the underground injection of oil-drilling wastes or saltwater.

The Texas Clean Air Act of 1967 empowers the TACB to issue permits to any facility that may emit contaminants into the atmosphere. This agency also implements the provisions of the Federal Clean Air Act. The TACB administers the state plan for improving air quality in Air Quality Control Regions which do not attain national ambient air quality standards. For example, in 1980 the TACB established nitrogen oxide limitations for large facilities located in the Dallas-Fort Worth and Houston-Galveston areas, which do not attain these standards.[34]

New energy facilities are required to meet stricter emissions standards than are older facilities. New power plants are expected to extract as much as 80% of the sulfur content of the fuel they burn. Facilities locating in regions which have cleaner air than the national standard must certify that they will not significantly reduce air quality.

During the 1970s, utilities in Texas began a massive shift from nearly total dependence upon clean-burning natural gas to coal and lignite. By 1983, about 25% of the state's generating capacity utilized lignite, and about 40% of all electricity was generated by this fuel. By 1992, these figures are expected to be about 34% and 50%, respectively.[35]

The Texas lignite belt extends from the northeastern corner of the state to the southwest, beyond San Antonio. Because lignite is bulky and costly to transport, power plants are being built at the mines. The expansion of lignite combustion raises a potential threat of (1) emissions of sulfur and nitrogen oxides; (2) competition for scarce water between mining/electric generation, and other sectors; and (3) groundwater contamination from the lignite cycle.

The power plants planned for the lignite belt are situated in areas that currently meet national ambient air quality standards for sulfur and nitrogen oxides. Preliminary analysis suggests that the construction of all of these plants can be achieved without a significant deterioration of ambient air quality standards with a fifty-kilometer radius of the plants.[36] However, there may be significant impacts from emissions of particulates, radioactive traces, or from the long-range transport of sulfur and nitrogen oxides.

The long-range transport of these oxides has been associated with increased acid precipitation in the eastern part of the United States.[37] The consequences of acid rain are complex, and it may even benefit vegetation in zones with alkaline soils, like West Texas. There is considerable evidence, however, of the damaging effect of acid precipitation on lakes, forests, and farms with soils that are naturally acidic. This may be the case in the Piney Woods of East Texas.

The lignite belt overlays aquifers that are significant sources of water.[38] Water is withdrawn in nearly all stages of lignite electric generation. Water is consumed in strip mining and reclamation, ash handling, and scrubbing. Steam electric power plants require water for cooling, ash handling, and scrubbing. Cooling involves the temporary withdrawal of water for later discharge at a higher temperature. In all phases of the lignite cycle, the amount of water withdrawn and consumed is minor relative to the available supply in the humid portions of the lignite belt.

The lignite cycle poses several potential threats to water quality. If mining extends below the water table, the normal recharge of the aquifer is interrupted. There is a risk that the water flooding the mine or runoff from the overburden may become acidified, but careful mining practices can avert significant impairment of surface- or groundwater. A more serious problem is the disposal of ash and scrubber sludge that is captured from air pollution control equipment. Unless these solid wastes are disposed of properly, they may contaminate the groundwater. Fortunately, proper disposal techniques appear feasible, including the recycling of ash as a construction material.

It is too early to determine whether fishing, lumbering, ranching, and farming in East Texas will suffer from the expansion of lignite electricity generation, but public officials and citizens should be alerted to the possibility.

Texas Energy Future

Petroleum production in Texas is likely to continue the decline that traces back to the 1960s. The value of this production, the royalties from public lands, the magnitude of severance taxes, and the future of the oil-service industries will all depend upon prices in world oil markets. Despite the apparent glut of the 1980s, nearly all observers expect the real price of oil (correcting for inflation) to increase by 1% to 3% for the rest of the century.[39]

While it is unlikely that the oil boom will be replicated, the long-run trajectory of oil and gas prices will provide the state with a solid, but relatively diminishing, economic base. The share of the state's output derived from petroleum extraction is likely to drop by half by the year 2010.[40] Regions which depend heavily on petroleum extraction will have to make painful adjustments to the new realities. The state treasury will have to depend less upon petroleum production taxes and the Permanent Funds less upon royalties. In the future, Texas will no longer be able to attract new industry on the basis of cheap and abundant energy. Electricity, gasoline, and natural gas are no longer much cheaper in Texas than elsewhere (Table 5–4).

Petroleum has financed a solid infrastructure of highways and universities. Petroleum has also sown the seeds for a highly dynamic, diversified economy. Texas will continue to be a major, although declining, petroleum exporter for the next few decades, but one new dynamo may be the petroleum-servicing sector drilling companies, seismic instrumentation manufacturers, petroleum engineering consultants, and construction contractors. Technological spinoffs from the petroleum service sector may serve as a further dynamo: microelectronics, computer systems, and genetic engineering. The petroleum-service sector may be the bridge to a future economy based upon worldwide export of high technology.

Notes

This chapter was prepared with assistance of Gerald B. Fritz, Douglas J. Manifold, and Barbara Durso.

1. T. R. Fehrenbach, *Lone Star: A History of Texas and the Texans* (New York: Collier, 1968), 667–69.

2. David Howard Davis, *Energy Politics* (New York: St. Martin's Press, 1978).

3. David Prindle, *Petroleum Politics and the Texas Railroad Commission* (Austin: University of Texas Press, 1981).

4. According to the Standard Industrial Classification (SIC), the petroleum sector comprises oil and gas extraction (SIC 13), petroleum and coal products (SIC 29), oil field machinery (SIC 3533), and gas distribution (SIC 492).

5. Texas Department of Water Resources (TDWR), *The Texas Input-Output Model, 1972* (Austin; 1978); idem, *The Texas Input-Output Model, 1978* (Austin; 1983). For a general exposition of the technique, see Chiou-Shuang Yan, *Introduction to Input-Output Economics* (New York: Holt, Rinehart and Winston, 1969).

6. Because of federal oil price controls, the increase in world oil prices in the 1973–80 period did not translate into commensurate increases in prices received by domestic producers.

7. *Texas Almanac, 1983*, 435.

8. The Federal Energy Regulatory Commission allows gas transmission companies to count the gas gathering tax as an expense, which is passed on to consumers.

9. Comptroller of Public Accounts, *The Petroleum Industry and the Texas Sales Tax*, Special Financial Report (Austin: April, 1983).

10. James R. Norvell, "The Railroad Commission of Texas: Its Origin and Relation to the Oil and Gas Industry," *Texas Law Review* 40 (1962):238–41.

11. The higher the rate of oil production, the greater the likelihood that water and gas escapes with the oil, thereby reducing field pressure. Lower pressures reduce the amount of oil that can be recovered without resort to expensive secondary recovery procedures; i.e., repressurizing the field by injecting gas or steam. See Stephen L. McDonald, *Petroleum Conservation in the United States: An Economic Analysis* (Baltimore: Johns Hopkins University Press, 1971), ch. 2.

12. Gary D. Libecap and Steven N. Wiggins, "Contractual Responses to the Common Pool: Prorationing of Crude Oil Production," *American Economic Review* 74 (March, 1984):87–98.

13. Prindle, *Petroleum Politics*, ch. 5. On the current status of slant drilling, personal communication from Rex King, Oil and Field Operations, Texas Railroad Commission, August 3, 1984.

14. Economic efficiency prescribes extracting oil from the cheaper wells first. Prorationing allows expensive and cheap wells to operate simultaneously.

15. James M. Griffin and Henry B. Steele, *Energy Economics and Policy* (New York: Academic Press, 1980).

16. *Texas Almanac, 1983.*

17. Anthony M. Champagne, *Congressman Sam Rayburn* (New Brunswick, N.J.: Rutgers University Press, 1984).

18. Edison Electric Institute (EEI), *Historical Statistics of the Electric Utility Industry through 1970* (New York: EEI, 1974), Table 61.

19. Edison Electric Institute, *Statistical Year Book of the Electric Utility Industry* (New York: EEI, 1980), Chart VII-B.

20. *Electric Light & Power* (June, 1983).

21. Edison Electric Institute, *Statistical Year Book*, Tables 57 and 58.

22. Michael A. Crew and Paul R. Kleindorfer, *Public Utility Economics* (New York: St. Martin's Press, 1979).

23. U.S. Department of Energy, *Monthly Energy Review* (March, 1980).

24. William Ramsay, *Unpaid Costs of Electrical Energy* (Baltimore: Johns Hopkins University Press, 1979).

25. Paul R. Portney, "The Macroeconomic Impacts of Federal Environmental Regulation," *Natural Resources Journal* 21 (July, 1981):459–88.

26. Committee on Nuclear and Alternative Energy Strategies, National Academy of Sciences, *Energy in Transition, 1985–2010* (San Francisco: Freeman, 1979), 161.

27. Federal Energy Regulatory Commission, *Typical Electric Bills* (Washington, D.C.: Government Printing Office, 1983).

28. Jack Hopper, "A Legislative History of the Texas Public Utility Regulatory Act of 1976," *Baylor Law Review* 28 (Fall, 1976):777–821; James E. Anderson, "The Public Utility Commission of Texas," *Public Affairs Comment* 26 (February, 1980):1–8; Greg A. Jarrell, "The Demand for State Regulation of the Electric Utility Industry," *Journal of Law and Economics* 21 (October, 1978):269–95.

29. Public Utility Commission of Texas, *1982 Annual Report* (Austin: 1983).

30. Merrill Lynch, Pierce, Fenner and Smith, *Utility Industry Opinions on Regulation* (New York: Merrill Lynch, September, 1983).

31. Peter Navarro, "Public Utility Commission Regulation: Performance, Determinants, and Energy Policy Impacts," *Energy Journal* 3 (April, 1982):119–140.

32. Patrick C. Mann and Walter J. Primeaux, Jr., "Regulator Selection and Electricity Prices," Bureau of Economic and Business Research, University of Illinois, Urbana-Champaign, BEBR Faculty Working Paper No. 887 (July, 1982).

33. Texas Energy and Natural Resources Advisory Council (TENRAC), *Guide to Texas Environmental Regulatory Programs* (Austin: June, 1982).

34. On compliance, see 31 TAC chap. 117, October 1, 1980.

35. North American Electric Reliability Council (NERC), *Electric Power Supply and Demand, 1984–1993* (Princeton, N.J.: NERC, 1984), 41, 79. Because they consume relatively cheap fuel, lignite plants are used almost constantly, to serve the "base" loads on the utility. Gas plants are used intermittently, to serve the "peak" loads on the utility. For this reason, the proportion of electricity generated by lignite can exceed the proportion of lignite-fired capacity.

36. U.S. Environmental Protection Agency (EPA), *An Integrated Assessment of Texas Lignite Development*, 4 vols., prepared for Texas Energy Advisory Council and U.S. Dept. of Energy, April, 1979; Texas Air Control Board (TACB), "Report on Feasibility Study of Locating Lignite-fired Power Plants in Texas, 1982–2000," prepared for TENRAC (November, 1982).

37. E. C. Krug and C. R. Fink, "Acid Rain on Acid Soil: A New Perspective," *Science* (August 5, 1983):520–25.

38. Herman W. Hoffman, "The Impact of Lignite Strip Mining and Use on Water Resources in Texas–A Brief Overview," Texas Department of Water Resources (October 19, 1978).

39. Sam Schurr et al., *Energy in America's Future* (Baltimore: Johns Hopkins University Press, 1979); Martin T. Katzman, *Solar and Wind Energy: An Economic Evaluation of Current and Future Technologies* (Totowa, N.J.: Littlefield Adams, 1984), 165–67.

40. Bureau of Business Research (BBR), *Texas Economic Outlook: Long-Term Forecast* (Austin: University of Texas, 1984).

Chapter Six

ASSESSING EDUCATIONAL *David Plank*
REFORM

Texas, the argument goes, has squandered its natural patrimony. The state has grown rich through the prodigal exploitation of its endowment of water, land, and petroleum, but these resources are rapidly being depleted and cannot be replaced. In the coming decade, therefore, the Texas economy will have to shift away from agriculture and oil toward high-technology industries and services if the state is to continue to grow and prosper.

This argument is often adduced in support of reform and improvement in Texas' educational system. In the future, the economy of Texas will be far more knowledge- and skill-intensive than it is at present. If the state is to remain competitive nationally and internationally, it will require a better-educated labor force, qualified to fill positions in the high-technology fields that will increasingly dominate the economy. It is argued that the quality of the state's educational system must be improved if entrepreneurs, engineers, and their high-technology firms are to be induced to settle in Texas, first, because a well-educated labor force is thought to be attractive to such firms and second, because excellent schools are necessary for the children of the entrepreneurs, engineers, and managers who decide where such firms are to be located.

This argument is open to serious question as a basis for educational reform. Though put forward as an argument in favor of broad-based educational improvements, it finally boils down to the need for well-educated workers and excellent schools in the handful of major metropolitan centers that might prove attractive to high-technology firms on other grounds: Houston, Dallas-Fort Worth, San Antonio, Austin. In fact, however, many communities in these areas are now served by schools which are as good as any in the country, and the continuing flow of interstate migrants to these centers combined with the output of local schools should ensure that a sufficient pool of well-educated workers is available to firms considering relocation. Other inducements, such as tax advantages, university support, and the proximity of other high-technology firms (all of which are present in Texas), are likely to be of considerably greater importance in the location decisions of particular firms than is the quality of the local public schools.

The argument also suggests that the shift of the national and state economies toward knowledge-intensive industries and services will produce a radical mismatch in the labor market, in which firms will face shortages of workers with the requisite levels of education and training, and in which workers lacking such education and training will be unable to find jobs. There are a variety of problems with this argument. It probably overestimates the labor requirements of the high-technology industries and it certainly overestimates the technical and intellectual requirements of most "high-technology" jobs. Moreover, it entirely rejects the possibility for on-the-job training of inadequately prepared recruits. As was noted above, the flow of interstate migrants to Texas combined with the output of the state's better schools is likely to be sufficient to avert any shortage of skilled personnel for Texas industries, and on-the-job training and national (or international) recruitment will be able to satisfy any specific shortfalls.

In addition, the advent of the "high-technology" era is likely to have effects on the labor market that are considerably less far-reaching than is often implied. Most Texans will continue to work in the occupations that have sustained them in the past, where education and skill requirements remain relatively modest, and most of the jobs created in high-technology industries will probably have education requirements not very different from those prevailing in the labor market today.[1]

The presumptive "crisis" in Texas' educational system is thus greatly exaggerated, as are most "crises" in the American public schools. The fact remains, however, that the state's educational system is among the worst in the United States, and there are at least two good reasons why improvements should be made.

First, improved education will enhance the productivity not only of those workers employed in high-technology industries, but also of all workers in the state's economy. Secretaries who can spell, mechanics who can read safety instructions, farmers who can calculate compound interest, and managers who can compose grammatical sentences perform their jobs more efficiently than those who lack these skills. The increases in productivity associated with improved education benefit the entire population of the state as well as the workers and firms directly involved, because of higher incomes and tax revenues and enhanced interstate and international competitiveness, among other things.

Second, the basic knowledge and competencies acquired in school are of increasingly great importance for the protection of individual rights and democratic values in a society that is daily becoming more complex. The failure to provide basic literacy and mathematical skills to all children is the single most important failure of the education system in Texas, not only because it restricts the future economic prospects of those without skills but also because it prohibits them from the free exercise of the most elementary rights of citizens in a democratic society. This failure is especially troubling when those who do not acquire these skills are disproportionately members of particular groups, including ethnic minorities, rural residents, and the poor.

A number of proposals for school reform have recently been put forward in Texas. These address four principal issues: the recruitment and retention of teachers; the integrity and rigor of the curriculum; the alleged excesses of previous educational reforms; and the quantity and distribution of resources for public education. Problems and reform proposals in each of these areas are examined in the following sections of this paper, in order to determine what changes are needed and what the effects of reform are likely to be. The concluding sections discuss the recent campaign for school reform in Texas.

Texas School Reform

Regardless of whether the crisis in Texas' public school system is real or imagined, the perception of crisis is widespread, and the cause of educational reform has attracted a great deal of public attention and political support in Texas as elsewhere in the United States. A wide variety of reforms have been proposed, but the common theme of present reform proposals is the need to restore the quality of American education. The campaign for improved quality in public education has two main aspects: an effort to restore "basic skills" to a central place in the school curriculum; and a related effort to cultivate excellence (especially in mathematics and scientific and technical subjects) among average and above-average students.

The accomplishment of these goals may require a variety of changes in the public school system, but four areas (the teaching force, the curriculum, special programs, and school finance) have received particular attention. In this section we examine each of these areas in turn, looking both at the dimensions of the problem and at the solutions that have been proposed.

Teachers Teachers have been the subject of many of the current proposals for educational reform in Texas. Two related problems are recognized. On the one hand, the competence of the present and future teaching force in Texas is questioned. Teachers are disproportionately recruited from among the least talented students in the state's colleges and universities, and their mastery of the subjects they teach and even of rudimentary literacy and numeracy is often uncertain. The training provided to prospective teachers bears only a tangential relationship to the occupational requirements of the teaching profession, and many new teachers find themselves unprepared for the conditions they encounter on the job. Excellence in teaching is seldom recognized and almost never rewarded, and the best teachers are consequently tempted to move into administrative posts or to leave the profession entirely in search of higher salaries and improved working conditions.

On the other hand, a serious shortage of teachers is anticipated in Texas in the near future, especially in particular fields including mathematics and natural science. Shortages in these and other areas are already severe in some of the less wealthy rural districts in the state, and "emergency" certificates have been granted to unqualified teachers in order to staff courses in these subjects. This practice is likely to become more common in the future, with further negative consequences for the quality of education provided to Texas children. Moreover, the shortage of teachers is exacerbated by high rates of turnover, especially among teachers with marketable qualifications.[2]

These problems are clearly related; both may be traced back to the fact that teaching is a relatively unattractive occupation in American society. Teachers are held in low esteem, working conditions in schools are often bad and sometimes appalling, salaries are low, and prospects for advancement within the profession are limited. Under these circumstances, it is not surprising that prospective teachers are commonly less bright and less qualified than those who plan to pursue other occupations; or that present and potential teachers with marketable qualifications in mathematics, natural sciences, and technical subjects choose employment in business and industry over employment in the schools. What is surprising is that so many competent, dedicated people continue to choose teaching as a career in spite of its many disadvantages.

While these two sets of problems are related, they are not the same, and reforms aimed at improvement in one area may create new problems in the other unless their interrelationship is taken into account. A comprehensive approach to the recruitment and employment of teachers is required if the quality of the state's teaching force is to be significantly improved.

Various reforms aimed at the recruitment and retention of competent teachers have been proposed in Texas. These fall into two main categories: those concerned with teacher salaries, and those concerned with teacher competency. Included in the first group are proposals for across-the-board increases in teacher salaries, increases in the salaries of beginning teachers, monetary rewards for excellence in teaching (career ladders and merit pay), and salary differentials for teachers in districts and fields where shortages of personnel are anticipated. The second group includes proposals for competency testing of present and prospective teachers, additional requirements or more rigorous training for teacher education students, and extended periods of internship for new teachers.

In the scope of a brief chapter it is not possible to discuss all of these proposals in depth, but some general observations on the problems associated with specific proposals are nevertheless in order. With regard to teacher salaries, for example, the central question is whether the proposed reforms will have the desired effect of improving the quality of the teaching force in Texas. An across-the-board salary increase like the 24% raise originally proposed by Governor Mark White would have made the teaching profession marginally more attractive to prospective teachers (by raising the minimum salary for beginning teachers from $11,100 to $13,700, but its principal effect would have been to widen the gap between the salaries of beginning and more senior teachers, and to reward the present teachers of Texas without improving their competence or distribution by fields. More fundamentally, it is not clear how large a salary increase would be required to make teaching an attractive profession, or how much the citizens of Texas are willing to pay for improved schools.

An additional problem is the concerted opposition of teachers and teachers' organizations to salary differentials based on anything other than seniority and credentials. Whatever the possible advantages of merit-based pay plans as an inducement to excellence among teachers or as a strategy for retaining the best teachers in the classroom (and these are open to question), the practical difficulties inherent in the assessment of merit in teaching (for example, who will judge, on what criteria?) and the opposition of teachers to such schemes are likely to outweigh the advantages. Similarly, while salary differentials based on qualifications by field will almost certainly be required to avert future shortages of teachers in mathematics, science, and technical subjects, the opposition of teachers and the administrative complexity of such differentials may block implementation.

With regard to proposals aimed at raising the quality of the teaching force in Texas, the problems are potentially even more severe. Unless such proposals are implemented in concert with salary increases and other reforms aimed at making the teaching profession relatively more attractive, they are likely to make the prospective shortage of teachers worse, and so to *reduce* the average quality of the state's teaching force. This is most clearly the case with proposals for competency testing in the state, because the establishment of minimal standards of competence in reading and mathematics for present and prospective teachers will in all probability bar many would-be teachers from the profession. The recently administered competency test for teachers, for example, was failed by approximately 4% of those who took the exam. Teachers may retake the exam, however, and when results of the second examination are considered, only 9% of the state's teachers failed the competency test. Even with a high proportion of teachers passing the exam, the state will lose over 6,000 teachers. Of those retaking the exam 1,199 teachers failed; 676 failed the first exam and did not retake it; and 4,444 refused to take the exam. If meaningful standards are to be established and adhered to, the magnitude of the shortage of certified teachers may be greatly increased, and the number of teachers working on "emergency" certificates may increase as well.[3]

This is equally true of the many proposals aimed at making the preparation of teachers more rigorous or more thorough. While such efforts may be desirable in themselves, they necessarily require time and effort that might otherwise be devoted to academic work and subject mastery. Moreover, extensions in the length of training or the addition of an internship year to teacher training programs in effect raise the cost of becoming a teacher, and unless this increase in costs is compensated through the provision of higher salaries or other inducements, the consequence is likely to be a further decline in the size and average quality of the pool of prospective teachers, rather than the anticipated improvement.[4]

A further problem for reformers is introduced by the legal obligation in several big-city school systems in the state to ensure that the racial distribution of the teaching force in the system reflects the racial distribution of the student body. As prospective teachers from minority backgrounds perform less well on average than whites on most achievement tests, and as the pool of prospective nonwhite teachers is relatively small, the maintenance of hiring quotas requires these districts to employ teachers who are deficient in basic skills. In the absence of other changes, reform may require a choice between the desirable goals of racial representativeness in public school faculties and higher academic standards for classroom teachers.[5]

In its Special Session in June, 1984 the Texas legislature passed several measures that address these issues. The legislature approved an increase of nearly 40% in the minimum salary for beginning teachers, while providing smaller increases for senior teachers.[6] Stricter standards for teacher-training programs and a program of forgivable college loans for prospective teachers were instituted. The legislature introduced mandatory competency tests for present and prospective teachers and established a "career ladder" for educators, though the source of funds for the proposed salary steps and the procedures for placing teachers on the ladder have not yet been clearly defined.

These reforms will go some way toward improving the quality of the teaching force in Texas, as they do in fact address both of the problems noted above. The large increase in the salaries of beginning teachers and the provision of forgivable loans to prospective teachers should significantly increase the number of candidates for teaching positions in the state, while the introduction of stricter standards for teacher education programs and competency tests for teacher education students will raise the average levels of ability and training among prospective teachers. The problems of minority recruitment and shortages of teachers in specific fields remain, but the changes approved by the legislature in this area are likely to have a generally positive impact on the quality of the public schools in Texas.

Curriculum   Another area in which reforms have been proposed is the curriculum of the public schools. The schools are said to be doing a poor job of training students in basic skills and an equally poor job of providing students with the mathematical and technical skills that will be required in the emerging technology-based economy of Texas, and a variety of changes have been suggested. Proposals again fall into two broad categories: those aimed at the establishment of more stringent academic requirements and higher academic standards, and those aimed at restoring the integrity of the curriculum and returning extracurricular activities to their proper place outside of school hours. Under the former heading fall proposals to give more attention to training in basic skills in the primary grades; to stiffen requirements for high school graduation (that is, requiring students to take more English, mathematics, and natural science); to abolish social promotion; to lengthen the school day and the school year; to introduce "computer literacy" into the curriculum; and to assign students to "tracks" based on their academic performance and occupational goals. Under the second heading fall proposals to tighten the academic requirements for participation in athletics, to end the practice of granting academic credit for extracurricular activities, and to eliminate interscholastic competition in athletic and other activities in the elementary and junior high schools.

The deficiencies of the public school system in Texas are widely recognized, and there is a broad consensus in the state that the curriculum is in need of improvement, however, and specific reforms consequently encounter significant opposition.

The most notorious instance of such opposition emerged in response to efforts by H. Ross Perot and the Governor's Select Commission on Public Education to challenge the preeminence of football and other extracurricular activities in the public schools of Texas. Suggestions that extracurricular activities should be limited to after-school hours and should not receive academic credit, that academic requirements for athletes should be tightened, and that the trend toward greater emphasis on interscholastic sports and related activities in the junior high and elementary schools should be reversed stirred up a great deal of controversy when first proposed, and have continued to generate political and legal conflict with the implementation of the "no-pass, no-play" rule, even though the objective of such reforms, improved academic performance by Texas students, receives broad and enthusiastic support.[7] While the goal of improvement in Texas schools is acknowledged to be desirable, the specific steps necessary to achieve the goal are regarded as unacceptable by many groups and individuals in the state.

Other proposals have encountered a similar if generally less spirited response. While the need for change is acknowledged, the steps required to bring about change, whether the extension of the school day or school year, the abolition of social promotion, or the elimination of nonacademic courses from the curriculum, are regarded as being too difficult or too costly to implement. Alternatively, such reforms are viewed as inimical to the accomplishment of other desirable objectives, including the protection of equal educational opportunity or the protection of teachers' jobs.

Some proposals, in contrast, have been greeted enthusiastically and are already being widely implemented. Notable among these is the recent wave of interest in purchasing computers for Texas schools and adding "computer literacy" to the standard curriculum. This enthusiasm has waxed rapidly in spite of the fact that the applications of computers in classrooms have not been fully specified or tested, the meaning and significance of "computer literacy" remain vague, and the relevance of computing skills acquired in school to students' occupational goals is undemonstrated.[8] In contrast to most of the other reform proposals, however, computers and "computer literacy" can be incorporated into the curriculum without requiring major reductions in the quantity of resources and time devoted to other programs. (In the extreme case, which may not be all that unusual, computers may be purchased and installed in classrooms, but never used.) Such reforms require little or no change in the way schools function and do not challenge the interests of teachers or other groups, but they are unlikely to have much impact on the performance of the schools.

Changes in both of these areas have recently been approved. More rigorous curriculum standards for elementary and secondary schools were instituted by the State Board of Education prior to the Special Session of the legislature. Among other things, these increased the number of credits that a student must take to graduate from high school and laid down curricular guidelines for teachers in kindergartens and the elementary grades. The legislature went further. The reform bill approved during the Special Session introduced mandatory kindergarten and preschool and summer programs for disadvantaged children; abolished social promotion; established an extensive program of testing and remediation for students in the first, third, fifth, seventh, ninth, and twelfth grades; introduced an "exit test" for high school graduation; and restricted participation in extracurricular activities to students who achieve passing grades in all of their courses.

The immediate effect of these initiatives is likely to be negative rather than positive. Changes in the curriculum have generated confusion in a number of school districts, where teachers will have to be redeployed from elective to required subjects in order to comply with the new standards. The abolition of social promotion, the introduction of an extensive testing program, and the institution of strict limitations on participation in athletics and other extracurricular activities are all likely to raise the state's already high drop-out rate, and this may increase community dissatisfaction with the schools.[9] These effects may well persist for several years, but in the longer term the emphasis that the reformers have rightly placed on compensatory programs for disadvantaged children and on improvements in the state's elementary schools should result in improved education for the state's children, and in improvements in the state's economic standing as well.

Special Programs A third area in which reform proposals have been put forward is that of special programs for particular groups of students, including ethnic and linguistic minorities and the disabled. The cost of these programs is often cited as an obstacle to excellence in the education provided to other children, and their effectiveness in improving the academic performance of the children for whom they are provided is open to question. While many such programs have been subject to criticism, three will receive attention here: school desegregation, bilingual education, and equal education opportunity for the disabled.

Several aspects of the ongoing effort to desegregate public schools in Texas have come under fire recently. School busing aimed at the achievement of racial balance, affirmative hiring quotas for minority faculty, and compensatory "pull-out" programs for disadvantaged students have been criticized as needlessly costly and disruptive to the educational system, as ineffective in improving the academic achievement of minority pupils, and as inimical to the establishment and maintenance of excellence in public education. At its best, such criticism represents an honest recognition that programs that damage the organizational integrity and educational performance of public school systems are disproportionately harmful to poor and minority children, because such children do not enjoy the options of moving to the suburbs or enrolling in private schools, which are available to middle-class children. There is an emerging consensus that public school systems should aim at the provision of excellent education for *all* children regardless of race or status, and not at the attainment of an illusory representativeness in the racial composition of faculties or student bodies or the proliferation of well-intentioned but ineffective special programs.

At its worst, however, such criticism urges the abandonment of all efforts at desegregation or compensatory education in favor of improved discipline and a return to local control. Though well intentioned, advocates of this position may bring about a return to the injustice of the past, when the best teachers, the best facilities, and the most resources were provided in white, middle-class schools, and poor and minority children were obliged to make do with what was left over. While recent efforts to equalize educational opportunities have proved to be counterproductive in many instances, it is well to remember that the present problems faced by poor and minority students in urban schools are of a quite different order than those faced prior to the *Brown* decision and the beginning of school desegregation. One danger in the present reform movement is that the goal of excellence in education for *all* children will be abandoned along with the strategies, such as desegregation and affirmative action, that were adopted to achieve it. A "reform" that provides excellence in education to the best-off at the sacrifice of recent gains made by the poor and members or racial minorities is not in the best interests of Texas, as it will exacerbate the state's most pressing educational problems.

A second area in which criticism of special programs has been encountered is that of bilingual education. Federal regulations requiring native-language instruction of children from linguistic minorities are in force in Texas despite the fact that the objectives of such programs remain in doubt and their educational efficacy remains unproven. The cost of such programs for local school districts can be high, and the difficulties involved in finding teachers qualified to teach in each of the thirty or so languages spoken by pupils in the Dallas Independent School District, for example, are severe.[10] The provision of a bilingual education program is estimated to cost anywhere from $200 to $700 more per pupil than the standard educational program, and the federal government pays as little as 7% of the cost.[11] Critics of such programs argue that the cost of maintaining the programs is not justified by the payoff in academic achievement, that non-English speaking students perform just as well in classes where instruction is carried on largely or exclusively in English as they do in bilingual education programs, and that the education of non-English speaking children in bilingual classes retards their assimilation into American society. Proponents of bilingual education, on the other hand, argue that students taught in their native language feel better about themselves and about school than do students taught in English, and that they achieve more as a result. Some also deny that assimilation is a worthy objective and argue that native-language instruction is essential to preserve the integrity of minority cultures.[12]

From the point of view of the present debate over educational reform in Texas, the critical question about bilingual education programs is whether or not they improve the academic achievement of non-English speaking students, and the evidence on this question is equivocal. The future of bilingual education programs in the state is probably not in doubt, however; the political power of the Hispanic community is such that special programs for Spanish-speaking children will almost certainly be preserved and expanded, and the maintenance of bilingual education programs for Hispanic children will require their maintenance for other children as well. This will serve the interest of Hispanic politicians and bilingual teachers quite well, but the benefits to children have yet to be established.

A third area in which controversy over special program has emerged is the provision of equal educational opportunities for the disabled. While few would argue that children with mild physical or mental disabilities should be denied access to public education, the cost of such programs for local school districts is already large and potentially much larger, and funds allocated to such programs are necessarily unavailable for other programs and other students. "Mainstreaming" may require the provision of special materials and facilities and the employment of special teachers, nurses, physical therapists, counselors, and other noninstructional personnel. The cost of educating the average disabled child is approximately twice that of educating a child without disabilities, and may range as high as $25,000 per year in the case of severely disabled children. No limit to the responsibility of local school districts for the education of the disabled has yet been established, and the cost of such programs is largely borne at the local level. Though the federal government requires that such services be provided, federal revenues cover only a fraction of total expenditures.[13]

The number of children requiring special services in the public schools of Texas has increased rapidly in recent years, and the maintenance and expansion of such programs consequently represents a threat to the quality of the educational program provided for the general population of children in a school district. The critical issue with regard to education for the disabled is not whether such programs should be continued, but whether and how the costs of these programs can be controlled. This issue is less charged politically than either school desegregation or bilingual education, but it nevertheless requires attention.

As is often the case with school reform, the present campaign for improvement in the public educational system aims partly at the correction of some of the negative consequences of past reforms. While the salience of these unintended effects is not in question, it must be recognized that past reforms were implemented in order to solve problems which at the time seemed as pressing as the need for improvement in the quality of education seems today, and reformers must ensure that their efforts represent more than a simple return to the injustices of the past.

School Finance

Perhaps the most pressing and potentially contentious issues in Texas school politics are those concerned with public school finance. The debate on this subject revolves around two questions: How can the state continue to support its public school system at the present level and pay for needed improvements; And how can the resources available for public education in Texas be distributed more equitably? These questions are clearly related, and a successful reform of the system of school finance in Texas should address both simultaneously.

Texas provides less money for schools than most other states. Texas ranks forty-second in per pupil spending on schools, and forty-ninth in the percentage of taxable income allocated to educational purposes. Moreover, the distribution of the resources available to the public school system is extremely unequal: per pupil expenditures are as much as six times greater in rich school districts than in poor.

In a brief chapter it is impossible to describe the present structure of the Texas school finance system in detail. In essence, however, the system combines elements of flat-grant and foundation aid programs and allows unlimited local enrichment.[14] Revenues are obtained from ad valorem taxes levied on local property wealth; from a variety of sources at the state level, including the Permanent School Funds, the gasoline tax, and general revenues; and from the federal government. In this essay we focus on those elements of the system that contribute to the unequal distribution of educational resources across school districts.

The key to the distribution of school revenues in Texas is the unequal distribution of property wealth across the state. Some school districts have oil, and others do not; some districts have large tracts of valuable agricultural land and few people. Big-city and suburban districts are characterized by concentrations of residential and industrial wealth, while many rural districts are desperately poor. The value of taxable property ranges from approximately $25,000 per student to over $10 million per student across school districts in Texas.

The unequal distribution of property wealth has two main consequences. First, wealthy school districts are able to generate revenues equivalent to those generated by poor districts while taxing property at much lower rates. If one district has $50,000 per student in taxable property per student, and another district has $5 million per student, the first district has to tax property at a rate of $1 per $100 to generate the revenue that the second district generates with a tax rate of 1 cent per $100. Across the state of Texas, tax rates vary from less than 10 cents per $100 to more than $1.80 per $100. Second, the right of local school districts to supplement the legally specified minimum level of educational expenditure with unlimited local enrichment means that wealthy districts can generate and spend far more on their school systems than can poor districts, even when tax rates in the wealthy districts are lower. Annual expenditures per pupil thus range from approximately $1,600 to over $10,000 across Texas school districts.

The inequalities in educational resources that are created by the unequal distribution of property wealth are reduced to some extent through state aid, but the role of the state government is not nearly as equalizing as it might be, for several reasons. First, revenues from the Permanent School Funds (PSF) are distributed to all school districts in the state on a per capita basis. In itself, this is neither equalizing nor disequalizing, but in school districts that receive additional state aid the allocation from the PSF is "charged back" against the additional aid, so that the assistance to which the district would otherwise be entitled is reduced by the amount of the PSF allocation. In those wealthy districts that receive little or no additional revenue from the state, in contrast, the PSF allocation cannot be "charged back" against other assistance, and these districts therefore receive the full value of their allocation as a flat grant from the state.[15] Despite the apparent neutrality of the formula for distributing PSF revenues, these funds provide the greatest benefits to the wealthiest school districts.

Second, the level of the local fund assignment (LFA) in the Foundation Schools Program (FSP) remains low. The LFA represents the mandatory contribution of local school districts to the FSP; until 1984 all school districts were required to tax local property at a given rate, and the difference between the revenues generated and the established "foundation" level of educational expenditure was made up from state revenues. Setting the LFA at a low level ensured that only a handful of wealthy school districts could generate this "foundation" level of revenues through local effort alone, and so required that state contributions to the FSP be divided among a far larger group of districts than would be necessary if the LFA were higher. Most districts taxed property at a level far higher than the LFA required in any case, and the revenues generated by this additional taxation were regarded as "local enrichment" to be used at the discretion of the local district. The availability of such discretionary revenues allows wealthy school districts to employ better teachers and to offer far more extensive programs than poor districts do.

Third, the explicitly equalizing component of the school finance system, state equalization aid (SEA), is provided to all school districts with up to 110% of the average property wealth across districts in Texas, and was until 1984 limited by law to a maximum level of $350 per student. In a state where the richest school districts spend several thousand dollars more per student than the poorest districts, the provision of an additional $350 does not go very far toward equalizing revenues or expenditures, and the availability of SEA to the large majority of school districts in the state means that less is available for the poorest districts.

Finally, recent revisions in the system of public school finance in Texas incorporated "hold harmless" or "minimum aid" provisions, which guaranteed all school districts in the state *at least* the same allocation of state assistance that they received in the preceding year, regardless of changes in local wealth or revisions in the system of school finance. These provisions ensured that further equalization in public school finance in Texas would require the generation of new revenues through increased taxation; it could not be accomplished at the expense of the wealthier school districts. They also ensured that wealthy school districts would oppose reform, as such districts had a great deal to lose from changes in the current system.

Efforts to reform the system of public school finance in Texas had relatively little effect before the Special Session in 1984, though the issue came before the legislature in every session in the 1970s. The most significant attempt to change the system was made in the *Rodriquez* vs. *San Antonio Independent School District* case in 1971. Plaintiffs in the case argued that the Texas system of school finance was unconstitutional because it denied children resident in poor school districts the right to an equal education, and the Federal District Court ruled in their favor. The decision was reversed by the Supreme Court, however, and subsequent reform efforts were restricted to the legislature. These efforts resulted in some increases in the quantity of resources allocated to public education in Texas, and in the establishment of the SEA program, but in the final analysis they did little to improve or equalize the quality of education provided in the state.

In its Special Session in 1984 the Texas legislature approved a variety of changes in the distribution of state revenues for education that make the system of school finance in Texas significantly more equitable, both by increasing the level of state aid to poor school districts and by reducing the level of state aid to wealthy districts. The legislature did not go nearly as far as it might have in equalizing educational resources across districts; that it chose to address the issue at all is nevertheless to be welcomed.

The legislature made four particularly important changes in the system of school finance.[16] First, the "hold harmless" provisions in the previous law were repealed, which made possible a reallocation of state revenues from wealthy to poor school districts. Second, the local share of the FSP was increased for wealthy school districts by replacing the measure of LFA based on a mandatory tax rate with one that varies with the ratio of local property wealth to state property wealth. Districts with greater-than-average property wealth will consequently pay a significantly larger share of the FSP than districts with less-than-average property wealth.[17] Third, the amount of state equalization aid (SEA) to poor districts was increased. Finally, additional state revenues were made available to districts with special needs, including those with large populations of children who require compensatory educational services.

Many of the disequalizing features of the previous system of school finance were left intact, however. The mechanism for distributing Permanent School Funds revenues was not changed, nor was the right of wealthy school districts to retain all revenues in excess of the local fund assignment for local use. State equalization assistance will continue to be provided to all districts with up to 110% of the average property wealth across school districts in Texas.

The changes introduced by the legislature will have two principal effects: they will increase the level of state assistance to poor school districts, and they will oblige wealthy school districts to tax themselves at somewhat higher rates in order to maintain the quality of their school systems. The changes do little to make the system of school finance in Texas more equal, but they do make the system more equitable, and this will work to the benefit of many of the state's children.

The Politics of School Reform

The recent campaign for school reform in Texas ended in a triumph for reformers. The campaign addressed most of the problems considered in this paper, but finally turned on two issues: the cost of educational excellence, and the assignment of responsibility for the problems of the state's schools. On the first question, the reformers argued that the economic future of Texas required educational reform, and that the cost of improving the schools would be repaid in increased productivity and continued economic growth. Budget constraints had to be respected in the short term, but the cost of reform would finally prove smaller than the cost of failure to act. The opponents of reform argued in response that increasing taxes to pay for education would hinder efforts to balance the state's budget, damage the local business climate, and overburden the citizens of Texas.

On the second question, the reformers asserted that blame for the crisis in the Texas public school system should be borne by the arrogant and self-serving "educational establishment" (of teachers, administrators, Texas Education Agency officials, and State Board of Education members) in charge of the system. The reform campaign was periodically enlivened by Ross Perot's intemperate assessments of the motivations and competence of educators, and the reformers' call for the replacement of the elected State Board of Education by an appointed board was the source of much of the controversy in the Special Session.

The various constituencies of the educational establishment answered these charges with several different arguments: there was no crisis in the educational system; the crisis was not the fault of educators; educators were doing all that could be done to end the crisis; the solution of the crisis only required more money for education and those employed in the schools. Their efforts to justify their administration of the educational system, to counter proposals for change with defenses of the status quo, and to insist upon the need for higher salaries for themselves as prerequisites to educational improvement tended to confirm the justice of the portrait painted by the reformers, and in the end worked to the disadvantage of educators.

Whatever the merits of the perspective arguments of the reformers and their opponents, approval of the school reform bill and passage of the tax increases needed to finance educational improvements appeared doubtful until the final days of the Special Session. An unlikely but powerful coalition of educators, antitax and fundamentalist conservatives, and representatives of wealthy suburban school districts (who stood to lose state aid under an equalized school funding formula) worked together to block reform; an equally diverse coalition, comprising big-city and rural school districts, minority representatives, and leaders in the business community, worked to win approval. The opponents of reform appeared to have the better of this contest in the opening weeks of the Special Session, but the personal commitment of Governor White and the leaders of the two houses of the legislature to the cause of reform finally ensured the reformers' victory.[18]

Conclusion

The reformers' accomplishments in the Special Session exceeded expectations on virtually all accounts, and the changes that they have introduced into the Texas public schools are likely both to improve the quality of the education provided to the state's children and, in the long run, to contribute significantly to the economic well-being of Texas. There are nevertheless two important reasons why this optimistic conclusion should be qualified.

First, the implementation of the reforms approved by the legislature is in the hands of teachers and administrators who by and large opposed the reformers' efforts to bring about change in the schools. The abolition of the elected State Board of Education and the appointment of a new commissioner of education ensure strong support for reform at the top of the educational system, but the day-to-day administration of the reforms in the schools and in the Texas Education Agency will be carried out by officials many of whom worked hard to defeat the proposals they are now asked to implement. Ross Perot has expressed confidence that the classroom teachers of Texas will get behind the reform program and ensure its success, but it remains to be seen whether his confidence is warranted.[19] Many of the changes that have been approved will improve the state's schools regardless of who supports or opposes them, but others depend for their effectiveness on the willingness of teachers and other educators to work for their success, and it is an open question whether this willingness will now be forthcoming.

Second, the reformers' success has presented the Texas legislature with a dilemma. In the short run, the continuing decline in public revenues from oil and gas production combined with rapid population growth have created a large and growing budget deficit in Texas, which must be financed either through additional taxes or through cuts in services. Having raised taxes for the first time in thirteen years to provide additional funds for education and highways during the Special Session in 1984, many members of the legislature are reluctant to further jeopardize the state's business climate or their own political futures by raising taxes again. There has consequently been talk of diverting some of the new revenues provided for education to other purposes, though so far cuts in educational spending have been successfully resisted.

In the long run, though, the economy of Texas is in transition, as the reformers argued. As reserves of oil and water run dry, the state will increasingly come to depend on services and light industry for its economic well-being, and a well-educated labor force will be an important determinant of continued prosperity. The reforms approved by the Texas legislature increase the resources available for the education of children throughout the state, and may be regarded as a prudent and timely investment in the state's economic future. This investment will only begin to pay dividends in a decade or so, however, and politicians are understandably more concerned with the short run than with the long run. Whether the legislature will leave the reforms and the resources needed to implement them in place long enough for this investment to pay off has not yet been decided.

Notes

1. The likely consequence of the advent of the high-technology era for employment in the United States are discussed in R. Rumberger and H. Levin, *Forecasting the Impact of New Technologies on the Future Job Market*. Project Report #84-A4 (Stanford, Cal: Institute for Finance and Governance in Education, 1984).

2. Data on teacher salaries and teacher turnover are presented in "A Policy Statement: A State in Motion in the Midst of a Nation at Risk," approved by the Texas State Board of Education on June 11, 1983. Projections of the impending teacher shortage in Texas are included in Texas Education Agency, "A Study of the Availability of Teachers for Texas Public Schools," Staff Report to the State Board of Education (Austin: Texas Education Agency, 1982).

3. Competency tests in basic academic skills have been mandatory for prospective teachers in Texas since March, 1984. A one-time-only competency test for currently employed teachers was administered on March 10, 1986. Fewer than 60% of those taking the test for prospective teachers in June 1985 received passing scores (*Dallas Times Herald*, October 12, 1985). Such figures suggest that the shortage of teachers in the state is likely to grow worse, at least in the short- and medium-terms. Results on the statewide competency testing are reported in "Most Texas Teachers Pass Test on Second Try," *Dallas Times Herald*, (August 1, 1986).

4. The program of forgivable loans for college students who agree to teach in the public schools introduced in the 1984 Special Session should help to maintain the size of the pool of prospective teachers.

5. This is necessarily a problem only if tested competence in basic academic skills is regarded as the sole or determining criterion of teacher competence. If other criteria are taken into account, minority teachers may do as well or better than whites. At present, however, tested competence in basic academic skills is widely viewed as the minimum criterion for excel-

The constitutionality of the "no-pass no-play" rule has subsequently been upheld by the U.S. Supreme Court.

8. These issues were discussed in a recent issue of *Education Week* (January 22, 1986).

9. At present, public dissatisfaction is focused not on the problems of dropouts, but on the problems of football teams deprived of star athletes and on the possibility that the state's "exit test" is too easy (*Dallas Morning News*, December 19, 1985).

10. The DISD currently faces a shortage of approximately three hundred bilingual education teachers (*Dallas Morning News*, October 25, 1985).

11. Data on the costs of bilingual education programs are from the *Dallas Times Herald* (December 16, 1983).

12. The debate over bilingual education is summarized in Twentieth Century Fund, *Making the Grade* (New York: Twentieth Century Fund, 1983), 109–19. The debate has recently been revived by proposals for reform put forward by Secretary of Education William Bennett. See *Education Week* (February 12, 1986).

13. For a discussion of the costs of education for the disabled, see Twentieth Century Fund, *Making the Grade*, 122–26. See also the *Dallas Times Herald* (December 16, 1983).

14. The Texas system of school finance is described in great detail in Stephen B. Thomas and Billy Don Walker, "Texas Public School Finance," *Journal of Education Finance* 8 (Fall, 1982):223–81; and in Billy Don Walker, *The Basics of Texas School Finance* (Austin: Texas Association of School Boards, 1982). Statistical data on Texas school finance are published annually by the Texas Research League.

15. See Thomas and Walker, 227–78; and Walker, 19.

16. Recent changes in the school funding formula are discussed in Sherry Strain, "School Finance Equalization: Progress in Texas?" paper presented to the annual meeting of the American Educational Research Association, Chicago, April, 1985; and in Deborah A. Verstegen, Richard Hooker and Nolan Estes, "A Comprehensive Shift in Educational Policymaking," in Van D. Mueller and Mary P. McKeown, Eds., *The Fiscal, Legal, and Political Aspects of State Reform of Elementary and Secondary Education*, Sixth Annual Yearbook of the American Education Finance Association (Cambridge, Mass.: Ballinger, 1986), 277–306.

17. This change is discussed at greater length by Verstegen, Hooker, and Estes, "Comprehensive Shift," 290–91; and in Texas School Finance Policy Research Project, *The Initial Effects of House Bill 72 on Texas Public Schools* (Austin: Lyndon B. Johnson School of Public Affairs, 1985), 6–7.

18. The politics of Texas school reform are discussed at greater length in David N. Plank, "The Ayes of Texas: Rhetoric, Reality, and School Reform," *Politics of Education Bulletin* 13 (Summer, 1986):23–27.

19. The continued opposition of the state's major teachers' organizations to Governor White and several of his reform initiatives provides no ground for optimism. See Molly Ivins, "White Getting a Bum Rap from the State's Teachers," *Dallas Times Herald* (February 18, 1986).

Chapter Seven

FUNDING HIGHER EDUCATION

Lawrence J. Redlinger
Margaret Barton, and
Philip DiSalvio

While there are numerous and varied issues in Texas' higher education, four factors are fundamental: the highly political nature of Texas higher education; its essentially public nature; its economic relationship to annual state budgetary surpluses and deficits; and its role in the continued prosperity of Texas. In the coming decades, Texas must move away from its traditional severance tax/oil/natural gas and agricultural (especially cattle) revenue base and toward other bases. In this respect it will begin to resemble other areas of the country. However, in order to support such a move, the state needs an effective, efficient, and dynamic higher education infrastructure to supply the labor necessary to diversify and shift to other and newer areas. It is apparent that future labor needs are not in unskilled or semiskilled areas, but in needs for skilled and professional/managerial labor. Trained professionals are an asset that companies and industries need and the presence of such talent is a factor in location decisions. Texas to be competitive must meet the challenge of providing this talent.

Yet the solutions to these problems are played out in a politically created and sustained environment in which legislators must attempt to maximize the beneficial policy effects for their districts and in which a large number of special-interest groups desire benefits without incurring costs. The complicated nature of higher education in Texas promotes the different clusters of universities as "special interests" much as other groups which intensifies the political nature of higher education. Since about 90% of all enrollment is in the public sector, decisions in the legislature and the state capitol, in general, have immediate impact because of the manner in which funding is awarded to colleges and universities. As legislative decisions are made, schools will have to live with them in spite of the logic or consequences. In the tight budgets of the 1980s, there will be intense scrutiny of higher education. But coupled with this review will be a set of decision rules about how to divide up a pie that in previous years was always growing and always consumed. The state did not plan, as is now painfully obvious, for "rainy days."

The debate about how to divide a shrinking pie will be intensely political. Legislators will attempt to keep funds within their districts; systems will fight for their components; administrators will fight within the systems; faculty will fight with administrators; and the Coordinating Board (the state coordinating agency) will seek increased hegemony over the whole affair. That the Coordinating Board will seek greater power stems from its goals (albeit conflicting) of effecting *efficient* distribution of resources while providing *equal access* to citizens of the state.

How the political decisions are made and what solutions are proposed will have consequences for the distribution of talent in Texas and for communities because the higher education environment in Texas is unevenly textured. Urban metropolitan areas such as Austin, Dallas-Fort Worth, and Houston have a greater share of educational resources than other areas, and underlying the distribution of educational resources are population and economic dynamics. Those communities with quality educational institutions will have a comparative advantage over those that lack such a resource; that advantage can be translated into economic prosperity and increased quality of life.

At the root of higher education issues in Texas are economic concerns which because of higher education's essentially public nature are issues of *funding* played out in the political arena rather than in the marketplace. As we discuss later, during the economically prosperous mid-60s, public education in Texas proliferated in an apparent attempt to provide better postsecondary educational access to citizens. However, differences in the quality of educational opportunities did not decrease; better access is not necessarily equal access to education of similar quality. Resource investments were (and are) still greater in the dominant higher education systems (the U.T. and Texas A&M systems) and universities (U.T. Austin and Texas A&M), which during fiscal stress have more resources to fall back on and more resources to use to forge links to new resource bases.

Issues of school consolidation and closing are currently being discussed because of the economics of fiscal stress. The norm of equitable access which led to the proliferation of public higher education may not be as powerful as funding constraints. Similarly, for example, the goal of eradicating the discriminations of the past that left a residue of "separate but equal Negro colleges" cannot be accomplished in a fiscally strained environment. Sufficient funds either must be created or diverted. Fundamentally, fiscal matters, issues of funding, are central and critical to any policy discussion of higher education. It is for this reason that we focus on funding issues and policy in this chapter.

In the following sections we will briefly review the fiscal and historical contexts of funding higher education in Texas and examine current issues in relation to community college and senior institutions. Finally, we will consider possible future developments, policy problems, and their implications.

Context

Throughout the late 1970s and early 1980s, oil and gas severance taxes became an increasingly important part of Texas' tax receipts. From FY82, severance taxes rose at a 25% annual compounded growth rate and grew from 19% to 27.5% of the total tax collections.[1] However, the decline of severance taxes in FY83 and FY84 saw an end to this spectacular growth, leading Governor White to say, "It appears we may not be able to count on sufficient revenue from current sources to fund some programs that we would like to,"[2] and "I happen to be the first Governor in many years, maybe ever, who has seen a declining revenue estimate."[3]

Partially as a result of the budgetary commitments entailed in public higher education, the declining revenue estimates, and perceived duplication of educational programs the state would appoint a select committee on higher education. The Select Committee, which had a broad mandate to plan the higher education needs of the state through the twenty-first century and recommend action to the legislature which could have included restructuring the higher education system and closing and merging institutions, issued a draft report in December, 1986. The Select Committee bowed to pressure from system and university lobbies and pressure to not close or combine educational facilities and not to significantly re-vamp the governance structures. The Committee essentially endorsed the current configuration of higher education and asserted the dominance of the norm of equal (more or less) educational access. The Committee skirted the issues of how higher education is to be funded even as the state's budget problems worsened.

In August of 1986, Mark White, then Governor, responded to estimates of an approximate $3.5 billion budget deficit and called the first special session of the legislature which was to be followed by a second session.[4] In an election year, the general rhetoric aimed at balancing the budget through cuts in services, including higher education; however, the ultimate result was to impose two "temporary" taxes and make other short-term adjustments. Governor White lost the election to Governor Bill Clements who must now face the serious budget shortfalls. Governor Clements has proposed keeping the "temporary taxes" imposed by the special session and in addition expanding the sales tax base. Even so, the magnitude of the deficit suggests that at least in the immediate future, higher education in Texas will be making choices based not on sound educational policy about what is best for Texas, but on the basis of fiscal stress.

These developments in Texas' revenue picture were not without forewarning. In June of 1981, the Texas 2000 Commission projected that sometime during the early 1990s (perhaps *before*), the state would begin running into problems,[5] and correctly predicted that the legislature would at first "patch up the system–probably by modest rate increases in several existing taxes."[6] The commission went on to say, however, that the problem "might get large enough ... [to] require major definitive action."[7]

On December 5, 1984, Bob Bullock, state comptroller, announced his revised estimates: "If I had to tell the Legislature today what they can expect, I would say a revenue shortfall of $900 million."[8] This estimate was quickly increased to a $1.2 billion and Bullock added, "It might get worse before it gets better."[9] Governor White reacted to these revisions by proclaiming, "I think you're going to find there's going to be a thrust for across the board cuts" and that we need to see "how we can do more with the fewer dollars we'll have."[10]

Bullock's estimates of total state revenues are important because they carry the weight of law. The comptroller must certify that any spending measure approved by the legislature has enough projected revenue to finance it. Shortfall estimates continued to grow worse and by late July, 1986, the comptroller estimated a $3.5 billion state revenue shortfall.

A $3.5 billion shortfall should demand widespread fiscal rethinking. Texas is a low-tax (no state income tax) state, forty-fourth in taxes paid per capita, and forty-ninth in tax effort (the measurement of how much a state's potential revenue it is currently raising). Only in 1961 did Texas enact a sales tax. Tradition rejects large increases or changes in tax structure and suggests, rather, the dual policies of retrenchment or sales tax modifications which is what newly elected Governor Bill Clements proposed.[11]

Texas government, like many state governments, traditionally budgets incrementally. That is, items or programs to be funded are

added each session to create a steady addition. When the state budget operated with a surplus, such a budgeting model created little
problem. However, when a budget deficit occurs and there is a need
for retrenchment, the incremental model loses its power and its relevance. Faced with less funds, Texas politicians are attempting to
shift to a decremental budgeting model. Rather than finding funds,
they must first look at the total funds available and work backward
to determine how resources will be allocated. In the past, incremental budgets required little planning effort because only the increment
and not the base needed negotiation. Agencies and, in particular,
powerful higher education systems like U.T. and Texas A&M operated rather autonomously. Now in a retrenchment mode, the entire
budgetary commitment must be examined, and ironically, many legislators who believe in individual liberty and minimal government may
be faced with also supporting collective state planning.

Thus, the inherent nature of decremental budgeting suggests a
more conflict-laden and politicized environment. Agencies and institutions must jockey with each other for their shares and legislators
must answer to their constituents about cutbacks in their districts.
Budgetary discussions become couched in rhetoric and positions
change weekly. For example, in January of 1985, 26% across-the-
board cuts in public higher education were called for and the governor simultaneously publicly opposed tuition increases that might
blunt such drastic measures as well as any tax increase. By March,
a number of alternative proposals had been offered as the forces of
public higher education as well as private sector companies that need
trained talent pressured elected officials. The governor changed his
position on tuition increases, the 26% decrease faded, and cuts of
6% to 8% were anticipated. Later, rumors spread of no cuts at all but
rather a freeze at last year's funding level. There were proposals to
close institutions with low enrollments. On the other hand, university
systems officials (as well as legislators from those districts in which
the closings would take place) continued to work to put funding for
those schools back into the budget, and by the end of the session
funding for both schools was back in the budget. More recently,
proposals to close the schools were revived in the Select Committee
which, bowing to pressure, voted to recommend to the legislature to
keep them open (largely on the basis of equity in educational access).

Any cut in the Texas budget will undoubtedly affect the basics.
Education, employee, and teacher retirement and the Big Three agencies (highways, prisons, mental health and retardation) account for
three-fourths of the total budget. A federal mandate to remedy the
prison system, the need for continued support for the highway sys-

tem, a commitment to reform elementary and secondary education, and demand for a comprehensive water policy program will force a closer look at some aspects of the higher education budget. Indeed, while appropriations for higher education rose $184 million between the 1984–85 and 1986–87 biennia, funding for public four-year colleges and universities actually declined by $91.7 million. And further declines, given the tenor of Texas' fiscal climate ought to be expected.

While politicians have a tendency to talk of fat and waste in government, there is, in fact, a natural aversion to cutting. Every item has a vocal constituency. Whether or not the master plan of locating university and community college campuses in most senatorial districts was designed to make them safe from political attack, such an outcome is consistent with the political nature of higher education in Texas. Where in the past, everyone received a share of the pie under the incremental mode, in this new era of decrementalism, everyone might be asked to take a share of the decrement or at least publicly appear to be tightening the belt.

Higher education in Texas exists in a politically created and sustained environment that has become even more politicized because of fiscal stress and legislative responses to that stress. This is not to ignore other important factors such as institutional sunk costs, location, population shifts, inflation, changing preferences for kinds of education, and current market demands for different degrees. It is to say that changes in the structure of higher education and its funding will come about more so through political decisions than through market mechanisms. This is because in Texas today higher education is predominantly *public* education. Texas higher education is characterized by the importance of two factors: its essentially public nature, and the degree to which it is politicized. These factors are highlighted by the current budgetary stress and by the recognition that for the Texas economy to be competitive and ensure continued prosperity, it must have high-quality education facilities.

History

The Texas system of higher education ranks third in size and in appropriations for the United States.[12] Approximately 89% of all students are enrolled in public institutions that are located throughout the state. However, it has not always been this way.

Even though in the last 110 years there has been a steady growth in the number of public institutions, it was not until the mid-1960s that the state committed itself and its citizenry to an essentially *public* higher education system. With the mandate of the 1876 Texas Constitution to establish and support a "University of the first class"[13] higher education in Texas has become increasingly public.[14] By 1900, six public institutions existed (one had been previously private). By 1920 nine additional colleges and universities had been created (three were absorbed from the private sector). The Depression and World War II slowed the process and only three additional public institutions were created (one was absorbed from the private sector). In the early 1960s four private or municipal colleges were shifted to state control.

A 1964 special governor's committee examined the state's higher education system, "found it lacking and recommended it be moved to top priority for planning, funding, expansion, and enhancement of quality."[15] Underlying the expansion was the premise that education is essentially a public good and as such the state should improve access to and opportunities for education. While this premise does not automatically foreclose on private provision, it does legitimate a public "solution" for higher education; further legitimating a public solution is the provision of public education at lower levels.[16] However, in the political processes that were at play, more stress was placed on issues of equity such as statewide access to local educational facilities, rather than on access to excellent higher education.

The Coordinating Board, Texas College and University System, was established in 1965 as the state regulating agency. Its expressed directive was to strengthen the state system of higher education and assure efficiency in public colleges and universities. By 1968 it had (1) adopted a statewide plan for the development of public community junior colleges in Texas;[17] and, (2) recommended that enrollments be stabilized at existing public senior institutions and that appropriate new units be authorized.[18] In the years that followed, the number of public senior colleges and universities jumped from twenty-three to thirty-seven. Similarly, with state support and local voter approval, forty-nine community college districts were created and now operate over sixty campuses.[19]

The statewide plans for the development of community colleges and the expansion of senior universities were intended to accomplish three objectives. First, they were to improve access to educational opportunities for all Texans. Second, with enrollment stabilization, there would be a more equal distribution of students among institutions which would, third, reduce the needs of existing institutions to build new facilities and hire new faculty and staff. The first of the objectives was clearly accomplished. However, with the state attorney general's ruling that the Coordinating Board lacked legal authority to impose enrollment ceilings, the second and third objectives have not been met. The large institutions have grown even larger, moderately sized campuses have also grown, but many of the smaller newly established institutions have not grown as fast as was expected. While perhaps reflecting student preferences, these unplanned variations in enrollment growth in the four-year institutions have led to uncertainties for educational planners concerning costs and quality.[20]

On the other hand, public community college enrollment exploded during the 1970s. Community colleges enrolled about one-third of all public college and university students in 1970; by 1979, the proportion had jumped to about half, an increase of 200%.[21] However, the growth has not continued into the 1980s and in the fall of 1982, public community colleges accounted for about 45% of public enrollment and 39% of the total public/private enrollment.[22]

While there are over forty private institutions of higher education in the state, they are dwarfed by public education both in terms of total appropriations and student numbers. Most of these institutions are church related, and while the largest enrollment is approximately 10,500 students (seven institutions account for over 50% of all enrollments), the vast majority enroll less than 2,000 students and quite a number less than 1,000. For comparison, statewide enrollment figures for 1984 indicate that of the 770,997 students enrolled in higher education, private higher education enrolled about 88,000 (11.4% of the state enrollment).[23]

Virtually all of the issues discussed below in the context of public higher education are applicable to private providers. Funding, increased costs, enrollment shifts, faculty salaries, and role and scope are critical concerns of private higher education. Moreover, private institutions are generally more vulnerable to changes in the environment of higher education because they depend more heavily on tuition to pay costs and lack significant public funding. Declining or stable enrollments in an era of increasing costs pose a serious problem. Tuition increases to pay for increased costs can trigger further enrollment declines as students choose relatively cheap public education as an alternative. This can lead to a vicious cycle of increases, declines, and increases which ultimately may close the institutions.

To circumvent this problem partially, private institutions have turned to the state for aid. The Texas Tuition Equalization Grant (TEG) provides subsidies to private institutions to help make up the difference between private and public education costs. In the 1982–83 biennium TEG paid $1,369 per student, and overall transferred about

$47 million in public funds to the private sector. In the future, how-
ever, such funds may not be as available to private schools, which
will increase pressures on private education.

Our focus in the remaining sections of this chapter will be on
the political nature of the funding issues in public higher education
in Texas today. All institutions in Texas face challenges and problems
in the remaining part of this decade. Yet each, by virtue of its history,
location, sunk costs, resource base, and political alliances faces a
vastly different set of options. It is well beyond the scope of this
chapter to examine individual problems and prospects except as they
illustrate larger issues. Further, we will not discuss in detail issues such
as minority education, student financial aid, and private education.
What we will do is survey the context for the present issues in public
community colleges and in senior institutions and consider possible
future developments and their implications.

Community Colleges: All Things to All People

The organization of community colleges in the United States and
Texas has evolved in response to a diverse constituency. They began
as junior colleges in the early 1900s. At first, the majority of U.S.
junior colleges were private, but by 1939 the majority were found
in the public sector, largely because of legislation that provided for
establishing and financing public junior colleges. Junior colleges were
generally organized as part of the local public school system and were
often located on high school campuses.[24]

In the years immediately following World War II, junior colleges
rapidly began to change. Demands from industry and communities
for vocational/technical training brought pressures for a broadening
in the role and scope of the traditional junior college. In addition
to preparing students to transfer to a four-year institution, community colleges began preparing students to enter the marketplace. This
dichotomy set up one of the most enduring issues in community college curricula: the demand for "parity" between vocational-technical
and academic programs.

By the mid 1960s further functions were added to commu-
nity/junior colleges. Communities wanted continuing education. As
conceived, continuing education had two purposes, both related to
the vocational-technical, academic dichotomy. On one hand, continuing education was designed to provide means to update skills (much

like contemporary inservice education/training done by corporations).
On the other hand, it was to furnish "cultural and public interest" programs that were a response to community interest or need. That is,
continuing education was to serve as a way both to keep abreast of
changes in one's occupational endeavor and to educate for "life"; it
was a means to continue learning past the traditional organization of
schooling. This significantly enlarged the perceived role and scope
of community colleges.

In relation to this dual purpose, most community colleges have
"open door" admissions policies. Irrespective of the continuing debate about whether education is a right or a privilege, community college admission policies are established on the premise that community residents should have equal access to postsecondary education.
For community colleges, this premise inevitably leads to charging little or no tuition. This makes community college education a kind
of public good supported by various financial arrangements involving
community college districts that tax residents and states that support
most or some of these community college activities.[25]

Community Colleges in Texas   Community colleges in Texas are
comprehensive educational organizations; that is, they offer the curricula for the first two years of college, vocational-technical training,
and continuing education. As we noted earlier, a state master plan
for community college development was adopted in 1968. By 1971,
the legislature recognized in statute the enlarged mission of the community college and "the obligation of open-door comprehensive institutions to provide appropriate programs for all eligible students."[26]

The public community college mandate stipulates that their purpose will be to provide

(1) technical programs up to two years in length leading to degrees
or certificates;

(2) vocational programs leading directly to employment in semiskilled and skilled occupations;

(3) freshman and sophomore courses in arts and sciences;

(4) continuing adult education programs for occupational or cultural upgrading;

(5) compensatory education programs designed to fulfill the commitment of an admission policy allowing the enrollment of disadvantaged students;

(6) a continuing program of counseling and guidance designed to
assist students in achieving their individual goals; and

(7) such other purposes as may be prescribed by the Coordinating Board, Texas College and University System, or local governing
boards, in the best interest of post secondary education in Texas.[27]

The "admissions policy" in point 5 above is the "open door" that assures that all people, in theory, have the opportunity to succeed or fail at education through their own efforts. The open door leads to compensatory education, or "watered-up" high school courses, such as remedial English and mathematics. It also leads to extensive testing and counseling programs designed to check the academic readiness of each enrollee. But, perhaps, more importantly, it places a burden on the local community college to close the gap between inadequate high school education and current labor market demands, and it means that resources must be committed to these tasks as opposed to other areas.

Revenue and Expenditures: Some Problems of Making Do   The central issue for community colleges in the 1980s is "how to maintain the open-door commitment, the diversity of opportunity and continuing access for all who can profit from further education at a time when financial resources are scarce and are being eroded by inflation."[28] Community college districts created by voters are responsible for all funds necessary for physical plant construction and maintenance as well as for supplemental funds for education programs. State monies are legislatively allocated by formulas on a biennial basis. These formulas are tied to enrollment numbers. Changes in enrollment alter the state allocation, while changes in student characteristics alter the internal allocation of funds to programs and services. For the 1984–85 biennium state appropriations totaled $880 million (an increase of 25.7% over the previous biennium); the 1986–87 allocation was over $889 million, a 10.8% increase. The total current increase for the two biennia is over 36% (although the special-session cut back approximately 10% of the 1986–87 increase).

With the implementation of the "open door" policy came a change in the nature of the student body. More students were in need of remedial work. While such students aid enrollment figures, they also require the administrative apparatus necessary to identify, teach, and counsel them. Moreover, students needing remedial work are not located at random in the landscape but cluster in some districts and on some campuses. The open door is de facto social promotion whether the lack of student readiness is the fault of the student, the schools, or the fabric of the social structure. Where resources are scarce and remedial programs are in heavy demand, other academic programs are likely to suffer.

It appears, too, that student demographics are changing. Community college students are, on the average, getting older. They also are more likely to be working and attending part-time. Thus, while the total number of students enrolled may be increasing, the total number of credit hours generated may remain constant or even decline. However, the base administrative costs per student do not decline, nor do general physical plant costs.[29]

These problems are exacerbated by the dual funding system. The amount of funding available is a function of the size of enrollment and the size of the local tax base. Where the local tax base is large and enrollment high, resources are less of a problem than they are for districts with a small tax base and small enrollments (the worst of both worlds).[30] Moreover, state funds are appropriated every other year. Formulas are applied to "base year" enrollment characteristics.[31] There are a number of effects that can result from this funding pattern. A dip in enrollment during a base year has negative effects for two years in the future. A change in base costs (for example, utilities) or inflation erodes a budget based on outdated information.

In addition, districts adding new programs may not see benefits from enrollment increases in the short term and must incur the start-up costs. For vocational-technical programs, this can be expensive. "The local district has to finance all new programs, including building and equipment. Usually, it takes at least two, sometimes three years before any state money is received, even for instruction."[32]

The importance of these considerations can be reflected in the percentage of income state appropriations represent. This percentage has been steadily climbing. In 1970, about 55% of the total educational and general income for all districts was state appropriations. By 1979, state appropriations made up 62.5% of the total educational and general income for all districts.[33] Moreover, for twenty-three of the forty-nine districts, state appropriations accounted for over 67% of total budgeted expenditures, and for nine of those districts, state monies provided over 75% of their funds.

There is, however, a wide range of state appropriations for community college districts. In 1983, for example, College of the Mainland in Texas City had only 43.3% of its budget made up of state funds, while at the other extreme, state funds for Angelina, Ranger, Tyler, and Clarendon Junior Colleges made up 75% of their total budgets. For the largest district, Dallas County Community College District, state funds accounted for 61.4% while Houston Community College and Alamo Community College districts received 66% and 68.4%, respectively. The 1983 average of state to local funds for public junior colleges in Texas was 61.7% state and 38.3% local. Obviously, reductions in state funding patterns would have an impact on districts such as Angelina and Ranger more than on those with less dependence.

The vastly expanded role and scope of community colleges during the 1970s was probably welcomed by many community college administrators. Now, however, in districts with leveling or declining enrollments, the problem becomes how to continue to meet the expectations of a diverse constituency.[34] While the Coordinating Board signals that overall enrollment growth may be slowing and resources leveling or even declining in real terms, other elements continue to use the community colleges as depositories for public solutions to perceived problems. The legislature, for example, continues to increase certification requirements for a variety of occupations from food handlers to real estate salesmen, and it is expected that community colleges will respond by offering both credit and noncredit programs in these areas.

The development of compensatory education programs forces community colleges to provide testing, counseling, and remedial services while simultaneously attempting to prepare other students for matriculation at four-year institutions and/or others for the job stream. More than one hundred occupational programs are offered in community colleges, and in some urban districts vo-tech, or job training, is the primary educational function they perform.

As resources wane or stabilize, something has to give. As the debate over the "crisis" in public education leads to reform of funding mechanisms and to increased taxation in whatever form, attention will come to focus on the community colleges. State legislators looking for continued means of conversation may in the future pass legislation that shifts more of the funding burden to local districts. Since local taxpayers pay for a share of local operations, they can simply resist increases and even demand decreases. What happens when local voters decline to authorize a sufficient local tax to support the operation and maintenance of the campus?

To what extent should the state subsidize those districts unable to carry their share of the financial burden? What happens when tuition costs rise sufficiently to force low-income students out of the school market, thereby threatening the goal of equal access? As population continues to shift, will new districts be formed? Will small districts merge? All of these questions demand answers and will undoubtedly be resolved in the political arena.

Funding Senior Universities

The rapid expansion of four-year institutions in Texas during the Sixties and Seventies paralleled the growth in the Texas economy. The

construction of new urban institutions was in response to the changing demographics of the state and needs of the citizenry. Yet this
growth was overlaid on the legacies of the past. These legacies included both major research universities with continued enrollment
growth and excellent funding and other institutions not so fortunate.
In addition, some of those not-so-fortunate institutions are located in
areas that have been largely bypassed by economic and population
growth. Furthermore, the Coordinating Board, created in 1965, covered a multiplicity of systems, boards of regents, and administrative
support staff. To fund the result, the 68th Legislature appropriated
slightly over $4 billion for the 1984–85 biennium for public senior
college and health-related units; the 69th Legislature decreased this
amount to $3.97 billion.[35] All of the funds cut came from public se-
nior universities. The current special session, particularly the Texas
House, aims to cut even more, perhaps over $510 million. The ques-
tion is not whether increases will continue. Increases are eventually
inevitable because of factors such as physical plant upkeep costs,
maintenance of national parity for faculty salaries, and a slow, steady
inflationary curve. The key question is therefore not how much but
how will it be funded?

Financing Bricks and Mortar   Two funds were constitutionally established for the support of construction, maintenance, and upgrading
of facilities. Both have been modified since their establishment, and
in November of 1984 were put before the voters of the state for further changes. At stake was the funding of not only construction, but
libraries, capital equipment, and upgrading of outdated facilities. The
first of the funds (the Permanent University Fund) was established in
the late 1800s for the "endowment, maintenance, and support" of
the University of Texas (Austin). When it was established, UT-Austin
was the only university in the UT System. In the 1930s, Texas A&M
was also allowed access to the PUF. The second fund, the Ad Valorem College Construction Fund, was established in the late 1940s
to provide other, smaller state college and universities with a means
to build and maintain facilities. Changes in funding went before the
voters in the form of a joint resolution (HJR 19), now called Proposition 2, in November of 1984. This proposition was passed at a rate of
almost two to one. A number of reasons sparked the changes, some
of which are discussed below.
    Permanent University Fund (PUF). The foundation of the Perma-
nent University Fund consists of over two million acres of land located
in nineteen West Texas counties. While early income was derived almost exclusively from grazing leases, the discovery of oil under the

lands in the early 1920s radically changed the nature of the fund. The PUF was originally established to construct and maintain "the" state university (UT-Austin) and its branches. Texas A&M, operating independently of the UT System, did not share in the income generated from the fund. However, this policy was changed in the early 1930s, and since then the Texas A&M System has been able to use income from the fund. Essentially, the Texas A&M System receives one-third of the income from the fund (called the Available Fund) while the University of Texas System receives the remaining two-thirds.

The PUF is an endowment account whose principal cannot be spent but only invested. It is the Available University Fund, or the income on earnings of the PUF, which is "available" for expenditure. The Available Fund (AF) is the accumulated net income from the PUF plus other income such as grazing leases, surface easements, etc. The first use of the AF is earmarked for academic enrichment, computer acquisitions, library acquisitions, and other remodeling projects at UT-Austin, certain other UT components, and the Texas A&M System. In 1982, the net income to the Available Fund was $149 million, of which approximately $6 million was nondivisible. The A&M System received $47.7 million out of the fund; UT received $101.3 million.[36]

The key issue regarding the PUF and the AF centered around the scope of application for the UT System. When the PUF was created there was, essentially, one university. Now there is a UT system with fifteen major participants. The UT and A&M boards of regents can, by law, issue bonds for construction purposes which are backed by the PUF. These bonds are limited to 20% of the values of the PUF exclusive of the values of the lands. While A&M has the authority to expend its bond proceeds for the entire A&M System, the UT System has authority to expend its bond proceeds only for selected components of the system, which excludes all other general academic units and some medical units. So as the UT System was expanded by the legislature, the PUF mandate was not expanded to cover them. Proposition 2 restructured the PUF while leaving the distribution of the AF essentially the same. That is, the AF would still be split between A&M (one-third) and UT-Austin (two-thirds).[37] However, with the passage of Proposition 2, all components of the UT and A&M systems are able to utilize the bonding capacity of the PUF to maintain and, when needed, expand facilities. In addition, bond proceeds can be used to acquire library resources, laboratory and teaching equipment, computers, and other capital equipment. Furthermore, the traditional arrangements for distribution of the Available Fund are retained and, it is argued, this assures both A&M and UT-Austin the needed resources for becoming and sustaining world-class programs. The perceived benefits are to provide for the whole systems a means to fund construction, libraries, and quality research programs without much additional cost to taxpayers. However, tied to the restructuring of the PUF as part of Proposition 2 was a proposal to assure funding for the other public colleges and universities, an issue related to the demise of the Ad Valorem Tax Fund.

The Ad Valorem Tax Fund and Proposition 2. From the late 1940s until 1979 the Ad Valorem Tax Fund provided monies for seventeen universities not part of the A&M or UT systems for new construction, land acquisition, and equipment. The basis for the fund was a statewide property tax that in the 1970s provided upwards of $50 million per year; however, in 1979, the legislature reduced the assessment of 0.001% (per $100), which effectively abolished the fund. The fund was formally repealed in 1982, which left the legislature with the problem of how to fund these public universities. In addition, since the creation (and repeal) of the fund, new institutions had been created. Faced with twenty-six universities, system administrations, and their components to fund, as well as the perceived need to restructure the PUF, the legislative proposed HJR 19 (Proposition 2) to amend the Texas Constitution.[38]

At the heart of the amendment is the annual dedication of $100 million "to be used by eligible agencies and institutions of higher education for the purpose of acquiring land, rehabilitation of buildings and acquisition of capital equipment, library books and library materials."[39] The fund is to be administered in a similar manner to the PUF. Furthermore, the legislature may allocate portions of these revenues toward creation of a dedicated fund (called the Higher Education Fund), the principal of which would never be expended. The income from the investment of the fund would be credited to the fund "until such time as the fund totals $2 billion," at which time the dedication of the $100 million annually would cease.[40]

That such funding is needed is obvious to educators and legislators alike. This is particularly the case in terms of physical plant renovation since a good third of all public senior institutions' buildings are over twenty years old. However, given current shortfalls and the projected shortfalls in anticipated state revenues, the current oil prices, the depletion of supply, and other such factors, the additional dedication of $1 billion over the next ten years might necessitate some sort of additional taxation. This is particularly true, given the expressed goals of the state of having both equitable access and a first-class higher education system and the necessary funding to achieve and sustain it.

Financing Operations   State appropriations to senior universities, like those to community colleges, are made every two years on the basis of formulas and are enrollment driven.[41] While enrollments grew 66% from 1970 to 1980, a continuation of this trend is improbable. Unlike in other parts of the country, Texas university enrollments on the whole are expected to increase. On the high side, enrollments are forecast to increase about 10% from 1980 to 1990; on the low side 4%. This growth, however, will not be uniform and neither will its consequences. In 1981, Kiest summarized the statewide picture this way:

> Among the 37 senior public colleges and universities in Texas, enrollment prospects are highly variable, and the consequences for institutional planning may be expected to differ sharply from one institution to another. While total enrollment in this sector of higher education will grow by 6.25 percent, nine of the 37 institutions will sustain decreases in enrollment below 1980 levels, the declines ranging from six to 16 percent. Of the 28 institutions whose enrollments will be stable or which are expected to grow, the growth in several will be significant, over 10 percent in four institutions.[42]

By 1985, Kiest's forecast proved to be optimistic. Eleven of thirty-seven universities (29.7%) had experienced enrollment declines below 1980 levels. East Texas State (-17%), Lamar University at Orange (-13%), Prairie View A&M (-16%), and the University of Texas, El Paso (-10%) had declines of 10% or more.

Several factors contribute to the mixed forecast for senior institutions. There is a predicted change in demographics. The 15–29 age group constitutes approximately 82% of the enrollment in public universities and about 71% in community colleges.[43] Between 1985 and 1990 it is anticipated that this age cohort will increase only 1.12% as compared to an overall population increase of 11%. Overall, then this traditional pool of students is diminishing and *ceteris paribus*, colleges and universities heavily dependent upon this age cohort for students are quite likely to experience declines. Add to this the fact that population changes are textured unevenly across the state. Institutions out of the mainstream in rural or nongrowth areas (for example, East Texas State) will have a more difficult time attracting students. Moreover, students outside this cohort are often part-time students who work and are therefore "place tied." Institutions not located where the jobs are will have a tougher time.[44] Finally, there will be changes in the larger economic and political environment (for example, alterations in government loan programs). Thus, there will be different decision mosaics and consequences at different institutions that will resist a statewide solution.

However, statewide policies in general and fiscal retrenchment in particular will greatly affect any given institution's capacity to cope with its situation. Enrollment declines may not be uniform across programs, and thus some programs might have to be eliminated. But this affects the very nature of the university. Are ideas and disciplines to be discarded when they appear to be economically depressed rather than when they are no longer tenable? Issues of adequate staffing and excess faculty are raised. The use of tenure is questioned.[45] In addition, while enrollments may slightly increase, stabilize, or decline, utilities, maintenance, and other costs increase. Appropriations for utilities now rank as the second largest funding item for public senior colleges and universities.[46]

On the other hand, the state's goal of having a first-class higher education system will require additional expenditures. Faculty salaries cannot be left to lag behind national averages because such discrepancies make it difficult to attract and keep the talent necessary for quality research and teaching programs.[47] Dedication of a significant amount of funds for research, especially matching funds, will be necessary, some would say critical, to continued quality education and to continued high-technology and industrial development.[48] In addition, maintenance of current operations will require appropriations increases (estimated at about $1.1 billion each biennium or a total state higher education appropriation for both community and senior colleges and universities to about $9 billion in the 1990–91 biennium).[49]

Given the 1978 constitutional amendment that ties the rate of appropriations from state revenues to the estimated rate of growth of the state's economy, the current economic climate and the tenor of the legislature, however, it is possible that higher education in Texas may face fiscal stress for a number of years. Even if the state freezes funding at FY1985 levels, the result will be real declines in appropriations. The results of such declines are difficult to precisely predict, but among the possibilities are a reduction in the quality of the faculty, reduced research output, reduced educational offerings (including restriction or elimination of summer sessions), a reduction in admission standards to promote the garnering of tuition-paying bodies, further increases in tuition, elimination of programs (including athletics), deterioration of physical plants including scientific equipment, and a deterioration of the quality of university libraries.

Alternatively, legislators will have to raise revenues and, in light of the continuing and increasing costs to reform elementary and secondary education, build new prisons and maintain old ones, maintain the highway infrastructure, support state law enforcement, and a host of other priorities, they may be extremely reluctant to do so. For example, in the past they resisted raising tuition at state universities and junior colleges, arguing that it would reduce access to higher education. When the fee structure was set in 1957, it only covered 16% of the cost of education. During the period between 1957 and 1985 (twenty-eight years) the unchanged tuition structure paid for less and less of the total educational costs until in 1984, it was estimated that tuition covered about 3% of the costs of education.[50]

Finally, primarily because of fiscal problems and secondarily because of quality-of-education issues, the tuition problem was addressed by the 69th Legislature. At first the governor resisted the idea of tuition increases, but because provisions were made for scholarships for the needy, the governor indicated in April, 1985 that he would support the increase since "there has been accommodation made for those people who are financially unable to otherwise take care of their education needs" (that is, equity in access).[51] The regular session of the 69th Legislature responded by passing HB 1147, which tripled tuition for residents from $4 per credit hour to $12 per credit hour and added modest increases thereafter until it reaches $22 per credit hour in 1993–94. It also raised the tuition for medical, dental, veterinary, and law students. Substantial tuition increases were mandated for out-of-state and foreign students. Even so, the new rates will not provide the funds needed to cover the basic costs of education let alone the costs of a high quality education.

Concluding Comments and Possible Futures

One way the 69th Legislature had to reduce the heat produced by the collision of the goals of equal access to education and achievement of an excellent higher education system (demanding increased funding needs) with shrinking revenues was to appoint a Blue Ribbon Panel much like the Perot Commission on Primary and Secondary Education to study the problem. This was, in fact, done. Approved by the legislature without controversy, the nineteen-member Select Committee on Higher Education, which includes the governor, lieutenant governor, and House speaker, was charged with examining higher education in Texas, planning the educational needs in the future, and making recommendations to the legislature when it next convenes in regular session.

On the agenda of the committee was a review of college and universities that because of declining enrollments and other factors might be closed. In addition, a number of suggestions for merger and consolidation of schools were to be examined. The committee and its staff examined four schools in terms of closure (East Texas State, Sul Ross, Texas A&M at Galveston, and UT-Permian Basin) and concluded that for the most part there were "no duplicative programs" in the areas covered by the schools and that a "concern for higher educational access" supports the need for the institutions.[52]

The Select Committee is still meeting on the various issues and problems. These include mergers (for example, all medical, dental, and allied health schools into a single system), rearranging the systems (e.g., by geographical region of the state), and other matters of governance. The Select Committee is considering whether mergers would result in better (or worse) education and what cost savings (if any) might result. However, the fate of the Select Committee's recommendations will become inextricably tied to the fiscal problems of the state. Will the norm of "equal educational access" (albeit to a fiscally stressed and perhaps gutted system) be considered more important than imposing new revenue measures? Will the convenient location of higher education facilities in virtually every district sway legislators not to make hard decisions concerning closures of both junior and senior institutions?

If there is an assumption one can confidently make, it is that the environment surrounding higher education will continue to change. Elements within higher education will change, too, partially in response to external changes, partially driven by their own imagery, internal forces, and goals. The pressures brought to bear and the specific participants involved will have a great deal to do with the shape of higher education in the 1990s.

Legislators faced with a changing Texas will have several options, some of which are depicted in Table 7–1. One option is to maintain a "steady state" of affairs. That is, they can keep expenditures steady (accounting for inflation), and simply continue allocating the same amounts of money in the same proportion as the previous years. Using only these two variables (level of expenditures and categories funded), legislators can be seen to have eight additional options to the steady state: expenditures can rise, relative to real costs, remain steady, or decline; categories of funding can increase in number, remain steady, or decline (see Table 7–1).

These "categories" are diverse. A category can refer to an entire university system (for example, the University of Texas System), or it can refer to a component or set of components within a system (for example, UT-Permian Basin). It might also refer to programs within a component (for example, intercollegiate athletics or research and development). "Categories" in their variant forms, therefore, can form a complex set of permutations ranging from change in program funding within a component of a university system to the university system itself. The nine strategies of category spending and funding provide a variety of scenarios, each with its own costs and benefits. Costs and benefits, here, refer not only to educational costs/benefits, but also social costs/benefits and especially political costs and benefits.

For example, an increase in categories funded with an accompanying increase in funds available for expenditure might seem more likely with an increase in revenue options, and a strong increase in state funding. In view of the present Texas economy, this may seem unrealistic (however, new institutions were proposed in the 68th and 69th legislative sessions).

A decrease in categories funded with an accompanying decrease in funds available for expenditure might have dramatic political ramifications. The long-standing tradition of higher education as a right rather than a privilege in Texas could be seen in danger of being compromised. The political implications of "taking away," particularly from minorities, the poor, and those in rural areas, mitigates serious consideration of this strategy in the long run. Actions such as shifting tax burdens, merging districts, and making community college no longer responsible for compensatory education are manifestations of this kind of strategy. The perceived Texas commitment to higher education appears to run directly opposite to these strategies and policies. However, for example, during the last special legislative sessions, the House proposed over a $500 million reduction in higher education funding. Had this reduction passed and, given continual fiscal stress, institution closure and shifting tax burdens would have eventually resulted.

Increasing funds available in the future for expenditure while decreasing categories funded would entail shifting resources. This might result in closing certain institutions, shifting the tax burden of community colleges, merging community college districts, or shifting remedial education to high schools. Decreasing funds available in the future for expenditure while increasing categories to be funded also involves shifting resources, but suggests different scenarios. Rather than closing certain institutions, expansion of nontraditional delivery systems might be likely with commensurate reduction in services among the traditional institutions (four-year state colleges).

A large number of issues previously discussed, and many others not examined, will play out their fates within these dimensions. In addition, despite the best intentions of educators and legislators, exogenous agents can intervene. For example, taxpayer resistance

Table 7-1. Strategies of Categories Funded and Expenditure Patterns.

TEGORIES BE FUNDED	FUNDS AVAILABLE IN THE FUTURE FOR EXPENDITURE		
	+ Increase	= No Change	− Decrease
rease +	*Raise tuition, increase fees *Proposition Two −Construct new institutions −Create new programs −Across-the-board increments (with equal access as a driving goal) *Testing incoming freshmen to improve educational outcomes and quality	*Matching private/ public funds for endowed chairs with interest-subsiding current costs −Decrements to existing institutions to sub-sidize new programs	−Private professional (e.g., pay as you go medical schools, medical schools as profit centers) −Across-the-board decrements but main-taining current long-term growth (with equal access as driving goal) −Expansion of non-traditional delivery systems (e.g. certificate programs)
change =	*Raise tuition/increase fees *Proposition Two *Increase funds for minority scholarship	Steady state	−Deferred Maintenance Program −Increase use of part-time faculty and lecturers −Short-term solutions to cutting expendi-iture (e.g., using endowment principle for current operating costs) −Decrease financial aid
crease −	*Raise tuition/increase fees *Proposition two −Shift remedial educa-tion to secondary schools via competency testing −Rent facilities/reduce construction −Shift program/elements to private sector *Eliminate degree *Close institutions −Eliminate TEG grants *Merge institutions/ systems	*Selected application of decrements −Eliminate off-campus course funding *Retrenchment −Eliminate Coordinating Board and/or Board of Regents *Close institutions *Consolidate systems *Merge institutions/ districts/systems programs	−Shift community college tax burden to local districts *Mergers to reduce administrative costs −Utilize existing secondary school facilities for community colleges *Close institutions

*Proposed by the 69th Legislature, or discussed by the Select Committee on Higher Education may lead to the repeal of revenue measures. The federal government can alter student loan and grants programs as well as a host of other programs. Demographic shifts can make it more difficult to attract students to certain schools. Changes in oil prices can further depress incoming revenue.

As noted previously, the legislature passed HB 1147, which raised tuition for the first time since 1957. Whether or not these increases result in a real increase in funds is still uncertain (expectations are that the increases will raise $285 million over the next two years). Further raises may be considered. Assuming a real increase, and assuming that other revenue is made available, a number of issues will vie for attention. While the list might be more comprehensive, three issues should be considered. First, increased costs of education may be seen as driving minorities out of the educational stream, a stream that traditionally has been thought of as a means of upward mobility. Adding fuel to this issue are the demographic trends in the state and in public education. By 2000 it is estimated that over 40% of the state's population will be minority and over 50% of the school population will be "minority." It is possible that the federal government could attempt to force adjustments in tuition for minorities nationwide on a state-by-state basis. Second, the Coordinating Board and other organized higher education interests might push for increases in faculty salaries to bring them in line with national norms and allocations to make faculty development leaves possible, key issues in attracting and retaining a quality faculty. Similarly, those same interests in concert with private industry will push for increased allocations, perhaps matched by the private sector, for the basic research and development necessary to fuel a change in the Texas economic base. Finally, newly authorized community college districts in burgeoning urban areas will need funds, as will already established districts. All of these issues involve powerful interest groups and will result in intense political infighting.

The legislature can respond in a number of ways. It can expand categories of funding; it can leave them at their present levels; or it can reduce the categories funded, thereby increasing the monies available. This last option is improbable under expanding revenue conditions, but is much more probable under declining revenue conditions. Where funds remain the same, pleas for increased funding are, on the whole, likely to fall on deaf ears. It would take a great deal of political pressure to succeed under these circumstances. More probable is that categories will remain the same, be reduced in amounts appropriated, or be eliminated altogether. For example, some universities located outside urban areas teach a significant percentage of their graduate courses off campus inside the urban area. They receive state funding for such activities under current law. Prior to 1972, virtually all courses taught off campus were self-supporting, paid for by students, not the state. Legislators could return to this position or alternatively reduce significantly the state support for such efforts. The net effect of such reducing efforts, generally, is either to generate a few dollars more (raise funds available), or close the revenue-expenditure gap because funding is falling behind.

But what options are available when funds decline? As a general rule one would not look for categories funded to increase but rather to decrease. In the extreme, the legislature might decide post-secondary education is a privilege, not a right, close all schools, and privatize higher education. This is most unlikely. On the other hand, the current level of in-state tuition make schooling relatively costless. One alternative is to accelerate tuition increases as a way of narrowing the deficit. There are a number of reasons for the appeal of this approach.

First, for out-of-state and foreign students some of the burden is shifted from the shoulders of Texas taxpayers to beneficiaries beyond the state's borders. This practice of "tax exporting" is politically convenient. It permits benefits for state residents at someone else's expense. All states do it (although some are no doubt more successful than others).

A second reason why it is expedient to raise tuition is that tuition is a user charge, a charge paid by the beneficiary for the privilege of enjoying the service. Public higher education is, of course, subsidized by appropriations from general revenues. That is, taxpayers who do not directly benefit from higher education pay taxes which support it. But students benefit directly in the form of higher lifetime earnings. Why should they not pay more for their education, particularly medical students, whose expected earnings are so high?

User charges are undesirable for precisely the same reason. That is, higher tuition fees require the student to pay relatively more while the subsidizing taxpayer pays relatively less. On the other hand, higher tuition fees may deny some low-income people access to higher education. In addition, many feel that the benefits of higher education accrue to the whole state and thus tuition should not be raised. Revenue should be raised in other ways.

For community colleges, the state can shift the tax burden to local districts and let local voters decide how much education they are willing to support. Legislators, having reformed elementary and secondary education, might eliminate compensatory education from community colleges. They could close schools and convert them to prisons or sell them to private individuals.

Given the predicted population increases and the state's commitment to education, it is unlikely that drastic cuts in funds will occur in the long run. It is likely that more scrutiny will be brought to categories funded, which is more politically palatable. In this regard, because of the dual funding system, community colleges will be especially vulnerable since there is always the option of shifting the tax burden to local districts. A mixed strategy for funding quality education in an era of tightening resources seems appropriate, but it must be remembered that any strategy will be formulated in a highly politicized arena.

The continued fiscal stress of the state may raise serious questions about the role of higher education and about the scope and missions of junior colleges and universities. The driving norm of equitable access to higher education has led to a proliferation of institutions statewide. The commitment to excellence in education to ensure a prosperous future demands differentiation in roles and missions of those institutions, particularly in light of fiscal stress. To reduce the scope of an institution, however, is in fact to reduce equity in access. Moreover, raising tuition reduces equity in access and as demographic changes put more minorities into the school-age population, this will become a more serious issue. That such issues are raised is important, that they are raised primarily because of fiscal issues rather than educational policy is perhaps unfortunate. Texas will need an excellent higher education system to fuel the future and such a system will cost a great deal but return even more. However, a commitment to excellence may entail a serious rethinking of the ideal of equity in access, particularly in light of current and future fiscal realities.

Notes

1. Bob Bullock, *Annual Financial Report of the State of Texas, 1978–1984* (Austin).

2. *State of Texas Executive Budget 1984–85 Biennium: Executive Summary*, i.

3. *New York Times* (June 8, 1983), A14.

4. *Dallas Morning News*, (August 9, 1986).

5. Texas 2000 Commission, *Texas Past and Future: A Survey* (Austin: June, 1982), 122.

6. Ibid.

7. Ibid.

8. *Dallas Times Herald* (December 5, 1984).

9. Ibid.

10. *Dallas Times Herald* (December 7, 1984).

11. Indeed the 1/8 cent boost in the sales tax to finance primary and secondary educational reforms serves to illustrate the lack of enthusiasm in dealing with shortfalls. The small boost was "just enough" and attached to a single issue, another legislative trend.

12. New York and California are larger. Given population shifts, it can be argued that as Texas' population grows, so will higher education.

13. *The University of Texas System Financial Report* (Austin: 1982) 2.

14. This development is not unique to Texas. In the 1880s most colleges were private institutions founded by religious orders. With the passage of the Morrill Act (1862), largely aimed at establishing colleges of agriculture and industry, public higher education increased in numbers of institutions. In 1890 Congress passed the second Morrill Act, which mandated regular appropriations for further support of these institutions. These appropriations were increased through additional legislation throughout the years. In addition, more funds were coming to education from the states. Together, these provided a powerful stimulus for the development of public institutions that has as its base the premise of equal access to education by all citizens.

15. Texas College and University System, Coordinating Board, *Informing the Future: A Plan for Higher Education for the Eighties* (Austin: 1981), 1:64.

16. In this regard, Texas is certainly not unique. Education in the United States is based on the assumption that all citizens should have access to equal shares of education. In theory, then the only variable that can account for difference in student outcomes is their abilities, aptitudes, skills, etc. Second, it is generally believed that a democratic, market-oriented, industrialized society must have a large stock of well-educated citizens for at least two reasons. First, the political and social freedoms currently enjoyed are dependent upon an enlightened citizenry; and second, education enhances the productivity of the society, which aids in sustaining and raising the standard of living.

17. Texas College and University System, Coordinating Board, *The Community Junior Colleges in Texas*, rev. ed., reissued (Austin: Coordinating Board, December, 1969).

18. See Texas College and University System, Coordinating Board, *Informing the Future*.

19. The effect of this growth and the number of educational institutions has led to an extraordinarily complex governance structure of higher education in the State of Texas.

20. By not allowing the Coordinating Board to stabilize, hence plan, enrollments, the attorney general introduced, albeit limitedly, elements of a market. Not just student preferences, but urban location and a number of other factors come into play.

21. Texas College and University System, *Informing the Future*, 78.

22. *Texas Almanac, 1984–85* (Dallas: A. H. Belo Corporation, 1984), 556.

23. Private sector enrollments constituted 11.65% of statewide enrollments in 1978, 12.1% in 1980, and 10.8% in 1982. See Texas College and University System, Coordinating Board, *1983 Statistical Supplement* and *1984 Statistical Supplement* (Austin); also see *Texas Almanac, 1986–87* (Dallas: A. J. Belo Corporation, 1985).

24. See Edmund Gleazer, *This Is the Community College* (Boston: Houghton Mifflin, 1968), 31; and William Ogilvie and Max Raines, eds., *Perspectives on the Community-Junior College* (New York: Appleton-Century-Crofts, 1971) on this point. Junior colleges were designed to offer the first two years (freshman and sophomore) of college work for transfer to a four-year institution. They allowed students to stay at home and gain postsecondary education; they also allowed students who were either financially unable, scholastically unprepared, or both, to gain some education.

25. See Gleazer and Ogilvie and Raines. On the effects of the "open door" policy, see Robert Palinchak, *The Evolution of the Community College* (Metuchen: Scarecrow Press, 1973); and Burton Clark, *The Open Door College* (New York: McGraw-Hill, 1960).

26. Texas College and University System, *Informing the Future*, 1:79.

27. Ibid., 79–80.

28. Ibid., 82.

29. One way to reduce costs is to invest heavily in part-time employees, a strategy that may have short-term gains but long-term negative implications. When fields advance rapidly, it is possible for community college curricula to lose ground; part-time faculty only add to this risk. Enrollment surges are handled by adding a section or two of a course. If the enrollment reaches a satisfactory number the section is taught. If, however, it does not, then the part-time faculty are not paid and the section dissolved. Part-timers can be paid less per course, need not be involved in tenure problems, etc.

30. For example, Laredo Junior College has a district of only 13.6 square miles (a very small area) that is, in addition, one of the poorest in the state.

31. See Ralph W. Steen, "Texas Formula System" (Austin: Coordinating Board, Texas College and University System, 1979), for an overview of the Texas formula system.

32. Robert Clinton, "Public Community College Programs: Development and Involvement for the 80's," in Texas College and University System, Coordinating Board *Informing the Future*, 2:180.

33. Staff Working Paper, "Public Higher Education Finance," in Texas College and University System, Coordinating Board, *Informing the Future* 2:200.

34. In data presented to the Select Committee on Higher Education in July, 1986, sixteen junior/community colleges were shown to have enrollment declines from 1980 to 1985. Seven of these have declines above 10% and two, Navarro and Ranger, over 25%.

35. Total funding for the 1984–85 biennium was over $5.8 billion of which 69% goes to the public senior colleges and universities and health-related units. Public junior/community colleges were appropriated $880 million while the rest went to "all other agencies." The 1984–85 biennium appropriation was an increase of $1.057 billion over the previous appropriation, or 22.3%, despite a $3.2 billion shortfall in anticipated state revenues. The 1986–87 total appropriation was actually $184 million higher than the 1984–85 appropriation despite the state's fiscal problems. The total 1986–87 appropriation was $5.989 billion. See Deborah Bay, "Texas Higher Education," *The Texas Almanac 1984–85*, and *The Texas Almanac 1986–87*.

36. *The University of Texas System Financial Report* (1982), 14–15.

37. Proposition 2 provides that for ten years beginning upon the adoption of the amendment, $6 million of UT's share shall be used by Prairie View A&M, one of the state's "black" universities that is part of the A&M System. At the end of the ten years, the provision expires.

38. The universities or components that could participate in this fund are East Texas State University including East Texas State University at Texarkana; Lamar University including Lamar University at Orange and Lamar University at Port Arthur; Midwestern State University; North Texas State University; Pan American University including Pan American University at Brownsville; Stephen F. Austin State University; Texas College of Osteopathic Medicine; Texas State University System Administration; Angelo State University; Sam Houston State University; Southwest Texas State University; Sul Ross State University including Uvalde Study Center; Texas Southern University; Texas Tech University; Texas Tech University Health Sciences Center; Texas Woman's University; University of Houston System Administration; University of Houston-University Park; University of Houston-Victoria; University of Houston-Clear Lake; University of Houston-Downtown; University System of South Texas; Corpus Christi State University; Laredo State University; Texas A&I University; and West Texas State University.

39. See Texas Legislature, *House Joint Resolution (HJR) 19*, (Austin: Texas Legislative Services), Section 1.

40. Ibid., subsection 17j.

41. See Steem, "Texas Formula System."

42. William Keast, "Faculty Tenure in the 1980's: Problems and Opportunities," in Texas College and University System, Coordinating Board, *Informing the Future*, 2:71. Actually, the slowing of enrollment growth began in 1977. In 1979, nineteen university campuses out of thirty-seven experienced enrollment declines.

43. See *Enrollment Forecasts 1985–95*, Texas Institutions of Higher Education Study Paper 27 (Austin: Texas College and University System, Coordinating Board, revised January, 1984).

44. Indeed, some institutions have begun offering numerous off-campus courses, in effect moving part of the university to where the students are.

45. It is beyond the scope of this chapter to discuss tenure and its merits and drawbacks. The best discussion of tenure and contracts systems for faculty can be found in *Faculty Tenure* by the Commission on Academic Tenure in Higher Education, (San Francisco: Jossey-Bass, 1973).

46. Texas College and University System, *Informing the Future*, 2:193.

47. One policy option is to raise salaries selectively and a good method is to use endowed chairs. Endowed chairs allow for the appointment of prestigious faculty. Through creative use of matching funds, endowed chairs have grown to 700 at UT-Austin, but not, however, without criticism. See John Schwartz, "UT Endowment Raises Questions of Priorities," *The Texas Observer*, no. 9 (May 4, 1984): 15–16.

48. In 1977 Texas A&M and UT-Austin ranked 18th and 19th, respectively, in total R&D expenditures. A&M spent $51.8 million of which $2.7 was federal monies; UT-Austin spent $47.7 million of which $30.1 was federal funds. *Together*, their total R&D was less than the University of Wisconsin-Madison ($103.5 million) and MIT ($102 million). In all, six California Universities (5 public, 1 private) placed in the top 25. Research capacity appears to be critical to the location of high-technology industries and other industries that rely on research. See National Science Foundation *Expenditure for Scientific Activities at Universities and Colleges. Fiscal Year 1977*, NSF 78–311 (Washington, D.C.: National Science Foundation, 1978).

49. Forecasting appropriations is, of course, difficult because forecasts must be based upon assumptions that may not hold in the future. The most conservative estimate of appropriations, based on a straight line projection, would be an increase of $1.1 billion per biennium. The $1.1 billion is derived from averaging the increase for the last two biennia (1980–81, 1982–83). The average increase, based on those two periods, is actually $1.7 billion. Appropriations could go higher or lower based on a number of factors, most of which would point toward the necessity of higher appropriations.

50. Bay, "Texas Higher Education," (1984), 556.

51. "White Supports Senate Bill to Raise University Tuition," *Dallas Morning News* (April 19, 1985).

52. From memoranda to the Select Committee on Higher Education on "Results of the Criteria Analysis," July 10, 1986.

Chapter Eight

HIGHWAY POLICY

Glenn A. Robinson

For over half a century, highway policy has stood as an exemplar of successful public policy in Texas. By the early Eighties, 272,500 miles of public highways had been constructed to form the nation's most extensive road system, 100,000 miles greater than second-ranking California.[1] The state's highway department (now officially named the State Department of Highways and Public Transportation) has been continuously admired for its technical innovativeness, its economy, and, in a business elsewhere riddled with corruption, its integrity. The legitimacy of highway building as an appropriate function of government warranting vast expenditures has been continually endorsed by the legislature, with the significant initiatives originating in the Highway Department itself. An extensively organized highway lobby has offered in turn almost unqualified support for the department's initiatives. Perhaps most importantly, policy success has been registered in the *continuity* and *resiliency* of the state's approach to conducting highway business, an approach fundamentally unchanged since the early Thirties.

The purposes of this chapter are to explain this tradition of success in Texas highway policy and to forsee how this tradition will cope with basic changes under way in Texas transportation. Obviously, Texas, especially in its urban areas, faces substantial challenges in transportation. I shall argue, however, that these challenges are neither radically different from previous challenges to highway policy nor likely to produce a crisis that would precipitate a dramatic change in the state's approach to transportation.

Explaining the Tradition of Success

At first blush, the reasons for success seem obvious. Texans are attached to and dependent upon personal automotive transportation. Their cars, vans, pickups, and motorcycles are metamorphosed horses allowing them a freedom consonant with their individualism. In addition, they are economically dependent on personal transportation. Historically, their railroads were constructed to get across Texas to more significant destinations such that to this day Texas railroads are primarily more oriented to interregional and international transportation than to intra-Texas needs.[2] Water transportation requires rivers and harbors, of which Texas is in short supply; the assiduous, repeated efforts of Houston to develop its port yields the exception that proves the rule.[3] Personal transportation became an economic necessity. To this day, it remains a relatively expensive necessity with transportation expenditures in Texas consuming a significantly greater share of gross state product than obtains for the nation as a whole: 25% of gross Texas product versus 20% of GNP for the United States.[4] A predisposition for personal transport and the seeming economic necessity for personal transport would appear to support an extensively developed highway system.

This reasoning could be applied to most areas of the country. On such statistical indicators as automobiles registered or percentage of males with drivers' licenses, persons using private autos to and from work, percentage of freight delivered by truck, Texas rates are close to national averages. History further erodes this reasoning. State involvement in highway policy was a direct response to federal policy. Texas created its Highway Department in 1917 to qualify for federal grants-in-aid.[6] As other chapters of this volume indicate, federal intrusions are often resisted by Texas politicians and administrators, as the examples of public welfare and criminal justice clearly indicate. Yet by the end of World War II, the Texas Highway Department emerged in the vanguard of states seeking federal assistance for massive road-building projects.[7] Texas, in short, embraced federal policy in a way it would not in any other domestic policy area.

Alternatively, one might plausibly argue that the state's success reflects an ability to link the mission of state highway policy (intercity/interregion highway transport) to a specific plan of highway projects. In recent years, this linkage served as the keystone of the 1976 McKinsey and Company study for the Highway Department,[8] which has been subsequently incorporated in the legislatively mandated twenty-year Operational Planning Document Study.[9] To many analysts, such a plan, whether implicit or explicit, would make a difference. An outsider provided with a map of Texas railways would likely design without additional input an interregional network of highways closely approximating the contemporary network of highways. Distinctive competency in plotting the Texas highway system, in contrasts to less successful experiences elsewhere, fails to account for Texas' success.

It seems that a tentative explanation can only be rendered when we begin to examine the *obstacles* to success, which policy scientists lump together as "implementation problems" but which may, in the case of Texas highway policy, reflect more strategic problems. Two problems figure prominently: the local controversiality of highway projects, and the intergovernmental complexity of highway policy in a federal system.

Local Controversies   In principle, Texans, like most Americans, support improvements to the highway system. Yet they are rarely united on *specific* improvements. The limited access beltway loop which promises to divert interregional traffic away from local congestion at the same time foreordains the economic decline of highway "strips" with their motels, gas stations, and restaurants oriented towards the long-distance traveler. Along similar lines, roadside merchants and real estate developers have a tangible, financial stake in frequent freeway exit and entrance ramps, which slow down traffic flow to other destinations, such as business districts and industrial areas. Highway policy during the Fifties and Sixties sought, through a radial-circumferential design, to minimize the damage of strategic bombing on centrally located transportation complexes; yet as Patrick Moynihan suggests, it had the unanticipated consequence of dispersing both business and residency away from the central city to suburban complexes.[10]

This policy thus invoked a zero-sum game between interests of the central business district and suburban developers. Neighborhood residents along busy highways variously react to the noise and air pollution, the isolation and destruction of traditional neighborhoods,[11] and the consequent decline of housing values: their reactions are at loggerheads with proponents of regional mobility. Trucking companies, quick to cite their tax contributions through highway user charges, promote policies in disagreement with the safety and convenience of the urban commuter, the tourist, or the occasional user. Rural residents, for whom an extensive road system is vital to the prosperity of their farms and ranches, have little in common with the interests of users seeking to traverse "barren" territory as quickly as possible.

Highway policy thereby gravitates trenchantly and divisively into *particularistic* policy. Local conditions and local decisions determine victors and victims, winners and losers, for whom the material stake may be substantial. These particularistic interests in turn possess formidable defenses, ranging from political lobbying to judicial injunctions, to thwart publicly beneficial projects. Prescriptively, one might encourage sensitivity to local conditions. But, if our reckoning is correct, local controversies, where citizens and businesses within a region disagree over details of a state's highway plan, make up the critical environment within which state highway policy must function. Hence, it is important to explain how Texas has defused local controversies to implement a statewide plan.

Intergovernmental Complexity   Highway policy involves a complex web of federal, state, county, and municipal jurisdictions. From the start, Texas highway policy has promoted interdependencies among jurisdictions. In other policy areas, such as municipal affairs and social services, Texas policymakers have sought an explicit division-of-labor and separation of responsibilities. Highway policy, by contrast, historically has promoted greater and greater interdependency.

The Highway Department was created in 1917 to qualify for federal grants-in-aid and thereby absorbed both road condition responsibilities and finances from the 254 counties.[12] Six years later, in 1923, it gained nominally dedicated funding in the form of a fuel tax designated for highway construction.[13] This nominal funding was subsequently, in 1946, constitutionally guaranteed with the voter ratification of the Good Roads Amendment to the Texas Constitution dedicating funding of state roads through a motor vehicle tax.[14] At the county level, the Colson-Briscoe Act of 1949 promoting farm/ranch-to-market roads granted the Highway Department discretionary authority to assume responsibility for nonarterial roads, to be partially financed through biennially appropriated funds from general state revenues.[15] At the federal level, the Federal-Aid Highway Act of 1944 and the Federal Highway Act of 1956, established incentives, inducements, regulations, and sanctions, the net effect of which was to induce compliance with federally set standards and policy goals.[16] At the same time, home-rule provisions constitutionally adopted for Texas cities and towns granted autonomous taxing, bonding, and expenditure capability to thousands of jurisdictions, empowering them to negotiate continuously with the state with regard to a division of responsibility.

These actions variously reflect the *interpenetration* of responsibilities between federal, state, region, county, and city and flout any systematic division of responsibilities. The stakes for which jurisdiction ultimately accepts responsibility happen to be material. At the federal level, federal highway designations determine the difference between 90%, 50% to 75%, and zero funding of highway projects. State absorption of county roads has, over the years, been transformed from shared-funding arrangements to 100% state funding.[17]

As a general rule, federal and state officials have been prepared, at the expense of their budgets, to absorb responsibility for funding highway projects. Yet politics frequently intervenes. Who ultimately finances specific highway projects may, on occasion, reverse even the most publicly proclaimed intentions of public officials.[18]

Texas is not immune from the foregoing conundrums. Its exposure, indeed, may be more extreme, given a traditional reluctance to intervene in local problems and an equally traditional desire to impose sharp demarcations separating levels of government. These obstacles in other states have paralyzed highway policy. By contrast, Texas has used issues of local controversy and intergovernmental complexity to promote statewide objectives. How has it done so?

Administrative Expertise and Political Control

Highway projects quintessentially involve pork barrel politics by providing direct, tangible benefits to a local region and, more specifically to a few individuals and businesses within the region.[19] These benefits were borne by a much larger polity. Thus, one might anticipate political conflict between beneficiaries, potential beneficiaries denied specific benefits, and a larger public expected to finance specifically beneficial projects. An individual highway project thus is likely to benefit a minority of citizens, while a log-rolling of projects designed to assure a majority nonetheless presumes considerable public dissent.[20] These suppositions are largely irrelevant to Texas highway policy, and their irrelevancy forces us to consider alternative explanations of how the Highway Department has successfully mobilized consent for its initiatives.

Thus, it is useful to invoke a dichotomy, originally suggested by Samuel Huntington for a radically different policy problem, to clarify the situation:[21]

> *Administrative expertise*: A professionalized agency establishes technical standards to manage and implement projects;
> *Political control*: the projects undertaken are chosen through a decision-making process in which elected officials are preponderantly influential.

This dichotomy suggests that the Highway Department establishes and applies technical standards demonstrated to be cost-effective in the implementation of highway projects. The choice of projects is retained by local, *elected* officials. The Highway Department thus retains the prerogative of deciding *how* to build a highway, an action which restricts the number of options available to local officials. But local officials decide *where* and *when* a project is to be undertaken. This division of responsibilities is idealistic, an ideal mode of operations which conceivably might be usefully applied. Its practice, in unraveling Texas highway policy, requires a historical argument.

Contemporary highway policy embodies the accomplishments of two individuals: Gibb Gilchrest and DeWitt Greer. Gilchrest served intermittently as state highway engineer from 1924 to 1937 before retiring to a distinguished academic career at Texas A&M.[22] DeWitt Greer, first hired by the Highway Department in 1927, served as engineer-director from 1940 to 1967 and as a member of the three-member Texas Highway Commission superintending the department from 1969 to 1981.[23] Longevity of tenure, when combined with the department's tradition of internal promotions has assured policy continuity extending to the current engineer-director, Mark G. Goode. Summarizing their respective contributions: Gilchrest established the autonomy of highway policy, setting it apart from other legislative and political considerations; Greer implemented a decentralization strategy that would leave the Highway Department invulnerable to political challenges.

The Gilchrest years are politically more important, for during his tenure explicit threats to the autonomy of both the Highway Department and highway policy were forthcoming. Twice during the era, Miriam and Jim Ferguson controlled the governor's office. During both terms, highway personnel were replaced by patronage appointments, many of whom showed no prior aptitude for highway administration. In reaction, the legislature became a forceful supporter of a professionalized highway department. Legislators had their own vested interests in the matter as their local supporters were frequently private contractors competing for road construction projects who in the long run were better off when political deals were not part of the contracting process.

Reform administrations were equally troublesome to highway policy. As governor, Daniel Moody, a former highway commissioner, proposed a massive bond program to finance a comprehensive roads program. And during the height of the Depression, James Allred suggested the diversion of highway user taxes to public welfare.[24] The Highway Department successively resisted both proposals. Highway finance remained on a pay-as-you-go basis. And highway user taxes were reserved for highway projects. Taken together, these measures dramatically restricted a governor's or a legislature's ability to affect highway policy for immediate political gains. Instead, the highway program was self-sustaining and self-financing. As an indication of this, the four-cent-a-gallon tax on gasoline, enacted in 1934, was subsequently raised only twice, to five cents in 1955, and to ten cents in 1984.[25]

Where the Gilchrest era established the political autonomy of the department in state politics, the Greer era established a conducive regime for implementing highway policy. When he became state highway engineer in 1940, the Highway Department had already assumed many county responsibilities for road construction. It was entirely possible for a centrally oriented highway administration to emerge with power concentrated in Austin. Indeed, Greer's strategy focused on decentralization, a policy which would have significant political and organizational implications.[26]

To Greer, the Highway Department's role was to establish statewide standards, specifically engineering and cost standards applicable to highway projects. District-engineers in each of the state's twenty-five districts were allowed to decide on the merits of local projects and, more importantly, to negotiate with county and city officials on proposed road construction. These negotiations at the grass roots yielded the stock of highway projects ultimately funded by the state. This hardly precluded "hidden-hand direction": both federal and state highway plans designated certain highway projects as of especial interest; and local highway projects were subject to approval by the Highway Commission sitting in Austin. Yet local consent was the critical determinant for new highway construction.

Today, decentralization continues to characterize highway planning. Typical highway projects might include the widening of a five-mile segment of freeway, building a new bridge, or upgrading a freeway interchange. While such capital improvements have an effect on other parts of the road system, this interdependence is only informally assayed. A major urban freeway in Houston or San Antonio thus consists of a dozen or more highway projects, each of which is costed and evaluated. This segmentation in part reflects the bidding process on new construction, thus expanding the opportunities for private contractors to bid on highway projects. But segmentation additionally reflects the prevailing political environment of road building.

Over one thousand county commissioners hold individual responsibility for county roads in their precincts. Home-rule cities and towns build and maintain city streets, while private real estate developers are frequently required to provide roads in new subdivisions. With the bulk of highway construction concentrated in urban areas, property owners and industry interests with stakes in specific highway developments are able to apply political pressures and threats of litigation. Thus, the Highway Department works with thousands of officials whose informed consent is necessary for local segments of the highway system.

At the regional level, transportation councils have been mandated to review and plan. For example, in North Central Texas, the Regional Transportation Council, organized through the North Central Texas Council of Governments, is a committee dominated by local elected officials which periodically revises a Regional Transportation Plan.[27] Traffic studies and projections by local officials represent the heart of the planning exercise. While most of these projects ultimately involve state funding, they are approved and prioritized at the local level. The North Central Texas Council recently imposed its own rule restricting approved projects to 150% of projected funding, thus curbing the tendency to promise projects with little hope of funding over the next twenty years.[28]

Comprehensive planning at the state level was initiated in 1977 in response to legislation mandating a Twenty-Year Project and Development Plan.[29] This resolution underscored the 1976 McKinsey study which concluded that the department was routinely approving projects very unlikely to be funded even in the distant future.[30] The resulting plan is an amalgam of twenty-five district plans. Each district was asked to identify current traffic problems based on existing traffic generators, current traffic delays, and identifiable safety hazards. Only the most casual efforts were made to forecast the direction or pace of urban growth, such that proposed projects are within the current limits of urban sprawl. Some major projects, such as the rebuilding of Dallas' North Central Expressway, were not included, pending a resolution of local controversies. Thus, the plan is basically a loosely prioritized shopping list of *existing* highway needs in each of the state's twenty-five districts, many of which can only be funded twenty or thirty years from now.

The significance of the Project and Development Plan should be noted: it affirms the long-standing objectives of Gilchrest-Greer highway policy. *Political control* for the recommendation of highway projects, in the determination of need, rests with local elected officials. The Highway Department at the district level merely facilitates the process. No attempt is made by Austin to weigh the relative benefits of a Houston expressway vis-a-vis an improved highway into San Angelo. While some projects are demoted to possible implementation beyond the twenty-year plan, virtually none are entirely rejected. Yet the department's *administrative expertise* remains unchallenged in designing the projects, in costing them, in establishing clear procedures for letting bids and monitoring construction, and in providing an independent evaluation of proposals which in turn can serve as a guide to local regional thinking.

These objectives carry associated costs. The planning exercises generates an inventory of projects which can be funded at current levels only in twenty or thirty years, thereby creating false optimism that solutions to existing highway projects are forthcoming. The allocation of funds among regions remains at the discretion of the department and the Highway Commission. Hence, anything from an especially entrepreneurial district engineer to a local campaign to "do something" about local congestion, can divert resources irrationally from one region to another. Finally, these objectives, premised on views of how to administer a low-profile, politically consensual highway department, intensify the question of highway finance to which we now turn.

Highway Finance: The Effects of Intergovernmental Complexity

The issues of highway finance can be usefully ordered in terms of two questions: who pays? and how much is enough? Issues relating to who pays for highways focus on the complex interrelationships among governmental units at the city, county, state, and federal levels. In the abstract, there are functional and programmatic divisions of responsibility which delegate financing to specific jurisdictions. In reality, the integrated character of a road system imposes more complicated patterns of cooperation and conflict. These patterns revolve around the readiness or reluctance of county commissioners courts, the Texas Highway Commission, or the Federal Highway Administration to assume financial responsibility either for specific highway segments or for general categories of roads. Issues relating to how much is enough arise from the likelihood that the present backlog of highway projects cannot be eliminated, given current funding restraints. Texans are unprepared to accept either the added taxes or the neglect of other public responsibilities to fund an extravagant highway program. Fiscal restraints on highway funding are not new. Thus, as we shall see, it is unlikely that a crisis in public policy will develop in coming years over problems in the Texas highway system.

Issues of highway finance can be illuminated by focusing on highway planning in Houston, the state's most chronic and complex highway problem. The 1982 Operational Planning Document envisions $14.1 billion to be spent by the state on prioritized road projects in Houston over the next twenty years. One might anticipate a roughly equivalent sum to be spent at municipal and county levels. If fully funded, these expenditures would approach $400 per capita per annum.[31]

The plan for the Houston area (District 12) is broken down into four distinct programs: interstate highways, $2,496 million; United States highways, $2,522 million; state highways, $5,583 million; farm-to-market roads, $3,511 million.[32] When originally enacted, each program had distinct purposes: for example, the interstate system sought nationwide mobility as a contribution to national defense, while the Colson-Briscoe farm-to-market program (1949) assumed county responsibilities for important rural roads. These public purposes have evolved dramatically to the extent that virtually all of Houston's projects relate to the problem of intraurban mobility.

Houston's interstate plans concentrate on two freeways, the Katy and the Gulf. No new interstate freeways are planned, and recently completed freeways, such as the I-610 circumferential, are not expected to be upgraded. The planned projects lie well within Houston's present, as contradistinct from its projected, metropolitan area. They reflect cost-conscious rather than aesthetically or environmentally pleasing solutions (for example, double-decking the Katy Freeway), which elsewhere in Texas, notably with respect to Dallas' North Central Expressway, have generated significant political opposition. While the Federal Highway Administration may provide 90% funding of interstate projects, federally required environmental-impact statements increase the risks of effective neighborhood challenges in federal courts and subsequent delays to construction.[33]

U.S. highways receive up to 75% federal funding. As these Houston freeways are indistinguishable from interstate freeways and given their contribution to interstate commerce, one might argue for their inclusion in the interstate system. To do so requires both an entrepreneurial congressional delegation and a covey of financially harassed local administrators;[34] but these conditions are at present absent in the Houston area. Federal financing significantly leverages state highway spending, and thus federal involvement remains a highly attractive way to pay for roads.

State highway plans in the Houston area are similarly focused on upgrading existing highways. Eighty of the district's top one hundred state highway construction priorities are devoted to the construction of additional highway lanes well within the geographical expanse of metropolitan Houston.[35] The only new highway planned is a controversial proposal for Beltway 8, a project sometimes cited as an example of the state's neglect of cost-effective criteria.[36]

Farm-to-market roads seem the least obvious of funding priorities for urban Houston. The original legislative intent in 1949 was to finance rural roads through a specifically funded farm/ranch-to-market program.[37] Consonant with this intent, many rural roads adjacent to urban areas were designated as farm-to-market roads and absorbed into the state highway system. As metropolitan sprawl advanced, these roads increasingly served suburban commuters. While Houston stands to benefit especially through this program, most Texas cities have substantial stakes in a program now oriented towards constructing four-, six-, and eight-lane roads throughout their suburbs. Thus, the farm-to-market road is hardly an anachronism continuing to divert monies to declining rural areas;[38] instead it finances highways used by homeowners and businesses throughout the suburbs.

Is the state highway plan for the Houston area implementable? The answer is no. Annual costs for Houston alone roughly equal or exceed 1982 statewide expenditures for construction or maintenance.[39] Federal financing, given the Reagan administration's dispositions and the projected federal deficits, is unlikely to increase in the future. Fiscal stringency within Texas, when linked with areas of acute public needs, such as an upgraded prison system and indigent health care, precludes projected demographic and commercial growth, and is more likely to increase in coming years.

This suggests a "crisis" for Houston and for other areas of the state, raising the specter of traffic gridlock and regional immobility. Obviously, congestion will remain a widely perceived problem by the public and occasion much hand-wringing among public officials.[40] But the gap between currently perceived needs and projects under construction to address those needs has *always* existed. Thus, we must propose reasons why current highway policy is likely to continue in the years ahead.

The key financing component, whether for Houston or Dallas or Waco or Muleshoe, involves an incommensurable. Present highway plans reflect an *engineer's* perspective, developed by traffic planners and local officials, that focuses on deviations from optimal levels of mobility and safety. Highway consumers, such as commuters, truckers, occasional users, and so on, may perceive instead a more *economic* level of efficiency. Where engineers and local officials seek to eliminate all sites of congestion or highway hazard, highway users may expect and accept as a fact of life periodic congestion and substandard highway conditions. They may either absorb the costs of delay or seek out roundabout routes or avoid travel at peak hours. Thus only a small percentage of drivers may be routinely subject to significant inconveniences. While virtually everyone may acknowledge and complain about inadequate highways, the groundswell of citizens prepared to take measures to accelerate highway improvements may fail to materialize.

At present, the state is favorably situated for whatever monies are available from the Federal Highway Trust Fund. Federal support has been actively sought for seventy years. Current per capita disbursements for Texas are below the national average, a lagged effect of the recent population growth of the state and the long lead time between commitments to build highways and actual construction.[41] As Texas highway standards meet or exceed federal standards generally, major redesigns of plans to conform with federal regulations are relatively infrequent. Finally, the Highway Department's inventory of projects has in the past been used to gain early access to new or expanded categorical grant programs.

Turning to state highway finance, it is generally known that highways and public education compose the two policy areas where tax revenues are constitutionally dedicated. Roughly three-quarters of the state's unit excise tax on gasoline is set aside in a special, nongeneral revenue fund for highway-associated expenditures.[42] This creates the impression that the Highway Department is flush with revenues, able to undertake virtually all highway projects and able to do so without the legislative restraints imposed on other state agencies.

The record suggests a different explanation. In 1955, the per-gallon excise tax on gasoline was raised from the four-cents-a-gallon tax passed in 1932 to five-cents-a-gallon, a rate that would hold until 1984.[43] Elsewhere gasoline taxes doubled between 1932 and 1971, prior to the inflationary crises of the seventies.[44] Texas gasoline thus came to be among the lowest in the nation. Even when Texas doubled the gasoline tax in 1984, Texas rates ranked only forty-third in the nation.[45]

Beginning with the mid-seventies, inflation ravaged the costs of highway construction, reaching 19% per annum, while growth in tax-revenues was sluggish as people turned to more fuel-efficient cars. At the same time, state revenues, notably from oil and gas production, created a substantial surplus. On paper, it might seem desirable that under these circumstances, the state would lower many of its taxes while raising the $200-million–$300-million shortfall in highway revenues through a higher gasoline tax. Instead, the legislature in 1977 passed House Bill 3 which appropriated from general revenues a sum sufficient to maintain highway expenditures at noninflationary rates.[46] Thus between 1977 and 1984 the department was assured a constant rate of real expenditure. Finally, the 1984 Special Legislative Session addressed education and highway finance by doubling the gasoline tax and raising motor-related fees. This promises the department about $500 million annually in new revenues.[47]

Constitutional dedication of revenues commenced with the 1946 Good Roads Amendment, which underscored the practice of earlier decades to devote highway-related taxes to Highway Department expenditures. The legislature retained the right to add or delete various programs from the Highway Department budget, for example, including part or all of the Department of Public Safety's budget in the Highway Department budget.

Instead, the Good Roads Amendment may have served to cap Highway Department expenditures over the long term. As Highway Department projects emerge from close collaborations between local officials and district engineers, they are highly conducive to pork barrel politics. Were the legislature to insist on line-item appropriation for specific highway projects, legislators would be especially subject to the intense, effective pressure of local officials seeking funds for specific highway projects. This pressure would likely balloon the budget and in the long run result in an over-capitalized highway system. It could be similarly attractive for individuals seeking to gain politically from an expanded roads program to replace the current pay-as-you-go approach by a bond-financed program where current expenditures would be paid off only in subsequent years.

The Texas Good Roads Association, the primary lobbyist for highways, has strengthened the department's hand. Founded in 1911, its primary financial backers consist of private highway contractors, trucking and bus line interests, oil companies with service stations, and so on, while its leadership has centered on local officials and civic notables.[48] As a peak association, it must straddle a welter of issues such as whether highway improvements desired by contractors are to be borne by added taxes on truckers. Thus, its most effective position is to support the initiatives of an already popular and highly respected Highway Department, especially on the critical question of how much is enough.

Historically, the major proponents of highway policy in the state have been concentrated among the more conservative factions of Texas politics, who share a similar interest in government frugality. One rarely associates the names of Dolph Briscoe or Allan Shivers or Preston Smith (all prominent highway backers) with unfettered expansion of government. Many of the highway lobby's backers, such as trucking companies, have sought special-interest legislation, but these efforts are quite different from efforts to promote a major spending department. Instead, the department's supporters have accepted the 1923 principle of a pay-as-you-go highway system financed from taxes infrequently raised to be paid for by highway users. And this has potentially capped highway spending at a lower level than might otherwise have been obtained.

Three-fourths of Texas roads remain the responsibility of counties and municipalities and thus an entirely different set of highway finance issues emerges. County government finance is virtually restricted to property taxation, and because of further restriction on general government expenditure, financing of highways is almost entirely supported by bond issues. Because state bond financing is negligible, being limited to the Texas Turnpike Authority's three modest projects,[49] counties float bonds in a better market that do their counterparts in other states, such as Oklahoma and Louisiana.

County government in Texas nonetheless mirrors the striking diversity of the state. Many rural counties have encountered continuous declines in population and real property value since the Fifties and operate under severe fiscal pressure. Other counties at present benefiting from metropolitan expansion, such as Fort Bend and Collin County, may readily justify bond-financed infrastructural improvements. Some counties are dissected by major intercity highways while others lack state-sponsored roads. Counties thereby face radically different needs and constraints.

In earlier decades, the state assumed responsibility for county roads when counties failed to promote construction of an effective statewide system. Today, with the interregion system virtually complete a different set of issues emerges. Many of the issues pertain to urban counties and who should bear responsibility for specific projects. Consider a Texas shopping mall, a traffic generator within an urban area. Merchandise from the mall's tenants is delivered exclusively by trucks engaged in interstate and interregional commerce, to wit, a justification for federal funding. While surveys may demonstrate that a majority of the mall's consumers live within the city and county where the mall is located, a large number of consumers will cross city and county lines. Who should pay for the augmented road system required to service the mall? Will additional property taxes indicate county responsibility? Will the incremental traffic generated by the mall increase congestion of interregional roadways? In most instances, there are few ways to allocate the burdens, such that the actual allocation depends on local Highway Department negotiations with county and municipal officials.

Many Texas counties are in a poor position to maintain, let alone reconstruct, their deteriorating road systems. Texas, like many Plains states, faces the prospect for state takeover of county roads. At the same time, urban Texas counties, responsible for the bulk of county road construction expenditure, have a financial incentive currently to expand their road systems to capture through higher property tax revenues the gains of regional expansion. In the competition for new industries and residential subdivisions, adequate road networks may prove decisive. Here, counties and municipalities may be encouraged to leverage their funds by seeking state assistance.

This diversity renders it difficult to fashion a statewide policy, such as the Colson-Briscoe farm-to-market road program of 1949. Legislative prospects tend towards a pork barrel approach, which recent legislatures have been reluctant to follow. Hence, some chronic problems may develop because of the difficulties of statewide legislation. Fiscally pressured counties will be unable to maintain present road conditions, while prospering counties may successfully shift the burden of highway finance to the state.

We must recognize the formidable accomplishment of the Texas Highway Department over past decades with respect to highway finance. Its budget, we argue, has been stable, a consequence of both constitutional dedication of taxes and of a reluctance to lobby for additional funds. Its focus on grass-roots decision making constantly threatens to assume greater and greater responsibilities for local roads. The changing economic and demographic composition of the state has occasioned a shift of its allocations towards metropolitan areas and away from the rural areas where one might expect its influence to be greatest. Overseers can complain the department has shortchanged its mission of developing an intercity/interregional road network.[50] Yet these restraints and reservations have not appreciably diminished the standing of the department. But the department's focus has unquestionably evolved. While it retains its bucolic image of planting wildflowers along the highways, it has concentrated its efforts on major reconstructions of urban arterial roads. While its grass-roots orientation of direct negotiation with local officials constitutes its leading premise, the department is one of the nation's most aggressive claimants for federal funds. While its Development Plan is fiscally unrealizable, traffic signs throughout the state provide evidence that the Highway Department is actively working to improve the highway system.

It may be useful to temper this positive perspective with a discussion of a challenge to current highway policy: public transportation. Even an honest and politically astute public agency risks becoming policy-irrelevant as the nature of issues changes. Public transportation is an issue which many Texans feel has been slighted in the past by the prohighway mentality of the state's leaders.[51] Does public transportation at present challenge highway policy?

The Public Transit Dilemma

Public transportation has made a comeback during the last decades both as an alternative to new highways and as a means to reduce pollution, overdependency on gasoline, the costs of accidents, and delays from congested highways. The lead was taken by state governments in the Northeast, which had inherited bankrupt municipal and private systems. State monies were ploughed into capital improvements, overhauling transit systems which had deteriorated over the previous fifty years. These same governments launched an appeal to Washington, resulting in funding for both existing and new systems during the late sixties and the seventies.

In Texas there was little initiative for public transit during these years. The state's one public transit program provides municipalities with part of the locally required matching funds for successful federal grant applications.[52] With the decline in federal activity during the Eighties, the state's Public Transportation Fund has become even more negligible.

Because public transit was viewed as a municipal or regional issue, state government held its distance. Traditionally, Texas cities have neither appealed to Austin for significant funding nor allowed the state to supersede their home-rule autonomy. Of course, highway policy had been closely intertwined with municipal and regional planning. But perhaps it is understandable that both municipal officials and state administrators were reluctant to weaken a clear-cut separation of authority.

Texas cities have also been relatively uncongested, even with very modest public transit systems, such that there was little urgency to promote massive expenditures associated with mass transit. There are few well-developed indicators comparing urban transportation among different cities. One of the more useful is the 1980 census reports of travel time and means of transportation to work for workers over age sixteen (summarized in Table 8–1). Commutation times for all cities seem strikingly low, and this only points up the fact that large numbers of workers travel only a short distance from their homes. Even in Houston, almost as many workers walk to work as take public transportation. Mean travel times in both Dallas and San Antonio are within five minutes of travel times in Amarillo, Odessa, Sherman-Dennison, Corpus Christi, or other mid-sized cities.

Of major American cities, only Detroit has as low a rate of public transit usage as Texas cities. Nonetheless, Texas cities compare favorably. In terms of travel time and percentage of workers traveling more than forty-five minutes, both San Antonio and Dallas are

Table 8–1. Average Travel Times to Work and Percentage of Workers Using Public Transit, Selected Metropolitan Areas, 1980.

City	Average Travel Time to Work (minutes)	% of Workers Traveling More Than 45 minutes	% of Workers Using Public Transit
San Antonio	20.4	6.8	4.6
Dallas	22.8	11.2	3.4
Houston	26.3	18.1	3.0
Detroit	23.0	11.4	3.7
Boston	23.5	21.0	15.6
Los Angeles	24.3	14.0	7.0
San Francisco/Oakland	25.3	21.8	16.4
Atlanta	25.9	16.3	7.6
Philadelphia	26.0	18.4	16.2
Chicago	28.2	22.6	18.0
Washington	28.5	21.4	15.5
New York	35.6	36.7	45.1

Source: U.S. Bureau of the Census, *1980 Census of Population. General Social and Economic Characteristics* (Washington: Government Printing Office, 1981), Texas: 205–207; District of Columbia: 87, Georgia: 117; Illinois: 191; Massachusetts: 158; California: 213–14; New York: 240; Pennsylvania: 193.

more favorably placed than other metropolitan areas. Houston workers face travel times comparable to those of Philadelphians, while Los Angeles fares a bit better than Houston; Chicago, Washington, and New York fare considerably worse.

These statistics hardly refute the case for public transportation. Public transit is a necessity for poor workers whose income hardly warrants the car per worker minimum seemingly required by an auto-dependent society; for senior citizens whose driving abilities have deteriorated and who might otherwise be immobilized were public transit unavailable; and for the young, who can experience urban society beyond the confines of their immediate neighborhoods. Public transit for many means the ability to see movies, to shop downtown, to gain access to parks, libraries, and museums.

Public transit may directly affect the vitality of central business districts. Certain activities, such as legal services, general government, finance, corporate offices, and education, appear to benefit from the close proximity which is available downtown. Thus American cities have quite generally seen a resurgence in central districts. But as these districts expand, parking facilities are at a premium and difficulties in recruiting capable employees mount. Thus a viable transit system connecting downtown with residential areas allows central business district development to continue.

There has additionally been a shift in the public's perception of public transit. Many Texas cities have approved the half-cent sales tax increase to expand transit systems or to create them from scratch (for example, Arlington).

Despite its lack of rapid transit lines, public transit in most Texas cities has noticeably improved. A rider on Houston's METRO or Dallas' DART bus system today encounters cleaner and more comfortable buses, operating on a more frequent and reliable schedule. A business executive arriving by air in Austin or San Antonio can board a frequent city bus for the trip downtown.

The costs of public transit are substantial. Even with a 50% increase in ridership over the decade, an average cashbox fare of $.49 requires a public subsidy of $.88 to cover expenses; and for each mile a bus operates, its $1.03 in revenues must be augmented by a $1.85 subsidy.[53] As these costs at present do not include the major capital expenditures associated with rapid transit systems, one presumably confronts larger subsidies in the future.

This leads to a dilemma confronting the growth of public transit in Texas. On the one hand, public transit can be presented as an alternative to highways; on the other hand, it can be viewed as a complement to the highway system. Each strategy has strengths and weaknesses.

An alternative strategy directly challenges new highway construction. It argues that additional lanes of highway construction can be traded in for land-efficient, cost-comparable public transit systems. In Dallas and Houston, where the costs of upgrading freeway facilities to projected levels of demand are frequently astronomical, due to cross bridges and buildings already in place, public transit may be a cost-effective solution. Yet for useful comparisons, planners must evaluate indirect costs and secondary consequences more systematically than is currently undertaken for either highways or mass transit facilities.

A complementary strategy focuses the objectives of mass transit differently from objectives for highways. Some may be economic in character, such as promoting downtown development; others may be social, such as providing service to the poor and the elderly. Such a strategy at least openly does not suggest a major diversion of travelers from automobiles to mass transit, for which evidence from other cities appears to be rather scanty. It allows a modicum of harmony between highway and mass transit interests, a good illustration of which is the planned redesign of Dallas' North Central Expressway, where the envisioned transit line has not reduced the number of planned traffic lanes. Yet it risks packaging public transit expenditures not with highways in a general transportation budget, but with other discretionary municipal and state expenditures.

Urban residents today widely support the principle of public transit, and this represents a major change of opinion. Texas transit systems have made modest gains which nonetheless constitute tangible improvements for users. Yet it is hard to forsee Dallas or Houston quintupling their riderships to approach the levels currently found in older American cities.

As Highway Policy Matures

One statistic encapsulates a transition under way in highway policy: 46% of the Highway Department's administration and engineering staff are eligible for retirement during the eighties.[54] This retiring cohort was originally hired to construct the Texas segments of the interstate highway system, the massive infusion of federal monies during the sixties. The last Texas segment of the interstate system, I-27 from Amarillo to Lubbock, will be completed in 1991.[55] New and expanded roles for the highway program have not been forthcoming during the seventies and eighties, as reflected in a lack of young recruits to the department. While Texas highway policy has not explicitly changed, it is fair to say it has matured.

Most highway projects today involve upgrading or rehabilitating established arteries, especially in urban areas. These projects consume an appreciably larger budget and furnish additional work to private contractors. Yet they do not add center-line miles of roadway, a criterion which casual observers can use to gauge accomplishment. Traffic through-put, in terms of traffic capacity or average speed during peak hours or numerous other indicators, is an intangible idea, not readily grasped by citizens or legislators. The complexity of reconfiguring crowded highway interchanges multiplies both the costs and the construction time required to complete projects. Thus, a contemporary project involving fractions of a mile may be as costly as twenty miles of open-road construction. The costs of success, in other words, have dramatically increased such that the general public enthusiasm accompanying completed projects is diminished from the heyday of the Sixties.

Highway maintenance has become a serious issue. The post-war highway system was designed with a finite useful life of forty to fifty years. The system preceded the use of heavy-load vehicles, which add to the wear and tear on highways. Large portions of the Texas system will reach the end of their expected life before the year 2000, and while this rarely means the complete replacement of a highway, it may require substantial reconstruction of bridges and overpasses.

Highway maintenance is performed by personnel of the Highway Department. Its activities range from resurfacing roads and widening shoulders to cutting roadside grass and planting wildflowers. As maintenance demands multiply, this work force is likely to grow.

The trucking industry poses a special set of problems. Trucks, because of wear and tear to highways, pay much larger user fees. Recent deregulation of the trucking industry has led more and more independent truckers to overload vehicles and to compete for carrying hazardous materials. In terms of citations issued, the Texas Department of Public Safety has a comparable record with the highway patrols in neighboring states. Yet the state does not routinely inspect trucks at fixed weighing stations. Officials argue that such weighing stations are impractical. Unlike Arkansas, where the bulk of truck traffic travels along specific interstate roads, Texas trucking is geographically dispersed. It is therefore easy for overweight trucks to avoid weighing stations. Nonetheless, safety and weight-limit enforcement is sporadic and ineffective.[56]

The effects of a maturing Texas highway system are impossible to assay. Engineering standards of road conditions record deviations from optimal highway conditions without regard for economic considerations. Thus, a bridge on which load limits have been applied or a low overpass requiring the latest generation of trucks to detour around is a candidate for infrastructural improvement, and when aggregated, suggest an astronomical expense. Costs-benefits analysis rarely would justify major reconstruction efforts. Road surfaces on many freeways are less than ideal, but the traffic delays encountered during repaving suggest that everyone might be better off waiting until the need is absolutely critical. Many of the construction projects in the Operational Plan replace deteriorating structures while upgrading the roadway to tighter standards and greater traffic flows. Perhaps what little can be said on the topic of road deterioration is that Texas faces obvious problems in the years ahead. Because it has historically overengineered its road system with higher standards than other states, Texas may encounter fewer problems and may be well situated to benefit from a national "crisis" brought on by deteriorating roads.

Past and Future: The Unintended Consequences of Success

Hindsight is more peripatetic than foresight. It is easy to "walk around" past policy problems, strategies adopted, and programs implemented and to consider alternative policies which might have yielded more desirable outcomes. Retrospectively, one can forcefully argue that "highway policy" per se is a conceptual misspecification. It might have proven more useful to think in terms of "transportation policy." In light of the urban emphasis that highway programs have taken over the past two decades, "urban location policy" might have been a more appropriate designation.

The unintended consequences of highway policy bear passing comment. Highways created the possibility of suburban sprawl. Older, compact suburbs like Dallas' Oak Cliff or Highland Park, both dependent on the central business district and on accessible public transportation, gave way to sprawling communities with their own decentralized workplaces, shopping centers, and amusements. Downtowns were abandoned and left to economically marginal merchants and socially disadvantaged ethnic groups. Only after decades of neglect has the comparative advantage been reversed, with downtowns viewed as indispensable for culture, education, art, sport, and commerce.

Intended to relieve congestion, freeways seemingly generate traffic. An empty freeway is an oxymoron. If the Highway Department's Operational Plan is any indication, a freeway without major construction under way will be a rarity over the next twenty years. For individuals, this means the costs of added travel time, not to mention of frustration and stress, of accidents and fatalities, and of the effects of pollution.

The most important financial consequence for Texas households is generally overlooked. Where once the "family car" was an American dream, today a personal automobile is almost indispensable for a vast majority of working Texans. Without public transportation and without the compactness of early suburbs where walking to shops, schools, and churches was the sensible mode of transport, Texas households require two or more cars, a substantial expenditure in all but the most affluent households. Where that expense is not possible, people are in effect immobile and isolated.

Retrospectively, it is easy to rewrite history, to suggest that a more balanced transportation policy would have served Texans better. One may specifically question Texas attitudes during the late Sixties and early Seventies. During this brief period, there was a brief burst of enthusiasm for mass transit. Northeastern cities in particular confronted a crisis where the horrendous costs and dislocations of projected freeways rendered them of dubious value, and a simultaneous crisis where existing mass transit systems, often built fifty to one hundred years earlier, faced bankruptcy or massive operating deficits. The response was to divert federal highway funds to mass transit and to establish a pattern of continuing federal/state funding of mass transit. At this time, Texas cities required only modest subventions to shore up their rickety transit systems, which appeared to play only a modest role in the overall transportation picture. Appeals to Austin and Washington were apostasy to believers in municipal home rule. Few transportation experts claimed that mass transit was a cost-effective option. Not surprisingly, the Texas Legislature's response was modest.

While Texas did not embrace America's brief fling with mass transit, what specifically was lost? The answer is federal pork barrel expenditures. Washington and Atlanta gained new transit systems; Philadelphia gained a rail link to the airport and a downtown commuter rail tunnel; Boston rebuilt and extended its turn-of-the-century transit system. All of them are splendid showcases which, alas, have only marginally diverted travelers off highways. It is doubtful that any of these improvements would be feasible in Texas municipalities with their longstanding skepticism of federal or state aid.

Thoughtful analysts of public policy, however, are surely chastened by the unintended consequences of a narrowly focused highway policy. The problems are far too obvious and some of the imperatives much too clear:

1. Public transit is an indispensable component of urban traffic problems. In recent years, Texas public transit has shown remarkable improvements: Houston's METRO and Dallas' DTS, previously among the worst of public services, now rank among the best. But conceptually, politically, and practically, there is no clear way to articulate the interface between mass transit and highways.

2. The impact of highways and public transportation on urban development, rather than the existing protocol stressing the impact of urban development on the need for highways, must orient policy decisions. This requires a change of philosophy. In Texas with its highly decentralized approach to highway policy, a rather profound reorientation of perspectives is needed, indeed, is possible given the professionalization of public servants.

3. The era of new roads construction has passed; the era of reconstruction of existing roads and their maintenance has begun. Texas will add few new highway miles in upcoming decades. There are no wildernesses to be spanned. Instead, the task is to upgrade ex-

isting facilities. The experience of the railroads in the first decades of this century is a chilling lesson of the prognosis for highway policy.[57] New projects can be simply justified in terms of prospective benefits. Improvements on existing projects, justified in terms of "throughput" or traffic flow rates, or average vehicle speed per mile, apparently require an engineer's sophistication to appreciate. Often these improvements cost more than the original highway, a prospect likely to confound ordinary citizens and legislators. Highway maintenance is a similarly prosaic, arcane agenda item. But unlike Roman roads, most Texas highways were built for a forty-year lifespan. Maintenance becomes the cost-effective means to minimizing long-term expenditures. Yet it is easily foregone in a budgetary crunch. In sum, Texas highway policy faces political obstacles quite different from what it previously encountered.

These are possibly surmountable challenges, especially given the Highway Department's track record in innovation, public relations, and political sensitivity. Yet if the state's highway policy has been previously "flawed," might not there be flaws in contemporary sentiments likely to produce unintended consequences in coming decades. What then are the risks?

1. Currently, no public transit system worldwide breaks even. Is a permanent, open-ended subsidy of public transit a legitimate charge on Texas communities?

2. To adopt a view treating highways and transport as a means of development and progress can readily lead to an overinvestment in transport facilities. Given a climate of scarcity in Texas' resources, would not a shift to a developmental perspective be fiscally perverse and counterproductive?

3. The reconstruction/maintenance program of the highway system may be hard to justify. The Federal Highway Trust Fund subsidies that reduced state costs to 10% or 25% have declined in recent years and could well evaporate in an attempt to balance the federal budget. Even the modest inflation of the mid-Eighties will oblige the Highway Department within five to ten years to seek a tax increase. It will do so under conditions very new to Texas: no new highway miles; congested freeways under seemingly continuous reconstruction; and the astounding costs common to urban reconstruction.

Conclusion

With respect to prevailing public policy analysis, Texas highway policy is an unqualified success. The Highway Department adopted a strategy and tactics to address thousands of problems, simultaneously winning legislative and local applause for its professionalism and service and winning as well the general confidence of the public. As the discussion in the previous section suggests, we may regret the unintended consequences and foresee a far different policy environment for the years ahead. Still, we should applaud success, the one policy arena where Texas leads the nation.

The keystone of Texas' past success in highway policy has been its grass-roots orientation, which has decentralized decision making to emphasize negotiations between local officials and district engineers. This decentralization has been fortified by strong claims of technical expertise at the state level and by an assiduous acceptance of political control at the local level. The Highway Department has been a bureaucracy that wants to survive, not by reacting defensively to counter assaults against its preferred choices and its rational decisions, but by actively promoting local interests.

By the same token, Texas highway policy has adopted an urban orientation more readily than can be accounted for by local interests or by mandates from either the legislature or the public. While legislative delegations from metropolitan areas potentially dominate the legislature, and while statewide candidates receive a majority of votes from metropolitan areas, an urban bloc of sustained political pressure has yet to materialize in Texas. Is it because from an engineer's standpoint, the needs of Dallas or Houston are significantly greater than rural areas? Is it because the potential for political attacks on highway policy is greatest in urban areas where mass media can flame the discontent of citizens? Is it because of the potential urban bias of members of the Texas Good Roads Association and other lobbying supporters of highway policy.

Historical evidence suggests that the shift is due to shrewd internal reckoning within the department itself. The urban shift is comparable with the assiduous pursuit of federal funding in the postwar years, in an environment where federal intervention was unpopular but where the tangible completion of public roads was considered a major accomplishment. Assumption of responsibility for nonarterial rural roads in the farm-to-market program, at the time a seeming deflection from the department's mission of building interregional roads, in fact intensified local contacts and added rural supporters of the highway program.

The underlying theme in these instances is that the department has adjusted its orientation before a problem has become politically critical. Thus, the type of crises which force revolutionary shifts in public policy have been avoided. Put a bit differently, the department has used its goodwill to win consent for new initiatives. With its integrity and technical competence established, it has reasoned with both its lobbyists and its legislative supporters to consent to its priorities. At the same time it has paid assiduous attention to local needs and has acted pragmatically to address those concerns.

Certain highway issues are obvious: increasing urban congestion, the high costs of urban highway construction, the role of public transit, the oncoming deterioration of highways built during the Fifties and Sixties, etc. None of these issues constitute at present a unique problem that might challenge highway policy. Highway policy is likely to remain intact. And the Texas highway system, while no longer an eighth wonder of the world, will remain one of the state's most valuable assets. Past success breeds future success.

Notes

1. U.S. Bureau of the Census, *Statistical Abstract of the United States: 1985* (Washington, D.C.: Government Printing Office, 1985), 591.

2. John Stricklin Spratt, *The Road to Spindletop* (Austin: University of Texas Press, 1970), 19–36.

3. Marilyn McAdams Sibley, *The Port of Houston* (Austin: University of Texas Press, 1968).

4. Texas Transportation Institute, Texas A&M University, "Transportation," in Texas 2000 Commission, *Texas Past and Future: A Survey* (Austin: Office of the Governor, 1981), 179–80.

5. *Statistical Abstract of the U.S.: 1985*, 596.

6. Dewitt C. Greer, "Highway Development in Texas," in Walter Prescott Webb et al., eds. *The Handbook of Texas* (Austin: Texas State Historical Association, 1952), 810.

7. Richard Morehead, *Dewitt C. Greer: King of the Highway Builders* (Austin: Eakin Press, 1984), 49–52.

8. State Department of Highways and Public Transportation, *Responding to the Changing Environment*, prepared by McKinsey and Company (Austin: 1976).

9. State Department of Highways and Public Transportation, *Operational Planning Document Study* (Austin: 1982).

10. Daniel Patrick Moynihan, "Policy vs. Program in the '70s," *The Public Interest* 20 (Summer, 1970):94.

11. A useful example is New York's Cross-Bronx Expressway. See Robert A. Caro, *The Power Broker* (New York: Vintage Books, 1975), 850–94.

12. General Laws of Texas, 35th Legislature, Regular Session 1917, Ch. 190, 416–27.

13. General Laws of Texas, 38th Legislature, Regular Session 1923, Ch. 134, 275–77.

14. Texas Constitution, Art. VIII, sec. 7-a.

15. General and Special Laws, Texas, 51st Legislature, Regular Session 1949, Ch. 51, 85–86.

16. Morehead, 49–50.

17. State Department of Highways and Public Transportation, *Texas Transportation Finance Facts* (Austin: 1982), 37.

18. The reversal of opposition to Westway is a classic example. See Edward I. Koch, *Mayor* (New York: Warner Books, 1985), 110–13.

19. For a useful description of this type of politics, see John A. Ferejohn, *Pork Barrel Politics* (Stanford, Cal.: Stanford University Press, 1974), 233–52.

20. For the type of dissent possible in Texas, see Texas House of Representatives House Study Group, *There's No Such Thing As a Freeway* (Austin: 1978), 17.

21. Samuel P. Huntington, *The Soldier and the State* (Cambridge: Harvard University Press, 1954), 80–98.

22. "Gibb Gilchrist," in Eldon S. Branda, ed., *The Handbook of Texas: A Supplement* (Austin: Texas State Historical Association, 1976), 338.

23. Morehead, 29, 44, 153, 169.

24. John B. Huddleston, "Highway Development: A 'Concrete' History of Twentieth Century Texas," in Donald W. Whisenhunt, ed., *Texas: A Sesquicentennial Celebration* (Austin: Eakin Press, 1984), 264.

25. Texas House of Representatives, House Study Group, *Key Issues of the June 1984 Special Session* (Austin: 1984), 18.

26. Morehead, 57–59.

27. North Central Texas Council of Governments, *Metroplex Transactions* (April, 1985), 5.

28. Ibid.

29. Senate Resolution 589, 65th Legislature 1977.

30. State Department of Highways and Public Transportation, *Responding to the Changing Environment*, ch. 2, 4–8.

31. Based on the 1980 population of the Houston SMSA.

32. Based on State Department of Highways and Public Transportation, *Operational Planning Document Study Appendices*, C-14–15, C-49–51, C-97–103, C-162–172.

33. See Alan J. Altshuler, "Changing Patterns of Policy: The Decision-Making Environment of Urban Transportation," *Public Policy* 25 (Spring 1977):171–203.

34. See Gary T. Schwartz, "Urban Freeways and the Interstate System," *Southern California Law Review* (May, 1976):406.

35. Based on the projects cited in State Department of Highways and Public Transportation, *Operational Planning Document Study Appendices*, C-97–103.

36. See the critique in State Department of Highways and Public Transportation, *Responding to the Changing Environment*.

37. Morehead, 56.

38. See Paul Burka, "The Bloody Billion," *Texas Monthly*, (March, 1985):56–57.

39. Based on the State Department of Highways and Transportation, *Annual Financial Report 1983* (Austin, 1984), 11.

40. Carolyn Barta, interview with Mayor Starke Taylor and City Manager Charles Anderson, *Dallas Morning News* (May 13, 1985).

41. *Statistical Abstract of the U.S.: 1985*, 594.

42. State Department of Highways and Public Transportation, *Texas Transportation Finance Facts*, 35.

43. *Special Issues of the June 1984 Session*, 18, 28–31.

44. U.S. Bureau of the Census, *Historical Statistics of the United States* (Washington, D.C.: Government Printing Office, 1975), 720.

45. State Department of Highways and Public Transportation, *Transportation News* (November, 1984):5.

46. Texas House of Representatives, *There's No Such Thing As a Freeway*, 8–14.

47. *Special Issues of the June 1984 Session*, 18.

48. Griffin Smith, Jr., "The Highway Establishment and How It Grew," *Texas Monthly* 2 (April, 1974), reprinted in Lawrence C. Dodd, ed., *Texas Monthly's Political Reader* (Austin: Texas Monthly Press, 1980), 194–95.

49. Texas House of Representatives, *There's No Such Thing as a Freeway*, 23–24.

50. State Department of Highways and Public Transportation, *Responding to the Changing Environment*, chs. 1, 3.

51. Smith, 201–202.

52. State Department of Highways and Public Transportation, *Texas Transit Facts* (Austin: 1984), p. 21. The citation for the Public Transportation Fund is *Vernon's A.C.S.*, Art. 6663c.

53. State Department of Highways and Public Transportation, *Texas Transit Facts*, 9, 11.

54. State Department of Highways and Public Transportation, *Five Year Automation Plan* (Austin: 1982), 17.

55. State Department of Highways and Public Transportation, *Transportation News* (September, 1984):3.

56. For a more extensive discussion of the issue, see Texas House of Representatives *There's No Such Thing As a Freeway*, 27–33.

57. For an illuminating account see, Albro Martin, *Enterprise Denied, Origins of the Decline of American Railroads* (New York: Columbia University Press, 1971):352-67.

Chapter Nine

CRIME AND CORRECTION   *Harry Mika and*
Lawence J. Redlinger

It is our intent to present an overview of crime patterns and policy, review correctional policy, and discuss possible criminal justice scenarios which could unfold in the coming decades. Crime, the responses to crime, the organization of criminal justice and criminal justice policy in Texas are understandable and logical outcomes of historical patterns, piecemeal policies, prevailing social changes, and legal institutions.

The contemporary "criminal justice system" in Texas is at best a loosely linked, fragmented response to social patterns including crime, political practicalities, legal constraints, and institutional capabilities. A casual listing of the number of agencies, commissions, forces, bureaus, departments, etc., involved becomes staggering. For example, one must include 254 county sheriffs; 500 plus police departments; 40 college and university police departments; countless constables, justices of the peace, and municipal, county, district, and state judges; the Office of the Attorney General of Texas; Texas Department of Corrections; Texas Commission on Jail Standards; Commission on Law Enforcement Officer Standards and Education; Board of Pardons and Parole; Adult Probation Commission; Juvenile Probation Commission; Department of Public Safety; Adjutant General's Department; Criminal Justice Policy Council; Alcoholic Beverage Commission; Board of Private Investigators and Private Security Agencies; Parks and Wildlife Department (game wardens); Texas Youth Commission; Court of Criminal Appeals; prosecuting attorneys at all levels; Prosecutors Council; State Law Library; and the Texas Judicial Council. We could show a schematic diagram of the "system" but the result would be overrationalized. What keeps components "hanging together" is the central input (crime), the technology of transformation (arrest and disposition), and the outputs, or products (convicts, probation, acquittals, and so on). To say each component does an efficient job would be as large an overstatement as to say all were ineffective. What is accurate, however, is to say that the criminal justice system in Texas reflects the historical accretion of local policy and practice, and strong political and social preferences for individual and piecemeal "solutions" to crime.

Crime Patterns in Texas

While we will briefly discuss arson and alcohol-related offenses, our discussion of crime in Texas will focus on the seven major felony offenses typically used to make up the Uniform Crime Index (UCI) both for Texas and for the United States.[1] The offenses are criminal homicide; forcible rape; robbery; aggravated assault; motor vehicle theft; theft; burglary; and arson.

As noted in the 1984 Governor's Office report on crime,

> In 1982, Texas ranked third in the nation in both population (15,280,000) and number of Index crimes reported (962,260). Texas ranked 12th, however, in the total index crime rate (the number of crimes per 100,000 population), and also ranked twelfth in both violent and property crime rates. The Texas crime rate for 1982 was 6,297.5 offenses reported for each 100,000 persons, compared to 5,553.1 for the United States. The statistics reflect the impact of the state's rapid growth in the last five years. Since 1978, the total number of offenses in Texas has increased 33.1%; the state population has increased 17.4%; and the crime rate has increased 13.3%. During the same period, the total number of offenses in the United States increased 15.4%, total population increased 6.2%, and the U.S. crime rate increased 8.7%.[2]

There is a relationship, albeit not linear, between total state population and the number of crimes. A large number of factors affect this relationship: unemployment, poverty, climate, religion, density of population, police behavior, to name a few. And although Texas was estimated to have gained about 450,000 people between 1982 and 1983, both the number and rate of crimes decreased (see Table 9–1). In addition, while the number of crimes may vary, the relative percentage of violent to property crime appears to remain quite similar. As Figures 9–1 and 9–2 present, the relative percentages of violent and property crime have not varied much over the last six years (1978–83). This pattern reflects the trend for the United States as a whole; that is, property crime outnumbers violent crime by about 9 to 1.[3] Within both violent and property crime categories, the percentage makeup by specific offenses has remained virtually constant over the past six years. Larceny (theft) has consistently accounted for 52% to 55% of all index crime; burglary accounts for 28.2% to 29.6%; motor vehicle theft, 8% to 9.2%; assault, 4% to 4.7%; robbery, 3% to 3.5%; rape, .68% to .71%; and murder .24% to .25%.

As one can see from Figure 9–2, total crime in Texas increased from 723,164 crimes in 1978 to 928,827 in 1983. However, there are fluctuations in the incidence of crime during this period. For instance, crime was less in 1983 than in 1982, with violent crimes decreasing by 8.6% and property crimes decreasing by 3%. A number of explanations for such decreases have been offered. One is that the population as a whole and particularly the postwar baby boom, is aging, and since younger people are most likely to commit crime, the rate of crime will go down. The postwar baby boom generation began to reach the "crime prone years" (sixteen to thirty) during the 1960s and generally crime has increased as a response. Now that they are getting older, the argument goes, crime should be declining. Another explanation emphasizes that a 3% drop in property crime is hardly a drop at all and the fact that crime in 1983 is still higher than in 1981. However, the total crime rate was lower in 1983 than it had been since 1978 (see Table 9–1), as were specific rates for murder, rape, robbery, burglary, and motor vehicle theft. A related argument is that vagaries of crime reporting could have caused a "statistical" rather than a "real" drop.

Since, however, crime is related to age and other demographic characteristics, one should expect future crime in Texas to reflect the demographic "mix" of the state's population. If there is one characteristic to choose as a predictor of crime, it is the percentage of males in the population thirteen to thirty-nine years old. In Texas, males account for approximately 83% of all arrests and males thirteen to thirty-nine account for about 68% of all arrests.

If additional demographic characteristics were picked as predictors of crime, one would choose ethnic/racial status and income. Ethnic/racial status and income are related to each other and to crime; that is, blacks and Hispanics in Texas have lower incomes than Anglos. Thus, we might expect that a higher percentage of low-income young males of minority status in the state would be associated with a higher rate of crime.[4]

Analysis of crime patterns in Texas over the last six years reveals a direct relationship between population density and the rate of crime. In Texas, 88% of all index crimes; 81% of the murders; 86% of the rapes; 94% of the robberies; 87% of the aggravated assaults; 85% of the burglaries; 90% of the thefts; and 88% of the motor vehicle thefts occur in urban areas. Dallas, Fort Worth, Houston, and Beaumont have the highest crime rates. In 1982, Houston ranked first in the state in murders, robberies, and motor vehicle theft. Dallas ranked first for burglary and theft; Fort Worth and Dallas were a close one and two, respectively, for rape. Beaumont ranked first for aggravated

Table 9-1. Estimated Crime in Texas, 1973-83.

Texas Estimated Crime Index: 1973-1983

Year	Population		Murder	Rape	Robbery	Agg. Assault	Burglary	Theft	Mtr. Veh. Theft	Total
1973	11,794,000	Number	1,501	3,006	16,765	23,723	149,358	241,904	40,954	477,211
		Rate*	12.7	25.5	142.1	201.1	1,266.4	2,051.1	347.2	4,046.2
1974	12,050,000	Number	1,646	3,521	19,420	21,931	184,562	269,900	44,787	565,767
		Rate*	13.7	29.2	161.2	182.0	1,531.6	2,405.8	371.7	4,695.2
1975	12,237,000	Number	1,639	3,430	20,076	22,658	203,821	362,665	47,388	661,675
		Rate*	13.4	28.0	164.1	185.2	1,665.6	2,963.7	387.2	5,407.2
1976	12,487,000	Number	1,519	3,666	17,352	21,885	193,280	400,767	43,871	682,340
		Rate*	12.2	29.4	139.0	175.3	1,547.6	3,209.5	351.3	5,464.4
1977	12,830,000	Number	1,705	4,336	19,552	26,714	205,672	383,451	51,018	692,450
		Rate*	13.3	33.8	152.4	206.2	1,603.1	2,988.7	397.6	5,397.1
1978	13,014,000	Number	1,853	4,927	21,395	26,475	209,770	398,923	57,821	723,164
		Rate*	14.2	37.9	164.4	218.8	1,611.9	3,065.3	444.3	5,556.8
1979	13,385,000	Number	2,226	6,026	25,636	33,909	239,263	411,555	72,687	791,304
		Rate*	16.6	45.1	191.5	253.3	1,787.5	3,074.7	543.0	5,911.7
1980	14,169,829	Number	2,389	6,694	29,532	39,251	262,332	450,209	79,032	869,439
		Rate*	16.9	47.2	206.4	277.0	1,851.3	3,177.2	557.7	6,135.7
1981	14,755,000	Number	2,438	6,816	28,516	40,673	275,652	454,210	83,244	891,549
		Rate*	16.5	46.2	193.3	275.7	1,868.2	3,078.3	564.2	6,042.4
1982	15,280,000	Number	2,463	6,814	33,603	45,221	285,757	501,312	87,090	962,260
		Rate*	16.1	44.6	219.9	296.0	1,870.1	3,280.8	570.0	6,297.5
1983	15,724,000	Number	2,238	6,334	29,769	42,195	262,214	503,555	82,522	928,827
		Rate*	14.2	40.3	189.3	268.3	1,667.6	3,202.5	524.8	5,907.1

Sources: 1972-1978-Federal Bureau of Investigation, *Crime in the United States*, (Washington, D.C., 1984) 1979-1983-estimated by DPS/UCR Bureau. Population from Bureau of Census provisional estimates as of July 1, except 1980 census.

Notes: The number of offenses shown were estimated from reports submitted to the Uniform Crime Reporting Program by Texas law enforcement agencies representing over 90% of the State's population. Traditionally, previous publications on crime in Texas have estimated crime in nonreporting jurisdictions based on an average of the reporting agencies in the same population group or by projecting yearly totals from agency reports covering less than twelve months; therefore the number of offenses were estimated for 100% of the state's population. The Census Bureau in 1982 revised all of the population estimates upward. The 1980 Texas population figure was finalized at 14,229,191.

* Per 100,000 population.

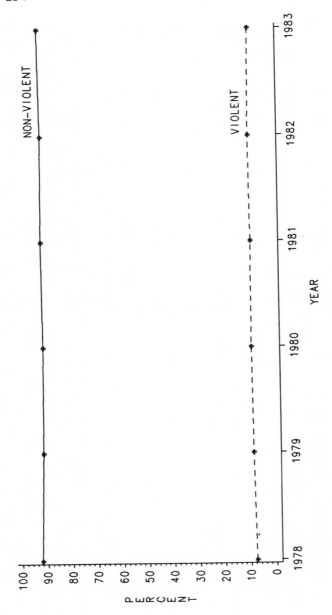

Figure 9–1   Statewide Percentages of Violent and Nonviolent Crime, 1978–83.

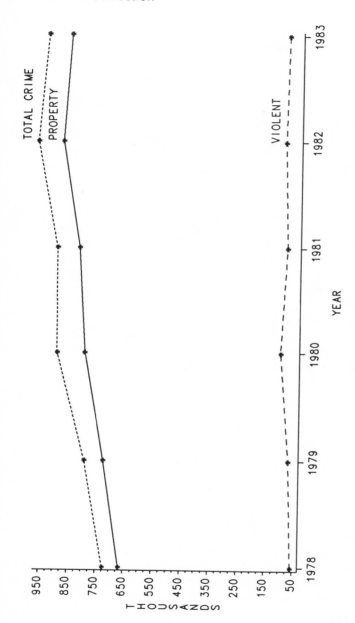

Figure 9–2   Statewide Offenses: Violent, Property and Total Crime, 1978–83.

assault (a position it has held since 1980).[5] Thus we would expect that as Texas' population becomes more urbanized and density increases, crime will also rise.

Violent Crime   In Texas, Hispanics account for about 34%, blacks about 31%, and Anglos about 35% of murder victims and all are most likely to be murdered by a member of their own ethnic group.[6] Men constitute 82.5% of the victims and 85.9% of the assailants. Roughly half of all victims and 55% of the assailants are between the ages of twenty and thirty-five. The most frequent circumstance precipitating murder is an argument with an acquaintance or a family member. The most likely weapon is some sort of firearm (66%), with handguns accounting for 44% of all weapons. However, the second most likely weapons are knives and other stabbing instruments (20%). Murders are most likely to happen on Fridays and Saturdays, with peak hours generally being in the evening until about 3:00 a.m. Statewide about 75% of all murder cases are solved (the highest clearance rate for any crime, state or nationwide) largely because of the circumstances involved. Clearance rates decline rapidly for other index crimes both in Texas and the nation, as Figure 9–3 depicts.

In 1983, there were an estimated 6,334 rapes in the state of Texas.[7] The number of rapes dropped 7% over 1982 and 1981 even though there was an increase in the state's population. Ninety-nine percent of those arrested for rape are men, and 58.8% are between the ages of twenty-one and thirty-four. Sixty-one percent are white while thirty-nine percent are black. Rape is much more likely to occur on the weekend, especially Saturday and Sunday between the hours of 9:00 p.m. and 5:00 a.m. Apartments and their adjacent parking lots are a likely spot about one-third of the time, followed by houses and highways/roads. In about four out of ten rapes strong-arm force is used. In 1983 for the state, police had a clearance rate of 58%; that is, they caught about six out of ten rapists.

Robberies in Texas are estimated to have resulted in the loss of $32,509,729 worth of property in 1983. This is $5.3 million more than in 1982 even though there were 3,834 more offenses in 1982. That is, while robbers in 1982 netted on the average $779 per robbery, 1983 robbers netted about $1,092. Ninety-one percent of those arrested for robbery are males and two-thirds of those are between the ages of seventeen and twenty-nine. Males in the same age range account for about half of the victims. Statewide, whites account for 52.5% of the arrests while blacks account for 47%. Robberies of individuals are most likely on the weekend between 8:00 p.m. and 2:00 a.m., pri-

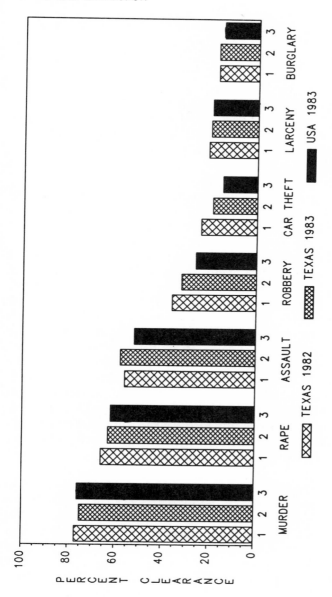

Figure 9–3   Clearance Rates 1982 and 1983 (in percent cleared) for Seven Offenses.

marily on Fridays and Saturdays. In contrast, it appears that business burglaries are most likely to occur between 3:00 p.m. and midnight Monday through Friday. Handguns and other types of firearms are much more common in business burglaries than in robberies of individuals; however, firearms still account for the greatest percentage in type of weapon used in individual robberies. Strong-arm robberies are much more likely with individuals than businesses. In general, robbery victims have a higher risk of injury from robbers who are unarmed or armed with sticks, bottles, or other weapons.[8] For 1983, the clearance rate for robbery was 32%, which was above the national average (see Figure 9–3).

There were about 3,000 fewer aggravated assaults in 1983 as compared to 1982; that represents a decline of 6.7%. Even so, there were over 42,000 offenses, and these did not include "simple" assaults, of which there were 58,414. Males between the ages of seventeen and thirty-nine accounted for three-fourths of those arrested and of those victimized. Statewide, blacks accounted for 27.4% of arrestees; white, 72.2%. Locally, however, statistics varied widely. In 31.2% of all offenses, "hands, feet and fists" were the weapons of choice followed by "cutting instruments" (25.8%) and firearms (23.4%). Aggravated assaults are most likely at night (8:00 p.m. to 3:00 a.m.), particularly on Saturdays and Sundays. Police cleared 63% of reported aggravated assaults in 1983.

Individually and as an aggregate, violent crimes have much higher clearance rates than property crimes. One primary reason for this is the higher probability of identification in rapes, assaults, and robberies. For homicides, the fact that so many involve acquaintances usually narrows down the possibilities considerably. Violent crimes account for 8.7% of all index crimes.

Property Crime   During 1983, police estimate that over $1 billion in property was stolen in Texas.[9] Forty-four percent ($434 million) of the thefts involved locally stolen motor vehicles; another $35.7 million involved motor vehicle parts and accessories. If one includes items stolen from cars, another $42.6 million can be added, and if we total the value of this theft, it accounts for over *half* of all property stolen, reflecting in an odd way our love of and preference for automobiles.

Motor vehicle theft accounted for an estimated 82,522 offenses in Texas in 1983. The average value per vehicle at the time of theft was approximately $5,300. Less than 20% of the offenses are ever cleared, and when the vehicles are recovered, about half (47.5%) are recovered in the same jurisdiction in which they were stolen. Automobiles are the targets of theft 60% of the time while trucks and buses are targeted in about 30% of the crimes; "other vehicles" make up for the remainder (for example, tractors, road machinery). Whites account for 73% of the cleared offenses; blacks, about 27%. Twenty-two percent of the thefts in Texas that are cleared are committed by juveniles. Friday and Saturday evenings (7:00 p.m. to midnight) appear to be a favorite time for car theft. Apartment parking lots are the most likely spots to have a car stolen, although there are a number of other parking situations in which cars are stolen. For parts and accessories, apartment parking lots appear to offer the best shopping for thieves, usually after 5:00 p.m. until 1:00 a.m., primarily on Thursdays and Fridays. This allows the thieves, one suspects, to use the parts for their work on the weekends.

The 503,555 estimated larceny-theft offenses for 1983 in Texas included motor vehicle part theft (discussed above). In 1983, it is estimated that $245 million of property was stolen. About one in five thefts were cleared by arrest. Theft over $200 accounted for 37.6% of all thefts, and the average value of goods stolen per theft was $486 (up from $429 in 1982). Both the percentage of thefts over $200 and the average value partially reflect the effects of inflation on the value of goods stolen. Of those arrested for theft, females accounted for 30.8%; whites, 71.2%; and blacks, 28.2%. Since theft is so wide-spread, it is difficult to say when and where it will occur. However, it appears that shoplifting is more likely to occur in supermarkets and department stores.

In 1983, 262,206 burglaries were estimated to have occurred in Texas, 65% of which were residential. For residences the favored time to burgle is during the day (6:00 a.m. to 6:00 p.m.), while for businesses, burglaries appear to occur more often at night. This, of course, makes sense, since burglars, in general, do not wish to be seen, confronted, or caught. For residences, it appears that many burglaries are committed in the morning hours and that the proba-bility of being burgled decreases in the middle to late afternoon. By far, single-family dwellings are the favored target, followed by apart-ments. In 1983, over $300 million in property was burgled, 70% of which came from residences. The average value loss for each burglary incident was $1,150.

For the state, 94% of those arrested for burglary in 1983 were males, 73% white, and 26.6% black. For major urban areas, however, the numbers of minorities arrested were much higher (for example, in Dallas in 1982, 61.6% of the arrestees were black and 12.1% were Hispanic). Of all index offenses, burglary is the least likely to be cleared by arrest (17%). One must keep in mind, too, that only the absence of the victim separates burglary from robbery.

Although not an index offense, arson is a special kind of property crime, one in which the goal is destruction of property with or without the intent to defraud. In Texas, there were 7,486 cases of arson in 1983—715 less than in 1982; however, the total value of property damage rose from $84.2 million to $92 million. For structures burned, incinerated, or exploded, single-occupancy residences are favored targets (46.3% in 1983; 45.4% in 1982). If one includes motor vehicles and other mobile property and crops, timber, fences, etc., single-family residences still account for 27% to 30% of all targets for arson. Between 1982 and 1983, the number of these offenses remained virtually the same (there were 7 less in 1983) and the property damage was between $25 million and $26 million. The real change in 1983 came in the area of apartments, hotels and other multiunit dwellings: although the number of offenses decreased by 12, the property damage increased by $8.5 million and for 1983 totaled $17.2 million. Although partially accounted for by inflationary factors, it is also evident that the damage done was more extensive. About 21% of arson offenses are cleared by arrest.

In our brief overview of crime patterns, we have focused on the major index offenses because of their perceived severity. Given the current controversy over the legal drinking age, however, it should be noted that alcohol and alcohol-related offenses (429,000 in 1983) accounted for 46% of total crime in Texas for 1983. Sixteen percent of these offenses were DWI's. If one adds, in addition, the number of serious offenses (for example, vehicular homicide) that have alcohol as a significant component, one can begin to understand the magnitude of the alcohol problem. While the monetary cost to the justice system is quite large and is ultimately borne by taxpayers, the social costs borne by citizens as a result of this problem is staggering. By far, alcohol abuse is the worst drug problem Texans have and will continue to have in the coming decades.

It is beyond the scope of this chapter to review thoroughly the workings of the criminal courts in Texas. Even so, we want to note that very few cases actually go to trial; that is, the vast majority are plea bargained. Plea bargaining, negotiating a reduced sentence for a guilty plea, has become endemic to national and Texas court systems. It is a policy issue involving police, prosecutors, defense attorneys, and judges. Proponents argue that it promotes efficient use of resources and protects the technical core of the courts, the trial process, from becoming overburdened. Critics argue that, among other issues, it denies defendants a right to a fair and impartial hearing and substitutes instead a negotiated agreement in which the defendant has the most to lose. It is an issue that is unlikely to disappear from the criminal justice landscape in the near future and as a result will periodically rear up in controversy.

In the next section we examine what for Texas is a vexing bundle of problems: what to do with those convicted of crime. We will examine a contemporary profile of corrections, specifically confinement, which will highlight some of the recurring problems of the correction system in Texas. Part of what makes solutions difficult is the number of different outcomes desired: revenge, correction, rehabilitation, or confinement.

Corrections in Texas

Public corrections is a multilevel system of probation, detention facilities, correctional institutions, and parole, which involves a variety of state agencies, commissions, and departments. The correctional system in Texas, particularly the institutional control of adjudicated criminals and juveniles, is distinctive on several levels. For example, the Texas Department of Corrections (TDC) in 1985 housed one of the largest populations of nonpolitical prisoners in the world, fourth only to the Soviet Union, South Africa, and California. A very high proportion, 94%, of the inmates in Texas prisons are confined in maximum security, even though the national average is only 52%. The extensive labor-intensive agricultural work program in Texas prisons is the largest existing plantation system in the United States. As we shall see, these and other significant features can be traced to the historical development of the criminal justice system in the Texas political economy.

Physical Incarceration   Despite the fact that three of every four offenders in Texas are under some form of community supervision (probation or parole) rather than under confinement, the physical incarceration of individuals in either short-term detention facilities or longer-term correctional institutions is the most visible, the most controversial, and, per offender, the most costly public response to crime and delinquency. It has been estimated that there are over seven thousand existing facilities which detain approximately 766,000 persons in the United States on any given day.[10] Such incarceration takes place on the local, state, and federal levels and involves both juveniles and adults. In Texas in recent years, considerable attention has been focused on state prisons (under the jurisdiction of the Texas Department of Corrections), particularly as the federal courts have increasingly intervened in the Texas prison system. While the TDC will be examined in detail below, two other distinct forms of confinement, youth institutions and jails, are reviewed first. Each is fundamental to the complex mosaic of incarceration in Texas.

Texas Youth Commission (TYC)   A national census of public juvenile facilities revealed that on an average day in 1982 more than 50,000 youths were in custody in the United States.[11] Approximately 45% of these juveniles were detained in short-term local facilities while the remainder were incarcerated in longer-term state schools or reformatories. The 1982 census identifies thirty-four county and state public juvenile facilities in Texas, with an average daily population of 1,980 youths and approximately 2,500 staff.

Of the nearly eighty-seven thousand juvenile (ages ten to seventeen) arrests in Texas during 1982, some fifty-four thousand were referred to juvenile probation departments throughout Texas counties. More than fourteen thousand juvenile court petitions were filed on the basis of these referrals and of these, 9,000 juveniles were judged to be delinquent or in need of supervision. While most of these juveniles were placed under some form of community probation, 1,461 youths were committed to the Texas Youth Commission.[12]

The Texas Youth Commission administers the state-level juvenile corrections system, exercising jurisdiction over adjudicated juvenile delinquents and those dependent and neglected children referred to TYC by the courts.[13] The focus of extensive publicity in the early 1970s, the TYC was the prime target of civil actions in federal court on aspects of the juvenile justice system in Texas.[14] In *Morales* vs. *Thurman*, 383 F. Supp. 53 (D. Tex. 1974), the court examined allegations regarding cruel and unusual punishment, abuse of procedural due process, and lack of treatment programs in TYC training schools. The court's intensive investigation of conditions at TYC revealed widespread patterns of physical and psychological brutality, lack of due process for juveniles placed in maximum security and solitary confinement, excessive regimentation and restrictions in institutional life, inadequate and insufficiently trained staff, and absence or deficiency of treatment-related programs, including assessment and placement procedures, education programs, and medical and psychiatric care.[15] The court, declaring that TYC institutions on the whole were incapable of offering adequate rehabilitative treatment, directed that two flagrantly abusive schools be abandoned,[16] that institutionalization be reserved as a last resort for youth found unsuitable for less restrictive rehabilitative programs, and that a system of community-based treatment alternatives be established. Ten years after the historic trial, the court dismissed *Morales* in April, 1984 after concluding that conditions had substantially improved within Texas Youth Commission facilities.[17] A stipulated agreement between plaintiffs and defendants details a broad range of present and future changes within TYC training schools.[18]

Currently, youth committed to the Texas Youth Commission are placed in three types of settings.[19] TYC contracts with more than ninety-five privately operated, community child care facilities. These include foster and group homes, halfway houses, and residential treatment centers throughout Texas. TYC has contracted bed space for approximately 400 youths in these facilities. A second community-based setting is halfway houses operated by TYC.[20] These eight halfway houses have a more structured environment than the residential contract child care facilities. The average number of youths in TYC halfway houses is approximately 190. The cost of services per youth in either contract facilities or TYC halfway houses is $33 per day.

The third setting, structured institutional confinement, includes five training schools at Brownwood, Crockett, Gainesville, Giddings, and Pyote, the Statewide Reception Center at Brownwood, and the residential treatment program for emotionally disturbed youth at Corsicana.[21] Most youths committed to the Texas Youth Commission reside in these institutions. Violent offenders are confined at the Giddings State School for a minimum of twelve months; those juveniles who have committed murder, capital murder, or voluntary manslaughter are confined for a minimum of twenty-four months. Typically, most youth in TYC institutions are fifteen to seventeen years old, most are male, and most have been adjudicated for felonies (crimes against persons and property, felony drug offenses, and so on), for violation of conditions of probation, or have had their parole revoked. The average daily cost per youth confined in TYC training schools is $54.

In addition to the residential programs, the Texas Youth Commission provides state parole services for youths on home placement following release from a TYC facility or contract program. Parole offices, located in more than twenty Texas cities, supervised thirty-six hundred youths in 1982.

Jails and the Texas Commission on Jail Standards   Jails, in theory, are designated for short-term detention of individuals awaiting hearings or trial, awaiting transfer to state prisons or other institutions, or serving short sentences (usually less than one year). The 1983 national jail census identified thirty-five hundred local jail facilities in the United States.[22] The majority of these are county administered while the remainder are administered by cities. The average daily population of these jails exceeded 223,000 in 1983. (In addition to jails, there are approximately fifteen thousand lockups in the U.S., all small, local facilities for short-term detention.) Nationally, the average stay in a jail is eleven days, and most (60%) jail residents have not been convicted of an offense. Jails hold one inmate for every two inmates incarcerated in state or federal prisons.

There are 254 county jails in Texas, ranging from ancient, rural outposts to the $75 million Harris County Jail opened in 1982. Some of these county jails are among the largest in the United States,[23] and the Harris County jails have the fourth-largest inmate capacity in the country.[24] Since 1975, county jails have come under the jurisdiction of the Texas Commission on Jail Standards, whose purpose is to standardize county jail facilities through promulgation and enforcement of rules and regulations. In addition to county jails, there are 303 municipal jails and lockups in Texas which, at the time of this writing, are under local jurisdiction.[25] These municipal jails usually involve the shortest term of incarceration, and like many county jails, are often antiquated facilities whose capacities have been outstripped by population growth. The average daily population in county and city jails in Texas was approximately fifteen thousand during 1983.

Jails loom as a very critical present and future problem for Texans. Despite spending $400 million between 1977 and 1983 on jail construction and renovation, overcrowded conditions in some jails are the rule, not the exception. In 1984, twenty-nine jail expansion projects were in various stages of development in Texas. This new construction would add space for sixty-five hundred inmates and increase Texas jail capacity to more than twenty-six thousand. However, the possibility of federal intervention in Texas jails could result in extraordinary additional costs for taxpayers.[26] In this regard, the Texas Commission on Jail Standards requested a study in 1981 to assess the liability for sheriffs and jail administrators. Comparing Texas minimum jail standards with existing U.S. constitutional standards for confinement, the report was critical of enforcement policy in the state and pointed out deficiencies in aspects of physical plant design, and a range of inmate services and programs.[27] In addition to the possibility that many of their own standards are inadequate with respect to the constitutional minimums established by the federal courts, fully 40% of the county jails in Texas do not even meet the standards of the Texas Commission on Jail Standards. Through 1984, no county jails in Texas were accredited by major national organizations, such as the National Sheriffs Association or the Commission on Accreditation for Corrections. In light of recent federal court actions involving standards for juvenile training schools and the prison system in Texas, possible future scenarios regarding county and municipal jails in Texas are sobering.

Texas Department of Corrections (TDC) There has been unprecedented growth in prison populations throughout the United States in the 1980s. In 1984, there were 419,968 inmates in state prisons. Texas alone accounted for 9% of this total, and with California and New York, housed over one-quarter of the nation's state prison population.

The continuing growth in the prison population can be explained in a number of ways. The most prison-prone population group is considered to be males, ages twenty to twenty-nine. The present size of this "baby boom" group is considerable: twenty-four-year-olds are currently the largest age cohort in the United States. Because the population is still quite young in terms of imprisonment potential, we might reasonably expect the rate of imprisonment to continue to increase throughout the 1980s. Other explanations for the increasing prison population involve changing laws and practices, which increase the number of persons incarcerated and more lengthy sentences. Forty-eight states now have mandatory sentences for some crimes, while six states have changed laws to allow only fixed, determinant sentences for offenses, and several states impose longer sentences for habitual offenders and for the use of a firearm in the commission of a crime. In addition, nineteen states have either eliminated parole release or curbed the discretion of parole boards and panels. The size of the "at risk" population, changes in laws which have generally increased sentence length, and a national decline in the use of parole, have all contributed to the explosive increase in the number of prison inmates in the United States. The pressures of this growth on state prisons are becoming more evident as prison resources are taxed to their capacity and beyond. Texas, with the second-largest inmate population in the country in 1985, is a dramatic illustration of the crises of large state prison systems.

Historical overview of TDC. Soon after Texas joined the union, the first legislature authorized the construction of the state penitentiary at Huntsville, a 225-cell unit which began operation in 1849. Modeled after the penitentiary at Auburn (New York), the Huntsville prison confined its prisoners in single cells at night and congregated inmates during the day to work in silence. During the period 1870 to 1883, the entire prison system was leased to a succession of private contractors who, in exchange for the labor of inmates, were to provide for the maintenance and security of the prisoners as well as pay a small stipend to the state. When the leasing system was abandoned in 1883, due to widespread abuses in the treatment of prisoners, a contract lease system was initiated. Convicts of the Texas prison system were leased out to railroads, planters, and others in exchange for food, clothing, housing, and a monthly stipend paid to the state. In operation until 1909, the contract lease system increasingly came under fire due to scandals and abuses and was finally abolished by the legislature in 1910.

A major investigation of the Texas prison system by the Committee on Prisons and Prison Labor in 1924 revealed a punitive system of cruel and brutal punishments, inefficient management, and generally inadequate care of inmates.[28] While most recommendations of the committee were ignored, the style of prison management was changed in 1927 with the establishment of a prison board of nine persons to oversee a general manager of prisons. This system remains largely intact today. The Osborne Association of New York conducted an intensive study of the prisons at the request of the Texas Prison Board. Among its findings were inefficient prison management, brutal disciplinary procedures, inadequate medical services, lack of rehabilitation programs, self-mutilation by prisoners, bad working conditions, and the like.[29] By the mid-1940s, the Texas Prison System was considered among the worst in the United States.[30] In the ensuing decades, there have been a great many changes that have affected prisons under the successive administrations of TDC directors O. B. Ellis, George Beto, W. J. Estelle, Jr., and most recently Ray Procunier. Such changes as modernization of the physical plant; increases in prison industries; changes in testing, classification, and rehabilitation procedures; establishment of educational and vocational programs; increased staff training; and expansion of probation and parole (alternatives to confinement) took place within the context of an ever-expanding prison system and inmate population.

While the quantity of changes in the Texas Department of Corrections cannot be disputed, their quality and significance certainly have been. In 1974, the Joint Committee on Prison Reform submitted its findings to the 63rd Legislature.[31] The report was critical of many aspects of institutional life in TDC; the living and working conditions of inmates; the classification of inmates for rehabilitation programs; disciplinary procedures; medical care; racial discrimination and segregation; educational and vocational programs; staff training; and parole were among the concerns of this legislative investigation. The Joint Committee's reform recommendations had negligible impact on the subsequent 64th Legislature; however, the prospects for reform and qualitative changes in the prison system would be enhanced by the external review of the Texas Department of Corrections by the federal court.

Federal intervention in TDC: Ruiz vs. Estelle. By 1983, forty-two states were either under court order or facing litigation due to crowding and other conditions of confinement and release in state prisons. Since the early 1970s, state and federal courts have been examining correctional facilities to ensure compliance with Eighth Amendment protections against cruel and unusual punishment. With the decision in *Ruiz* vs. *Estelle*, 503 Supp. 1265 (D Tex. 1980), Texas joined seven other states whose entire prison systems had been declared unconstitutional.[32]

Prisoner lawsuits are standard fare in federal courts. For example, during the period 1973–1983 (the tenure of prison director W. J. Estelle, Jr.), 19,696 cases were filed in federal courts by prisoners in Texas, some 20% of the total federal district court docket in Texas during that period.[33] Despite these many thousands of cases, the *Ruiz* case has been exceptional and controversial. From some points of view, it is extraordinary that the substantive allegations aired during the trial (October 1978 to September 1979) echoed over a century of legislative investigations and reports of prison conditions in Texas. Others argue that the court's decision undermines the ability of the Texas Department of Corrections to fulfill its public mandate, namely, to manage a modern prison system and to reform inmates.[34] Regardless of their view, *Ruiz* provides fundamental insights into institutional life and the endemic problems of a burgeoning, centralized, and complex prison system.

Ruiz vs. *Estelle*, a class action on behalf of inmates in the custody of the Texas Department of Corrections, initially began in 1972 as a test of the constitutionality of certain practices in the Texas prison system. After several years of investigations by experts in all areas of prison operations, and the active involvement of the U.S. Justice Department, the court heard testimony from 349 witnesses and accepted 1,565 exhibits into evidence during the longest prison trial in U.S. history. While the dimensions of the case are notable, the legal context of *Ruiz* includes both the many thousands of cases filed against the Texas Department of Corrections in recent years and increasing state and federal prison litigation throughout the United States. Indeed, the testimony in *Ruiz* consistently focused on recurring themes of such litigation, including crowding, security and supervision, health care, discipline, access to the courts, and the like. In its opinion of 1980, the court concluded that the Texas Department of Corrections had violated inmates' constitutionally guaranteed rights in these separate areas.

Finding that "overcrowding at TDC exercises a malignant effect on all aspects of inmate life,"[35] the court cited the incidence of assaults, rapes, and other forms of predatory behavior, disease, tension, stress, and depression that are related to both crowding and an inadequate system of classification and separation of inmates by their levels of dangerousness. The security and supervision of inmates was compromised, the court said, because the staff was too few in number and insufficiently trained. The use of building tenders to augment TDC personnel contributed to what the court described as a "routine" system of brutality practiced at all levels of prison security and supervision.[36] The provision of health care, judged inadequate, suffered from high rates of health staff turnover, use of unqualified personnel (for example, inmates), poor medical record keeping, and medical facilities dwarfed by the size of the inmate population. The system of medical and work classification, the testimony demonstrated, did not insulate sick and disabled inmates from work assignments that further endangered their health. Special provisions and accommodations for mentally and physically impaired inmates were largely nonexistent. Disciplinary procedures, including the use of solitary confinement and administrative segregation, were assailed both for the acute physical suffering which resulted and for the lack of procedural due process for disciplined inmates. The court found that inmate access to the courts and attorneys was blocked by systematic harassment of inmates (by staff or building tenders), and arbitrary rules limiting the use of legal materials. These and other aspects of institutionalization (for example, lax fire safety, unsanitary conditions in some areas, dangerous and unsafe working conditions) or what was described as the *totality* of prison conditions, were found to be unconstitutional by the federal court.

The variety of remedies proposed by the court, including limitations on crowding, an end to the building tender system, new classification procedures for inmates, establishment of smaller prisons nearer to urban areas, increased work furlough programs, and community corrections, have generated and will continue to generate litigation and controversy. The court's presence, symbolized by the appointment of a special master to monitor Texas prisons, was vigorously opposed by those prison officials who refuse to concede that "constitutional infirmities pervade the TDC prison system."[37] In 1985, plaintiffs and defendants in *Ruiz* began face-to-face negotiations which resulted in an agreement between state officials and prisoners' attorneys which was approved by the federal court. The major thrust of the settlement concerned prison capacity. The Department of Corrections agreed to reduce capacity at existing institutions from

40,042 (July, 1985) to 32,500 (95% of capacity) by 1990. This, it is proposed, will be accomplished in part by building new prisons which may not exceed 2,250 inmates (excluding trustees) per unit. The settlement agreement also stipulates the use of single cells for special categories of offenders (a five thousand-cell set-aside for violent offenders, the mentally ill or retarded, etc.), and the conditions under which trusty camps may be added to prison units. Specifications for new prison construction, detailed in the agreement, include an increase in cell space for inmates, and a prohibition against building new dormitories and double-bunking. Existing units must increase the square-foot-per-inmate allowance, construct recreation areas, improve visiting arrangements, and generally upgrade the basic necessities provided to inmates. To implement this agreement, the Texas Department of Corrections plans to build a new prison unit by 1988, and ten trusty camps by 1987.

Contemporary Profile of TDC. From its modest beginnings at Huntsville, the Texas Department of Corrections has become twenty-seven prison units, located predominantly in rural east Texas.[38] During 1983, TDC had approximately 7,500 employees. Of these, 4,231 were guards. By 1985, their ranks had swelled to 6,469 guards and supervisors.[39] The inmate population reached a historical peak of 38,000 in 1982 and 1985. The state prisons had literally closed in May, 1982, due to overcrowding, when as many as 4,000 inmates were held in tents.[40] During 1985, the inmate population was approximately 95% of prison capacity. The levels of overcrowding were reduced in 1983 and 1985 by granting early releases to inmates. For example, a record 7,198 inmates received early release in 1983, a figure which represents one-third of all early releases granted in the United States due to overcrowding in 1983.

Prison work programs in the Texas Department of Corrections are a major element and preoccupation within the system. Most inmates work: nearly one-half in agriculture, 10% in prison industries, 30% in institutional upkeep and service, and 10% in (prison) construction and building maintenance. From its initial purchase of twenty-five hundred acres of land in 1885, TDC has become an agribusiness, with more than ninety-two thousand acres of farmland under cultivation. The three major production areas, edible crops, feed crops and fibers, and livestock and poultry, rely on the intensive labor, primarily stoop labor, of many thousands of prison inmates. These agricultural operations meet the food and fiber needs of TDC inmates and some staff.

The manufacturing programs of the Texas Department of Corrections, begun in 1854 with operation of a cotton and woolen mill,

are more capital intensive. The twenty-five industrial facilities are located throughout the prison system, and produced $42.5 million in
goods and services in 1983: soaps, braille books, microfilms, metal
fabrications, dump beds, recapped tires, inmate and officer clothing,
shoes, dental prosthetics, highway signs, furniture, coffee. This diversity of production in the Texas Department of Corrections' factories,
plants, and shops is targeted at reducing TDC operating expenses,
reducing the operating costs of other Texas state agencies, *and* rehabilitating inmates. The productivity and scale of these agricultural and
manufacturing programs are distinctive nationally: the average daily
cost of an inmate to taxpayers in Texas was $14.57 in 1983, which is
the lowest cost in the United States. Most inmates in custody of the
Texas Department of Corrections come from the major urban areas of
Houston (28%) and Dallas (26%), and have not previously been confined in TDC (76%). Table 9–2 provides an overview of the inmate
profile in Texas prisons.

Crises and Reform in Corrections

Through 1985, the Texas Department of Corrections was again embroiled in controversies. The federal court, TDC's chief protagonist
during the previous decade, continued to challenge aspects of institutional life in Texas prisons. A report circulated in September, 1983,
by a special court monitor alleged that prison brutality by guards and
officials had continued unabated in the interim since the court had declared such practices unconstitutional. However, with the resignation
of TDC director W. J. Estelle in October, 1983, the court's activities
were overshadowed by increasing state scrutiny of the Texas Department of Corrections. The House Law Enforcement Committee, the
State Attorney General's office, and the Governor's Office began in-
vestigating a wide range of excesses and abuses in the operations
of TDC. Financial mismanagement, waste, and fraud in prison construction programs were said to have cost Texas taxpayers millions of
dollars. A multimillion-dollar lawsuit filed against a former TDC employee accused of rigging construction bids epitomized controversies
in the construction programs, which included cost overruns, excessive architectural and engineering fees, and the like. Such problems
as improper purchasing and accounting practices, questionable hiring
of professional consultants, excessive fringe benefits for officials and
staff, and conflicts of interest led to proposals in 1984 to change the
basic administrative structure of TDC.

Table 9–2. Inmate Profile.

SEX
  Male — 95.6 percent
  Female — 4.4 percent
  (August, 1983)

RACE
  Black — 43.7 percent
  Anglo — 37.5 percent
  Hispanic — 18.9 percent
  Other — .01 percent
    (May not equal 100 percent due
      to rounding)

AGE
  Average inmate age — 29.9
  Largest age group incarcerated — between 23 and 25 (16.9 percent)

SENTENCE
  Average sentence length in 1983, new inmates — 113.6 months
    (over nine years)
  Average sentence length, all inmates — 20.3 years
  Inmates serving less than three years — 5.2 percent
  Percent of inmates serving life sentences — 8.9 percent
  Previously confined at TDC — 39.4 percent
  Previously confined at other prisons — 11.5 percent
  Number of inmates on Death Row — 172 (second to Florida)

OFFENSE
  Crime with highest percentage of convicted inmates — burglary
    (26.3 percent)
  Crime with second highest percentage of convicted inmates —
    robbery (21.7 percent)
  Admissions — one inmate is admitted every 29 minutes

CONVICTION LOCATION
  Metropolitan Statistical Areas with highest inmate imprisonment
    rate based on conviction per 100,000 population —
    Beaumont (323.9), Houston (323.2) and Midland (312)
  Largest number of inmates sent to TDC by city — Houston (10,076),
    Dallas-Forth Worth (9,531) and San Antonio (2,028)

Sources: Texas Department of Corrections, *1983 Fiscal Year Statistical Report* and *The Correction Yearbook.*

The responsiveness of the Texas Department of Corrections to the federal court, which could only be described as sluggish, also appeared to be at issue. The clear sentiment of the court in *Ruiz* was that the type of prison construction in Texas (that is, large, maximum-security prisons) was endemic to the problems of TDC. While $300 million had been spent since 1979 for prison construction, the Texas

Department of Corrections asked that $674 million of its $1.5 billion budget request for 1984–85 be used for additional prison construction. This obviously struck a sensitive nerve in the state legislature, which halved the total TDC budget request and allocated only $12 million for construction programs. The problem of overcrowding in state prisons would be addressed by alternatives to the historical confinement solution in Texas (maximum security).

Of the more than 1,150 bills and resolutions passed during the 68th Legislative session (January 11–May 30, 1983), approximately 30% addressed aspects of criminal law and the criminal justice system. In the area of corrections, an unlikely coalition of budget-conscious conservatives and prison reform advocates succeeded in enacting a core of "reform" legislation. Faced with the twin pressures of the federal court order to reduce crowding and declining state revenues, a significant shift in correctional strategy became evident with the movement towards more "community-based" supervision. The distribution of appropriations in 1983 is some evidence of this change. Where the Texas Department of Corrections, which exemplifies the centralized, state confinement of offenders, had been receiving 76.5 cents of every corrections dollar, its share was reduced to 66.5 cents in 1984. Increased appropriations were targeted at agencies which might assist in controlling the state's inmate population through probation and parole.

The enabling legislation of the 68th Session touched upon several dimensions of the community-based approach. Two strategies were apparent: the first, to reduce the inmate population in the Texas Department of Corrections (conditions of parole); the second, to establish alternatives to imprisonment (conditions of probation). The former strategy included legislation to streamline the Texas Board of Pardons and Paroles, to allow good-time credit for confinement elsewhere, such as in county jails, to be counted towards parole in TDC, to reduce the inmate population in TDC during emergency overcrowded conditions by giving certain inmates additional credits for good time, and to establish community residential facilities, halfway houses, where low-risk inmates could be transferred up to 180 days prior to their parole date. Strategies to enhance probation included the use of community service work as a condition of probation, and the establishment of restitution centers. These residential centers would house certain inmates while they worked to maintain themselves and their families and to pay restitution to their victims.

Whether this legislation signals a substantive change in the future of corrections in Texas certainly remains to be seen. It is clear, however, that the correctional strategies of the past have disconcert-ing, if not dire, implications in the present. While Texans pay the least of any state for the upkeep of inmates ($6,951 per year in 1983) the total costs involved in the scale of the Texas Department of Cor-rections represent a significant drain of state revenues. The size of the inmate population, at its historical peaks in 1982, 1985, and 1987, bears both on those costs, and on the manner and quality of institu-tional life in prisons. These issues are at the heart of the federal court challenge to the state. It is an inescapable conclusion that not only the scale of maximum security incarceration, but the number of TDC inmates will have to be controlled.

A 1985 study of Texas prisons by the architectural firm of Hen-nigson, Durham & Richardson estimated that if no changes occurred in the sentencing structure and the rate of incarceration in Texas, the prison population would swell to ninety-two thousand by 1995. Even in the event that criminal laws are liberalized and alternatives to pris-ons are increased, there could be as many as fifty thousand inmates in Texas prisons by 1995. The study estimates that operating expenses in the coming decade could reach $1 billion per year for the Texas prison system. Perhaps the most controversial finding, however, was that Texans will have to pay $734 million to $872 million between 1985 and 1995 to bring the present prison system into compliance with federal court directives. By mid-1985, Texas had already paid in excess of $5 million in legal fees for *Ruiz*. One observer estimated in 1985 that the resistance to compliance with the federal court (*Ruiz* was both the longest prison case and the longest civil rights case in U.S. history) had cost Texas more than $146 million in inflation alone during the previous twelve years of litigation.[41]

While skepticism about the TDC operations and rankling over the affronts of the federal court had not disappeared, the Texas Leg-islature placed state prisons high on its list of priorities for the 69th Legislative Session. The 1985–86 budget for the Texas Department of Corrections was $539.1 million while the 1986–87 budget was $428.8 million. The two year total amounted to $967.9 million. A significant portion of these funds were targeted for upgrading prison facilities and operations. However, manifestations of a prison system in crisis continue to erupt. For example, in 1984 Texas recorded the second highest amount of prison violence, second only to the bloody 1980 New Mexico prison riot, since such national records have been kept. Twenty-five inmates died in Texas prisons at the hands of other in-mates and more than 400 inmates were stabbed, a rate of violence that continued in 1985, when 27 inmates were murdered and 219 were stabbed.[42] Such problems suggest that the task of simply *main-*

taining the Texas Department of Corrections, much less changing it, in the present and the future will be a formidable one.

Concluding Comment

A coherent criminal justice policy for Texas (or any other state) appears highly improbable given the number of powerful interest groups who profit from current arrangements. These groups, cherishing their own interests more than those of the larger public, evaluate every proposal for reform in terms of the potential loss or gain to their agencies and continue to view other components of the criminal justice system with distrust. Legislators support this state of affairs, which is also supported by jurisdictional boundaries (for example, municipal and county), past legislation, and legal limitations. The general public appears to prefer current criminal justice policy as well. Therefore, we can expect a continued fragmentation of the criminal justice system, the continuing problems that result, and the piecemeal, cosmetic solutions that follow. The controversies, however, will not go away because many of them have existed for so very long and because the nature of the larger Texas society is changing much more rapidly than any reform of the criminal justice system can handle.

Population analysts tell us that Texas will be the second most populous state by 1990. Since research suggests that the rate of crime appears related to the number of people, their density, and the age profile of the population, we can expect crime to increase as the population increases. This is especially so when the number of males thirteen to thirty-nine in the population increases. More people have more things, go more places, and provide more opportunities for crime. Criminal justice planning at local and state levels is reactive to population trends and thus always behind. And being behind is costly and forces us to focus on short-term solutions to pressing problems. How will Texans defend themselves against crime? What will we do with those convicted?

One solution is to decriminalize certain offenses de facto or de jure. De facto decriminalization has virtually occurred in some jurisdictions with vehicular homicides, particularly when the guilty party can be sued and damages collected. Possession of small amounts of marijuana in many urban and suburban jurisdictions has become nonoffensive, as has the illegal possession of alcohol. However, even if select laws were repealed, there would still be an oversupply of offenders, and there would still be confusion about what to do with them and where to put them.

The manifestations of crime and the organization of justice and corrections in Texas are a systemic part of preferences for ways of living, and thus what is considered tolerable in terms of laws, enforcement, and consequence. To be sure, the number of principles involved is large, as are the social factors they reflect. For example, the desire to move about freely, to live in loose connection to the community, to live in relative isolation from one's neighbors, to not have one's property or oneself openly watched is considered "freedom." But part of the result is that greater opportunities for crime also exist; with the "freedom" come the increased risk and the genuine lack of a support system. Moreover, watching is not the responsibility of neighbors; it is the responsibility of the police. Yet, there aren't enough police to watch because who wants a police state?

Police, for their part, are hamstrung by the publics they serve, by their fragmented jurisdictions, their jealous rivalry, and by legal limitations. Police pressure in one jurisdiction on one kind of crime merely disperses the action to other areas. When the "temporary heat" is off, crime returns. Scarce resources and allocation patterns make it virtually impossible for the heat to be on all of the time. Thus, police symbolically enforce some laws, and some, deemed less important, are not enforced at all. Urban sprawl, limited resources combined with radio transmission, and automobiles have changed police patrol strategy from watching to prevent crime to waiting to respond to crime. Indeed, Texas cities everywhere tout "response time" as a measure of police performance without ever questioning the logic behind the strategy and the consequences.[43] Concentrated foot patrol is both too costly and too passé and without it, the possibility of mediation and conflict resolution before escalation is lost.[44]

If there were one set of statistics that supported active changes in the law, enforcement, and sentencing it would be those relating to alcohol and crime. Alcohol is involved in a large number of homicides and about 20% of all arrests are for driving while intoxicated (DWI). Public drunkenness accounts for another 30+% of arrests. Yet, alcohol is the only crime-generating commodity that is legally sold and taxed. And until recently offenses such as DWI were treated quite lightly by Texas officials. Recent pressure form both private groups (MADD) and the federal government through the Department of Transportation (loss of highway funds) appears to be forcing the legal drinking age upward, but whether this will result in a reduction of alcohol-related crime remains to be seen.

While alcohol abuse may be a disease, the only apparatus set up in Texas to handle drunks, drunk drivers, and the like is the criminal justice system. Yet it is unlikely that the system will move any farther than it can be pushed. Why? Because police generally do not see public drunkenness as an enforcement priority and people arrested for it have a remarkable tendency to view the arrest as police harassment. Similar feelings abound for spot checks of motorists leaving bars, nightclubs, and liquor stores. Purveyors of alcohol are not particularly interested in being held accountable for the havoc which results from the drugs they have sold, and the liquor industry does not want any additional restrictive regulation. The result is a potent combination of powerful forces for the status quo.

There is no shortage of ironies and contradictions to muddle correctional policy in Texas. Historically, the state has had a penchant for exiling its convicts to maximum security steel and concrete cells regardless of the cost, the effectiveness, or the short- and long-term consequences. Despite the rather remarkable historical consistency in institutional conditions for both juvenile and adult offenders, the underlying rationales for incarceration which animate the citizen, victim, practitioner, and politician suggest a historical schizophrenia. The often conflicting and contradictory explanations for why we react to social trouble as we do, through retribution, reprobation, revenge, deterrence, and rehabilitation, are amply articulated in correctional policy and practice in Texas. Problems in our juvenile training schools, jails, and prisons are to be expected and will not, as is often suggested, be resolved by fine-tuning institutional management or reciting anew the tired punitive theories of correcting moral failures of some Texas citizens.

While it is never clear what Texans want from their correctional system, just as it is never clear what that system is capable of doing, there is little question about what Texans are willing to do. We pay billions of dollars. And it is likely that Texans will continue to spend hundreds of millions of dollars each year to incarcerate only 5% of those individuals who commit serious crimes (80% are never even arrested and continue to live amongst us). The predicted glut of sentenced offenders in the coming years poses a significant "management" problem for the state. Strategies which might reduce or maintain the inmate population in abeyance represent a broad sweep of philosophical positions on the nature of deviance and social control. Contemporary and future Texas public policy can be significantly affected through reallocation of resources to local community alternatives, including increased use of pretrial diversion, alternative sentencing, probation and parole (supervision in the local community), and community corrections and detention (for example, halfway houses, restitution centers, house arrest). Broader strategies could also have an impact, such as shifts in the targeting priorities of police and prosecutors, reduced use of detainers, and changes in the criminal law. And of course, we could choose to build more prisons, both public and private, in lieu of or in combination with other alternatives. However, we must not forget that correctional institutions are representations in miniature of all the dynamics of the larger society of which they are a part. Community-based alternatives to incarceration in Texas will succeed *only* to the extent that the local community has vitality in Texas and embraces, rather than shuns and acquiesces to, the responsibility for its errant members.

Finally, in part as a result of an increase as a percentage of Texas' population, relative position in the economic structure, and demographics, we are likely to see more Hispanics and a continued high percentage of blacks as offenders and as inmates. This will occur more rapidly at the offender level and will greatly exasperate ethnic and racial tensions both inside and outside criminal justice institutions. Again, these conditions will accurately reflect the real social conditions of the larger society.

Notes

1. The following definitions of index crimes are used in the Uniform Crime Reporting Program:

Criminal Homicide. The willful (nonnegligent) killing of one human being by another.

Forcible Rape. The carnal knowledge of a female forcibly and against her will.

Robbery. The taking or attempting to take anything of value from the care, custody, or control of a person or persons by force or threat of force or violence and/or by putting the victim in fear.

Aggravated Assault. An unlawful attack by one person upon another for the purpose of inflicting severe or aggravated bodily injury. This type of assault usually is accompanied by the use of a weapon or by means likely to produce death or great bodily harm.

Burglary. The unlawful entry of a structure to commit a felony or a theft.

Larceny-Theft. The unlawful taking, carrying, leading, or riding away of property from the possession or constructive possession of another. (Includes theft from a motor vehicle.)

Motor Vehicle Theft. The theft or attempted theft of a motor vehicle.

Arson. The willful or malicious burning or attempting to burn, with or without intent to defraud, a dwelling house, public building, motor vehicle or aircraft, personal property of another, etc. Includes violation of state laws and municipal ordinances relating to arson and attempted arson.

(Texas Department of Public Safety, *Crime in Texas: Calendar Year, 1985*).

2. From the Office of the Governor, State of Texas, "An Overview of Crime in Texas" (Austin, 1984), 4. (Mimeographed.)

3. See U.S. Department of Justice, Bureau of Justice Statistics, *Report to the Nation on Crime and Justice: The Data* (Washington, D.C.: U.S. Department of Justice, 1983).

4. There are a number of interpretations for this pattern, which occurs both statewide and nationwide. Blacks, nationwide, account for about 12% of the population but 46% of the arrestees for violent crimes and 31% for property crimes. Hispanics constitute about 6% of the U.S. population but 12% of the arrests for violent crime and 10% for property crimes. See Bureau of Justice Statistics, *Report to the Nation*, 31.

5. See Texas Department of Public Safety, *Texas Crime Report 1982* (Austin: Department of Public Safety, 1982); also idem, *Texas Crime Report 1983* (Austin: Department of Public Safety, 1983).

6. Unless otherwise noted, the data for this section are derived from ibid. (1983).

7. Statutory rapes are not included in this category.

8. On this point, see Bureau of Justice Statistics, *Report to the Nation*, 15.

9. Unless otherwise noted, the data for this section are derived from Department of Public Safety, *Texas Crime Report 1983*.

10. Unitarian Universalist Service Committee, "Cage Count," *Jerico* 37 (Fall, 1984):7.

11. U.S. Department of Justice, Office of Juvenile Justice and Delinquency Prevention, *Children in Custody: Advance Report on the 1982 Census of Public Juvenile Facilities* (Washington, D.C.: U.S. Department of Justice, 1983).

12. A substantial discrepancy between the reported number of TYC commitments for 1982 should be noted. The Texas Juvenile Probation Commission, which draws its data from county juvenile courts, reported that 1,461 juveniles were committed to TYC by the courts: This figure is used here to retain consistency with other statistics on juvenile arrests, referrals, and adjudication also supplied by the county courts to the Texas Juvenile Probation Commission. The Texas Youth Commission, on the other hand, reported 1,964 delinquent commitments in 1982. See Texas Juvenile Probation Commission, *Texas Juvenile Probation Statistical Report: Calendar Year 1982* (Austin: Texas Juvenile Probation Committee, 1983); also Texas Youth Council, *1982 Annual Report* (Austin: Texas Youth Council, 1983). The authors are unable to reconcile these disparate data with information provided by the respective agencies.

13. Jurisdiction over dependent and neglected children is shared between the Texas Youth Commission and the Department of Human Resources.

14. The Texas Youth Commission was formerly known as the Texas Youth Council.

15. The court additionally noted abuses of procedural due process for juveniles prior to their commitment to TYC, which had resulted in the release of about 865 youths in 1972 and 1973 by order of state courts.

16. The Gatesville State School for Boys and Mountain View State School for Boys were subsequently closed by TYC and transferred to the jurisdiction of the Texas Department of Corrections for use as adult female correctional facilities.

17. "Final Judgment," *Morales* vs. *Turman*, Civil No. 1948 (D. Tex. April 16, 1984).

18. "Second Amended Settlement Agreement," *Morales* vs. *Turman*, Civil No. 1948 (D. Tex. April 16, 1984).

19. See Texas Youth Commission, *Child Care Information 1984* (Austin: Texas Youth Commission, 1984); also Texas Youth Council, *1982 Annual Report* (Austin: Texas Youth Council, 1983).

20. TYC halfway houses are located in Austin, El Paso, Corpus Christi, Richmond, Dallas, Harlingen, San Antonio, and McAllen.

21. Dependent and neglected children committed to the Texas Youth Commission by the courts are placed in foster homes, relatives' homes, or independent living situations. Emotionally disturbed dependent and neglected children are confined at Corsicana.

22. U.S. Department of Justice, Bureau of Justice Statistics, *The 1983 Jail Census* (Washington, D.C.: U.S. Department of Justice, 1984).

23. These Texas jails are in Bexar, Dallas, El Paso, Harris (two facilities), Jefferson, and Tarrant counties.

24. Harris County is fourth only to the jail systems of Los Angeles County, New York City, and Cook County (Chicago).

25. During 1983–84, the Texas Commission on Jail Standards had been drafting rules to regulate municipal jails. In a series of public hearings held in Texas during 1984, local jurisdictions voiced apprehensions about mandatory rules on prison design (e.g., minimum square footage per inmate), which would require substantial expenditures to satisfy.

26. One such case, *Bush* vs. *Viterna* A-80-CA-411 (D. Tex, filed 1980), has been in the courts for several years. This case specifically challenges the adequacy of some regulations set by the Texas Commission on Jail Standards and claims as well that the commission does not uniformly enforce its own jail standards in Texas.

27. At the request of Texas Commission on Jail Standards Director Robert Viterna, Criminal Justice Consultants produced such a study, which is also referred to as the "Lonergan Report" for its principal investigator, Thomas F. Lonergan. See Criminal Justice Consultants, (Downey, Cal.), "An Evaluation of the Texas Jail Standards," 1981. (Mimeographed.)

28. Texas Committee on Prisons and Prison Labor, *A Summary of the Texas Prison Survey* (Austin: Texas Committee on Prisons and Prison Labor, 1924).

29. The Osborne Association, Inc., "Texas Prison Report," delivered by Austin H. MacCormack to the governor of Texas and Texas Prison Board in Austin, February 8, 1945. (Mimeographed.)

30. The name "Texas Prison System" was changed to the Texas Department of Corrections in 1957.

31. See Joint committee on Prison Reform, *Final Report of the Joint Committee on Prison Reform, 63rd Legislature* (Austin: Joint Committee on Prison Reform, 1974); also Citizens Advisory Committee, *Report from the Citizens Advisory Committee on Prison Reform, 63rd Legislature* (Austin: Joint Committee on Prison Reform, 1974).

32. Joining Texas are Alabama, Florida, Mississippi, Oklahoma, Rhode Island, Tennessee, and Michigan (male facilities only).

33. Data compiled from Administrative Office of the United States Courts, *Civil and Criminal Trials Statistical Tables: Twelve Month Periods (1961–1983)* (Washington, D.C.: Administrative Office of the United States Courts, 1984).

34. Texas Civil Statutes, 6166g.

35. *Ruiz* vs. *Estelle*, 503 F. Supp. 1265, 1277.

36. Building tenders are inmates with authority to supervise and in some cases, to discipline other inmates, usually in exchange for "special privileges."

37. *Ruiz* vs. *Estelle*, 503 F. Supp. 1265, 1391.

38. See Texas Department of Corrections, *1983 Fact Sheet* (Huntsville: Texas Department of Corrections, 1983); also Texas Department of Corrections, *1983 Annual Report* (Huntsville: Texas Department of Corrections, 1983); also Bob Bullock, "Prison System Faces Change," *Fiscal Notes* (November, 1984), 11.

39. Projected staff increases for 1985 include an additional fifteen hundred guards, and approximately eight hundred additional psychiatric workers and counselors.

40. Local jurisdictions were paid to temporarily house inmates under the jurisdiction of the Texas Department of Corrections.

41. Molly Ivins, "Pursuing Prison Cast Has Cost State Millions," *Dallas Times-Herald* (April 4, 1985).

42. Such violence includes guard against inmate (as detailed in the Special Master's Report in late 1983) and inmate against guard. As an illustration, cells at two prison units were searched in July and August, 1984 (an action precipitated by inmate violence), yielding 489 homemade weapons in the seventeen hundred inmate Coffield Unit, and 524 homemade weapons in the twenty-two hundred inmate Ferguson Unit.

43. A 1977 National Institute of Justice study measured the impact of response time on the probability of officers intercepting a crime in progress and making an arrest. It found that response time of two to twenty minutes made very little difference because citizens took so long to call the police

after the crime occurred. See Kansas City Police Department, *Response Time Analysis* (Washington, D.C.: National Institute of Justice, 1977).

44. Research suggests that a number of other benefits are lost. While studies differ on the effects of foot patrol on the actual level of crime, they generally agree that foot patrol reduced public fear of crime. In addition, foot patrol raised the public perception of order. Since there is some evidence that public disorder raises peoples' fear of more serious crime, and fear of serious crime is considered an important factor in business and residential flight from neighborhoods, reduction of the fear of crime can be seen to have a stabilizing influence in neighborhoods. In addition, at least one study found that police on foot patrol were more satisfied with their jobs. See Police Foundation, *The Newark Foot Patrol Experiment* (Washington, D.C.: Police Foundation, 1981).

Chapter Ten

WELFARE REFORM
IN PERSPECTIVE

Edward J.Harpham

Welfare is an issue that is not popular in Texas. Poverty. The dole. Dependency. All appear to fly in the face of the reality and the myth which is Texas. Texas is a state that champions success, whose people display their wealth conspicuously. Timber, cattle, cotton, water, oil, and high tech are the concerns that have shaped Texas politics for the last fifty years. In Texas, poverty has been a side issue, a problem to be solved by the further expansion of the economy. It has not been a matter of central concern to either policymakers or the public as a whole.

Yet poverty is a problem in Texas, a problem that has haunted the state as it has been transformed from a rural backwater dependent upon outside economic interests into a dynamic urban economy in its own right. The Texas success story has not solved the problem of poverty in the Lone Star State. Indeed, the state has barely begun to address it. The programs serving the poor in Texas have been among the most niggardly in the nation over the past fifty years. In the best of times, Texas has followed reluctantly the lead of other states in trying to meet the needs of poor people. In the worst, Texas has had to be compelled by either the courts or the federal government to meet what many considered to be a minimal level of subsistence.

In November, 1982, a constitutional amendment was ratified that transformed the conditions under which welfare policy was made in Texas. The amendment made possible a number of important welfare reforms in 1983 and 1984. This chapter assesses the significance of these reforms by putting them in the context of Texas welfare policy over the last fifty years. It argues that the early 1980s represents a new era of welfare policymaking in Texas. There is no simple explanation as to why Texas has provided in the past and still provides today such a low level of welfare assistance to its poor. Texas welfare policy has been dictated by a variety of interacting economic, political, and ideological factors. In order to assess the significance of the recent welfare reforms and to appreciate the problems confronting Texas welfare policy today, it is necessary to understand how these factors have worked together to shape welfare policy in Texas over the past fifty years.

The Poor In Texas

Some people find it difficult to believe that the land of cowboy dreams and high-tech realities could have a poverty problem. But it does. And it is a serious problem. According to the 1980 census, 2.0 million Texas live in poverty, approximately 14.7% of the state population, 2.4% above the nationwide poverty rate of 12.4%.[1]

As at the national level, poverty in Texas does not strike all groups equally. Some groups bear the burden of poverty much more than others. Poverty tends to strike minorities much more frequently than it does whites. In 1979, 11.5% of white Texans were poor. In comparison, 27.6% of all black Texans and 28.0% of Texans of Spanish origin lived in poverty. These figures differ significantly from national statistics, where it is calculated that 9.4% of all whites, 29.9% of all blacks, and 23.5% of all Americans of Spanish origin live below the poverty line.[2]

Poverty tends to afflict the very old and the very young more frequently than other groups in the population. According to the 1980 census, 39% of those living below the poverty line in Texas were under the age of eighteen, while 13% were sixty-five years and older. This compares with national figures that estimate the percentage of poor children at 37 and the number of elderly poor at 13.[3]

Poverty also has a regional component in Texas. Seventy-eight percent of the poor in Texas live in urban areas. Twenty-two percent of the poor live in rural areas. But poverty is not simply an urban problem. While 13.5% of those living in urban areas are poor, 15.6% of those in rural areas are poor. Moreover, 32% of all the elderly poor in Texas live in rural areas.[4]

The sheer size and diversity of the Texas economy has resulted in a skewed income distribution favoring certain sections of the state more than others. In 1980, the highest incidence of poverty was in the so-called Border region (the area along the U.S.–Mexico border from El Paso to Brownsville), where 29% of the population was classified as poor. Interestingly, three of the poorest metropolitan areas in the country are along the South Texas border. The second-highest poverty level in Texas was found in the so-called Central Corridor, where 17.4% of the population was poor. In East Texas, the poverty rate in 1980 was estimated to be 16.2%. The Plains region meanwhile had a poverty rate of 14.2% in 1980, while the Gulf Coast maintained a rate of 11.6%. The lowest poverty rate in Texas in 1980 was in the Metroplex (the Dallas-Fort Worth region), where only 10.3% of the population lived below the poverty line.[5]

Over the years a number of federal and state programs have sought to address the poverty problem in Texas. While in recent years the national government has assumed a much larger role in the antipoverty effort both financially and administratively, state efforts are still significant. For FY85 public welfare expenditures, excluding health, were 14.3% of the state budget.[6]

The Texas Department of Human Services (DHS), formerly the Texas Department of Human Resources (DHR), and the State Department of Public Welfare (DPW) administer most of the important public welfare programs in Texas, including Aid to Families with Dependent Children (AFDC), Food Stamps, Medicaid, and a variety of social services and child support services. The DHS is supervised by a three-member board, the Texas Board of Human Services. The board is responsible for adopting all policies, rules, and regulations for the DHS and for appointing a commissioner on human resources to formally head the department. While the board is somewhat limited by federal guidelines in what it can do, it is empowered to determine eligibility for public assistance programs provided by the state as well as the level at which payments and services will be made under particular programs.

By far the most important and controversial welfare program administered by DHS is the AFDC program. AFDC is a state-federal program that traces its origins back to the Social Security Act of 1935. Under the program, the federal government will contribute a certain amount of money to a state-sponsored welfare program that meets certain minimal federal standards. Significantly, the states retain the power to determine eligibility and payment levels under the AFDC programs. Texas officials have used this power to make the AFDC program in Texas one of the most miserly in terms of payments and one of the most difficult for which to become and remain eligible.

For FY83, AFDC payments totaled $189.6 million, 57% financed by the federal government, 43% financed by the state. Payments for the year averaged approximately $41.76 a month per person, about $1.39 a day. Texas, the sixteenth wealthiest state on a per-capita income basis, ranked second only to Mississippi, the poorest state, in providing the lowest level of AFDC benefits in the nation. Major increases in the AFDC program were appropriated for the 1984–85 biennium, raising total federal and state expenditures to $223.8 million in 1985. The average grant per month was still only expected to be $46.72, approximately 21.6% of the federally defined poverty level for a family of three. Benefit levels were increased again in 1985 and 1986. For FY86 benefit levels were averaging $57.57. But even with these increases Texas ranked only forty-sixth among the fifty states in its level of support for AFDC recipients.[7]

The level of benefits in the Texas AFDC program is only part of the story. Texas also has some of the strictest eligibility requirements in the nation for its AFDC program. In 1984, a mother with one child would not qualify for benefits if income exceeded $183 per month. There are strict financial limitations as to how much property an individual can own to remain eligible. An individual could not have more than $1,000 in assets, not counting a home and $1,500 equity in an automobile.[8]

One of the harshest features of the AFDC eligibility requirements in Texas is the fact that the program is largely limited to one-parent families. Texas does not participate in the federal government's AFDC-U program, which provides benefits to children where the primary breadwinner (generally the father) is unemployed. Half of the states have a similar restriction. AFDC benefits thus generally are not available to families where both parents are in the home no matter what their financial situation is. In order to get the family to qualify for welfare, a father might actually be forced to abandon the family.[9]

Along with these strict eligibility requirements, other factors such as political attitudes, access to welfare offices, and local staffing of welfare offices have played a major role in seriously limiting participation in the AFDC program in Texas. For example, Legal Aid lawyers contend that some regional DHS offices and regional judges are more hostile to prospective welfare recipients than are others.[10] According to one study, only about two-thirds of those eligible for AFDC in Texas actually participate in the program. In addition, while the poverty rate in Texas is significantly above the national rate (14.7% vs. 12.4% in 1980), the actual percentage of the population receiving public aid in Texas is significantly lower than the national average (3.4% vs. 6.0%).[11]

The Food Stamp Program is a federal program administered in Texas by the DHS. The value of food stamps made available to any particular family is directly related to the income and size of the family. The more a family earns, the less it receives in food stamps. Similarly, the larger the family, the more food stamps that are received. While the federal government is responsible for funding the program and determining eligibility requirements, Texas determines who is actually eligible. As is the case with AFDC, these requirements are quite strict.

For example, in 1984 a three-person family consisting of a mother and two children could not qualify for food stamps if its gross income exceeded $970 a month or its net income exceeded $705 a month. In 1984, an average of 397,765 households per month received a total of $665 million in food stamps for the year. While the number of households receiving food stamps dropped slightly in 1985 to an average 397,571 per month, the total amount of food stamps received by families in Texas for the year rose to $697.2 million.[12] Moreover, it has been estimated that only one-third of those potentially eligible to receive food stamps actually participate in the program.[13]

The third major welfare program aimed at the poor, Medicaid, finances medical services to those who participate in the AFDC program as well as the Supplemental Security Income Program, a federal public assistance program for the aged, blind, and disabled. Services financed by Medicaid include in-patient and out-patient hospital care, physician services, prescribed drugs, lab and x-ray services, radiation therapy, nursing home care, and family planning services. In 1985, two new programs were implemented, the Children and Pregnant Woman Program and the Medically Needy Program, whose goals were to extend medical care to individuals in groups not normally covered by DHS's programs and services. In FY85, an average of 691,501 people per month were provided health care services by DHS and approximately $1.6 billion was spent under the Medicaid programs in Texas, over half funded by the federal government.[14]

While it is difficult to measure the impact that these three welfare programs together have had upon the plight of the poor in Texas, some rough calculations are possible. One estimate has placed the total value of AFDC, food stamp, and Medicaid benefits for a family of three in Texas at $515 per month in 1985. But even this amount equaled only 69.0% of the federal poverty level.[15]

Popular beliefs to the contrary, most welfare recipients are not lazy able-bodied individuals, nor do they have large families in order to receive enormous welfare checks. Ninety-five percent of the adults on the AFDC program in Texas are women who head households with an average of two children. Their family income from welfare is less than one-quarter the federally defined level of poverty. Most of the women have neither a high school degree nor any substantive job skills. Approximately one-third have less than an eighth-grade education. Two-thirds of the families who get off welfare do not return.[16]

In light of these rather stark statistics, some rather simple questions emerge. Why has Texas failed to address the needs of its most impoverished citizens? Why has Texas consistently ranked near the bottom of those states willing to spend money to assist the less fortunate? But while the questions themselves might appear to be simple, the answers to them are quite complex, requiring an understanding of the policymaking process that has both defined and constrained the evolution of welfare policy in Texas.

Welfare and the Policymaking Process

There are a number of economic, political, and ideological factors that have played a major role in shaping welfare policy in Texas over the past fifty years. One of the most important economic factors is the simple fact that Texas has until recently been a relatively poor state. For many years, Texas could not afford an expensive set of welfare programs. The myth of the wealthy Texan to the contrary, Texas traditionally has lagged behind the U.S. average in per capita income. In 1929, per capita income in Texas was only $490, 68.1% of the national average. While this percentage rose in 1940 to 72.6 and to 90.2 in 1950, it fell to the mid-80 range in the late 1950s and early 1960s. The 1970s and early 1980s showed dramatic increases in per capita income in Texas. In 1970, it rose to almost 90% of the national average, and was a little above the national average in 1980. By 1982, the per capita income in Texas actually exceeded the national average by almost 3%, making it the sixteenth wealthiest state in the nation on a per capita basis. While per capita income in Texas fell slightly below the national average in 1984, dropping Texas to nineteenth, the real gains in per capita income continued unabated.[17]

Increasing wealth has not been accompanied by a corresponding increase in public expenditures for the poor in Texas. The liberalization of welfare programs has been inhibited by an ongoing desire to maintain a "favorable business climate" in Texas. In competing with other states for new businesses, Texas' economic and political leaders have stressed two features of the Texas economy: low taxes, and a traditionally low wage base. Not surprisingly, neither of these is particularly compatible with a liberal welfare program. Indeed, many business leaders would argue that the bare-bones welfare programs found in Texas are in and of themselves a positive feature of the Texas economy.[18]

But economic constraints are only part of the reason that welfare benefits have been kept low historically in Texas. There are important political reasons as well. One of the most important of these is the fact that up until the 1970s Texas was a one-party state dominated by a group of conservative Democrats from rural areas, the so-called Texas Establishment.[19] The Establishment has little use for either the poor on welfare or for minorities in general. Indeed, there were very few politicians who were willing to speak out for the poor on policy matters. The emergence of a liberal wing of the state Democratic party and the reapportionment of the state legislature according to the "one man-one vote" principle gradually has undermined the ability of the Establishment to dominate state policymaking totally over the past twenty years.

But until quite recently, these changes have had little impact upon welfare policy in Texas. For years, statewide leaders have refused to take up the banner of welfare reform in Texas. Crucial committees in the legislature responsible for drafting welfare legislation have been dominated by conservative individuals largely uninterested in addressing the needs of the poor. The House Budget Committee, in particular, has stood as a bulwark opposed to substantive welfare reform. As Molly Ivins, a columnist for the *Dallas Times Herald*, has noted, the attitude of most state legislators towards the poor has been a simple one over the years: "out of sight, out of mind."[20] It is revealing to note that the demands for the welfare reforms passed in the early 1980s did not originate out of either the conservative or the liberal wing of the Democratic party, but out of a broad-based non-partisan movement championed by elements of the religious community.

Negative attitudes towards the poor have been reinforced in the past by the inability of the Department of Public Welfare (today, the Department of Human Services) to speak out effectively on behalf of the poor or in favor of expanding welfare programs serving the poor. Part of this ineffectiveness was due to the fact that until the early 1980s, the department was prohibited by state law from engaging in outreach programs aimed at either broadening support for welfare programs or expanding participation in the state's welfare programs. Part, however, was due to preference on the part of the department's leadership. Beginning with John Winters, the executive director of DPW for over twenty-three years, DPW made a point of not getting embroiled in potentially controversial issues. While such a low profile orientation made some sense in light of the reigning attitudes towards welfare in the legislature, there also were serious costs; few individuals inside or outside the state capital fully understood the problems of poverty in Texas or how well current policies addressed these problems. By default public education was performed all too infrequently by a few organizations such as the Texas Social Welfare Association, a predecessor to the United Way.

Another factor that helps to explain why welfare benefits are so low in Texas is a budgetary one. There are no dedicated revenues committed to funding welfare programs in Texas. Instead, welfare is funded directly from the General Revenue Fund.[21] Significantly, there is a relatively narrow tax base from which this general revenue can be generated. There is no income tax in Texas. Moreover, the sales tax, which generates almost 40% of state revenues, is roughly comparable to other states. In 1982, the Texas per capita state level of taxation was $639.52 compared to a nationwide state average of $720.02. Among all the states, Texas ranked thirty-second in average per capita state level of taxation in 1982. While the legislature passed a three-year $4.8 billion tax increase in 1984, the first since 1971, much of the revenue was targeted for greater expenditures on education and highways in the state. Today, as in the past, welfare programs inevitably have been forced to compete with other state programs for rather limited tax dollars in the General Revenue Fund. When belts have to be tightened due to revenue shortfalls or to demands for lower taxes, the pressures to hold welfare spending down, or even to cut it back, often have proved to be overwhelming.

This budgetary factor is further complicated by the fact that state welfare spending for grants has been limited by a constitutional ceiling since the early 1940s. It is the only state that has had such a limit. Until 1983, the ceiling was a flat dollar amount that had been periodically raised over the years by constitutional amendment. In 1969, the limit for all welfare spending was set at $80 million. Beginning in 1983, it was set at 1% of the total state budget.

The significance of this spending ceiling to welfare policymaking in Texas has been threefold. First, it set strict limits upon how much money could actually be spent on the poor. Second, it built a curious ratcheting effect into the welfare system. If the welfare eligibility requirements were liberalized too much and too many new people were put on the welfare rolls, the benefits going to each recipient could actually decrease as the ceiling was approached. Finally, the ceiling placed an almost insurmountable barrier on substantive welfare reform. Amending the Texas state constitution is a difficult process at best, requiring a two-thirds vote in each house of the legislature as well as a popular referendum. Amending the constitution for purposes of increasing welfare spending has been something on which few politicians have been willing to expend political capital. Significantly, Medicaid and other social service programs have not fallen under similar constitutional spending restrictions. As a result, getting adequate funding for them has not proven to be as difficult or as controversial as it has for AFDC.

Along with these economic and political factors, ideology has also played an important role in keeping welfare benefits low. The mythos of the frontier, the idealization of the individual entrepreneur, the belief in self-help, and the idea that the government that governs least is the government that governs best all are well and alive in Texas in the 1980s. All have played a role in constraining a larger policy debate over the responsibility a society has for its poor. Indeed, the often-heard refrain, "Let's not make Texas into another welfare mecca," has been as difficult a barrier for welfare reformers to overcome as other more concrete economic and political ones.

The Evolution of Welfare Policy in Texas

The problems with welfare policy in Texas in the 1980s can be best understood by looking at them in light of the history of welfare policy in Texas throughout the twentieth century. For better or for worse, it is a history which is as unique as it is fascinating. As was the case in most other states, prior to 1935 public relief was a local responsibility to be dealt with by local government and private charity. But unlike most other states, Texas built this attitude directly into its constitutional structure. According to the Texas Constitution of 1876, the financing and implementation of welfare programs was left only to county governments. Article XVI, Section 8 stipulated that "each county must provide in such manner as may be prescribed by law, a manual labor poorhouse and farm, for taking care of, managing, employing and supplying the wants of its indigent and poor inhabitants."[23] County Commissioner Courts were given the responsibility for ultimately taking care of the poor. Significantly, the 1876 Constitution specifically prohibited the state legislature from making any welfare grants to individual citizens except to Confederate veterans or their widows.

In 1917, the state legislature permitted the County Commissioner Courts to grant aid to mothers caring for dependent children in their homes. Administration of mother's aid was local and no state funds were appropriated for it. While the program was liberalized in 1931, it remained very small, serving only a few hundred families across the state. Also in 1931, certain services were made available for the "local poor" in counties with a population over 350,000. Once again, efforts were minimal.[24]

The Great Depression was responsible for changing many popularly held attitudes about how welfare problems should be approached both at the national and the state level. New Deal programs such as the Emergency Relief Administration, the Civilian Conservation Corps, the Works Progress Administration, and the National Youth Corps helped to provide relief to people in Texas with neither jobs nor money. According to a study done by the Federal Emergency Relief Administration in 1933, 105,045 families in Texas were on relief, 7.1% of the state population. Interestingly, this figure was well below the national average of 10.3%. Of these relief families, 58% were white, 22% were Mexican American, and 20% were black. It was estimated that 5.4% of the white population and 8.8% of the black population in Texas was on relief at the time.[25]

New Deal programs required states to share some of the costs of the new direct relief programs. To meet this obligation, the Texas Legislature submitted to the voters a constitutional amendment to authorize the sale of $20 million in bonds for unemployment relief, so-called bread bonds. The constitutional amendment was ratified by the electorate on August 26, 1933. In addition, the legislature established the Texas Rehabilitation and Relief Commission to administer state and federal employment and relief programs.

The total amount of federal money funneled into Texas through the early New Deal programs was significant. The Federal Emergency Relief Administration alone is estimated to have spent approximately $50 million in Texas in 1933 and 1934. Prior to April, 1935, the national government contributed approximately $93 million to Texas for direct relief measures along with an estimated $21 million worth of surplus commodities.[26]

These programs were only a beginning. With the passage of the Social Security Act of 1935, welfare policy both at the national level and in Texas underwent a fundamental transformation. The Social Security Act established two major social insurance programs, Old Age Insurance (OAI, later OASDI for Old Age, Survivors, and Disability Insurance) and Unemployment Insurance, as well as a number of public assistance programs, including Aid to Dependent Children (ADC, later AFDC for Aid to Families with Dependent Children), Old Age Assistance (OAA), and Aid to the Blind (AB). The latter three assistance programs were state-federal programs aimed at a particular clientele. In order to receive federal monies for their program, each state had to meet certain minimal federal requirements. For example, an assistance program had to operate through an entire state, a single state agency had to administer the program, and opportunities had to be provided for fair hearings and appeals.

It took some time to implement fully the new state-federal public assistance programs authorized in the Social Security Act of 1935.

While OAA was established in Texas almost immediately, ADC and AB were not authorized until 1937 and money was not appropriated until 1941. The Texas Department of Public Welfare was not established to run these programs until September, 1939.

Much political controversy surrounded the implementation of both the DAA and the ADC programs in Texas. The idea of providing military pensions to veterans of the Confederate Army continued to receive state support well into the twentieth century. During the Depression, however, a new demand was championed throughout the country: pensions for all the elderly. At the national level, the Townsend Movement called for flat pensions of $200 for all people over the age of sixty-five. While most Texas politicians remained skeptical about such grandiose proposals to aid the elderly, there emerged a general consensus that some form of state assistance should be provided by the state for the elderly poor.[27]

The old-age pension issue took center stage during the 1934 election in Texas when the soon-to-be governor James Allred along with many other candidates called for the establishment of pensions for the elderly poor. In his 1935 message to the legislature, Allred referred to old-age pensions for the destitute as "just, humane, and inevitable." During a special election in August, 1935, a constitutional amendment was ratified authorizing the creation of an old-age assistance program for the elderly in Texas. The amendment stipulated that Texas' share of cash grants could not exceed $15 to people over the age of sixty-four. It also contained strong Texas residency requirements. It took the legislature some time to agree on exactly what the program would look like. Allred had to call two special sessions of the legislature before a pension act was passed.

The pension issue returned as a major theme during the 1938 and 1940 gubernatorial races. While campaigning on a platform comprising the Ten Commandments and the Golden Rule, W. Lee "Pappy" O'Daniel called for a liberalization of the pension program. Yet a serious liberalization of the program was difficult to achieve. There were limits, fiscal limits, to what the OAA program in Texas could provide the elderly poor, and politicians found themselves unable to move the program beyond them. Throughout the late 1930s, the state legislature had been unable to agree on an omnibus tax reform package that would put the program on a sound financial footing. From 1936 to 1941, the major revenue sources for OAA had been special taxes on such things as cigarettes and liquor. This funding proved to be inadequate and from 1936 to 1939 the program actually had to borrow money from a Dallas bank to pay benefits. Sadly, one of the first acts of the newly created Department of Public Welfare was to cut

OAA benefits by $6. In 1940, OAA monthly benefits were reduced $7.9 million in order to keep the program solvent. In 1941, they were reduced $5.1 million. While there were no cuts in monthly benefits in 1942, cuts took place again in 1943, 1944, and 1945.[28]

The financial problems experienced by OAA in its early years had two significant consequences. First, they caused many state politicians to lose their enthusiasm for the old-age pension issue. By April, 1941, the House actually called upon the federal government to take over complete control of the program.[29] Second, they taught key administrators of the program a valuable lesson—welfare issues that became too politicized could easily cost them their jobs. The firing of John S. Murchison, the first permanent executive director of DPW from 1940 to April, 1943, was due in large part to the uproar that followed his raising departmental salaries, including his own, while allowing benefits to be cut. In contrast, his successor, John Winters, lasted twenty-three years in office in large part due to his ability to stay in the background in Austin and to make as few waves as possible.[30]

A similar history plagued the early ADC program in Texas. On May 10, 1937, a constitutional amendment was ratified providing for state participation in the ADC and AB programs. While the legislature authorized later in the year an ADC program providing Texas' share of $8 grants per month for one child or $12 a month for a family, the program was not fully implemented until September, 1941 due to a variety of political and administrative complications. Like the OAA program, ADC had very strict eligibility requirements. Unlike the OAA program, however, a constitutional ceiling of $1.5 million was placed on the ADC program.

The implications of the constitutional ceiling for ADC were enormous. Twenty thousand needy families came into the ADC rolls in the early months of the program. As more families were certified as being eligible for participation in the program, pressures mounted to cut benefits. From September to November, 1942, ADC benefits were cut $10 per family. From December, 1942 through April, 1944, a rule was adopted by the Department of Public Welfare to limit aid to those who did not have sufficient income to meet 30% of their own needs. While the purpose of the rule, to provide aid to the most needy first, was laudatory, its effects were devastating. It was estimated that approximately twelve thousand families known to be in need were actually thrown off the rolls, about half of those on the welfare rolls at the time.[31]

A major consolidation of the welfare provisions in the constitution took place in 1945. Under the newly ratified Section 51a of Article III, the legislature was given authority to set limitations and restrictions on all categories of aid to the poor, residency requirements were modified, and a new constitutional ceiling was established which dropped the ADC ceiling and created a new ceiling of $35 million for OAA, ADC, and AB together. In addition, Section 51a mandated that state spending on welfare programs be limited to those matching federal monies. Texas thus could not supplement federal grants beyond the level for which federal monies were available. This constitutional provision put the state in the curious position of being unable to provide welfare relief to individuals except under the auspices of federal legislation with federal funding.[32] The amendment made state-led initiatives in welfare policymaking a practical impossibility.

With the passage of Section 51a of Article III, the broad features of welfare policy in Texas were firmly in place for the next twenty-odd years. Changes continued to be made at the margins. Between 1933 and 1965, sixteen constitutional amendments were ratified regarding welfare policies in Texas. Some raised the constitutional ceiling on spending. In 1954, the ceiling was raised from $35 million to $42 million. It was raised in 1957 to $47 million, in 1962 to $52 million, in 1963 to $60 million, and in 1969 to $80 million. Others broadened the programs and reflected changes in federal welfare policy. For example, mothers with dependent children became eligible for welfare payments under AFDC (formerly ADC) in the 1950s. In 1956, aid for the permanently and totally disabled was added in Texas. In 1961, Texas authorized funding of medical care for the elderly poor. In 1967, Texas began to participate in the Medicaid program. In addition, in 1965, provisions were made in the constitution empowering the legislature to rewrite sections of the constitution in order to bring it in harmony with changing federal regulations.

But despite these changes, welfare policy continued to be a dismal affair in Texas. Aggregate statistics appear to tell the story of a series of programs that were expanding to meet the needs of the poor from 1945 to the late 1960s. For example, monthly participation in OAA averaged around 171,000 individuals in 1945, rose rapidly to approximately 223,000 in 1950, leveled off through the mid-1950s, and began to decline slightly in the late 1950s and early '60s. Participation in AB averaged 4,640 per month in 1945, rose gradually to 6,569 in 1956, and fell to 6,383 in 1960. Participation in AFDC meanwhile rose from approximately 11,000 families and 24,000 children in 1945 to approximately 23,500 families and 80,000 children in 1967. Meanwhile, total federal and state spending increased in OAA from $47.9 million in 1945 to $141 million in 1960, in AB from $1.4 million in 1945 to $4.4 million in 1960, and in AFDC from $2.9 million in 1945 to $31 million in 1967.[33]

However, the expansion that did occur in Texas welfare programs took place in spite of, not because of, state efforts to address the needs of the poor. As a 1962 study of public assistance programs in Texas by the Texas Research League noted, "Texas has traditionally followed a policy of appropriating the minimum amount of state money necessary to get the maximum amount of federal money available."[34] It was the federal government, not the state government, that was responsible for expanding the program to include mothers of dependent children in 1950 and for creating incentives for states to establish certain social services to "rehabilitate" the poor in the early 1960s. Figures 10–3 and 10–4 highlight the impact of the federal government on welfare spending in Texas from 1945 to 1965. State expenditures on AFDC increased relatively slowly from $1.495 million in 1945 to $3.899 million in 1965. Federal expenditures, meanwhile, increased from $1.424 million to $16.594 million during the same period. In the OAA program, a similar story took place. State expenditures rose in the OAA program from $23.9 million in 1945 to $50.8 million in 1965. At the same time, federal spending increased over fivefold from $24.0 million in 1945 to $143.5 million in 1965.

It should be noted that the drop in OAA spending in 1968 was due in large part to the transferring of the Medical Vendor portion of the program (begun in 1961 in Texas) over to the Medicaid program, not a federal cutback per se. The drop from 1972 to 1974 reflected changes brought on by the liberalization of OASDI in the early 1970s and the establishment of Supplemental Security Income to replace OAA in 1971.

Even with the increased federal share, funding problems continued to plague the Texas AFDC program through the early 1960s. As in the early 1940s, periodic cuts in monthly benefits were made to keep the program within budgetary restrictions. Much smaller benefit cuts also were made in the OAA and AB programs through the mid-1950s. Despite the increase in the aggregate costs of each of its major welfare programs, Texas consistently ranked near the bottom among states in the average monthly grant per participant from the early 1940s to the mid 1960s.[35]

The late 1960s marked a watershed in the history of welfare policy both in the nation and in Texas. The War on Poverty transformed the way in which poverty was discussed and confronted by the federal government. It was no longer enough to provide assistance to the poor through the programs established under the original Social Security Act. Efforts were now made to rehabilitate the poor through a vast array of job training programs and social services sponsored by the federal government.

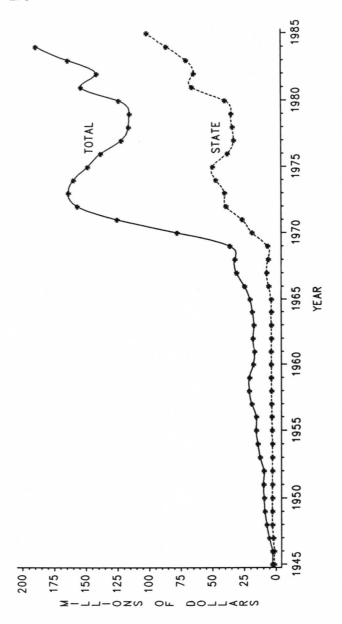

Figure 10-1. Aid to Families with Dependent Children Program in Texas. State and Total Expenditures, 1945-85.

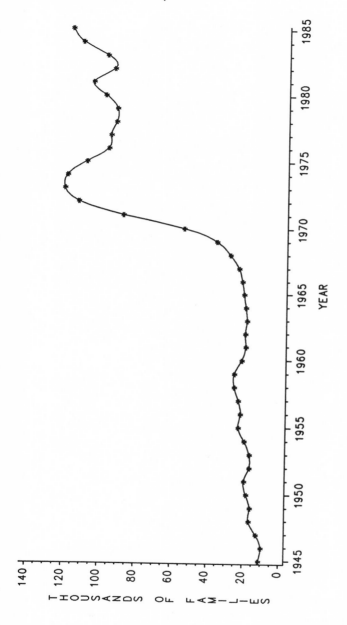

Figure 10–2. Aid to Families with Dependent Children Program in Texas. Mean number of Families per Month.

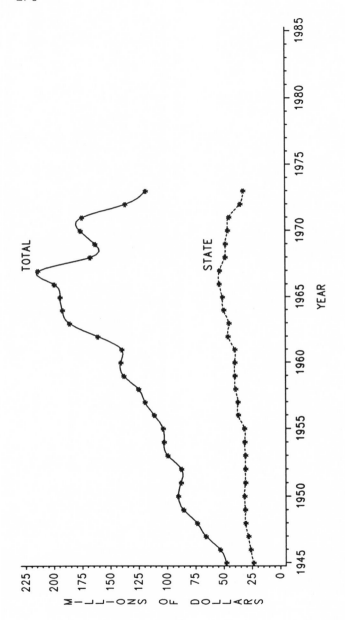

Figure 10–3.   Old Age Assistance Program in Texas. State and Total Expenditures.

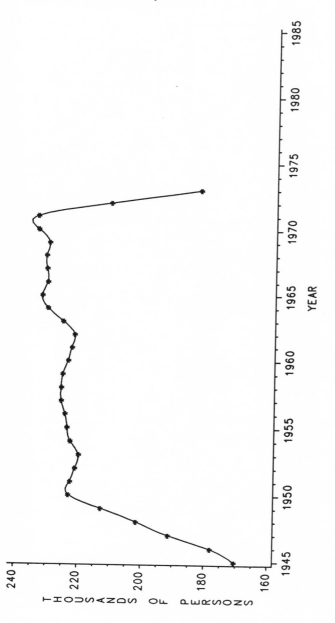

Figure 10–4. Old Age Assistance Programs in Texas. Mean Number of Persons per Month.

War on Poverty initiatives affected welfare policy in Texas along a number of interrelated dimensions. Important changes were made in the welfare provisions of the Social Security Act. In 1965, Medicaid was passed by the federal government. Texas began participating in the program in 1967. In addition, major changes were enacted for the AFDC program under the Social Security Act Amendments of 1967. War on Poverty efforts also stimulated the growth of a variety of social service and vocational training programs for the poor. Some of these programs helped to make the poor more aware of their rights to participate in Texas' welfare programs. Public-interest lawyers working out of the federally sponsored Legal Services Program played a major role in getting poor individuals to challenge some of the restrictions used by state and local officials to keep the welfare rolls down. Finally, there were a series of Supreme Court decisions between 1968 and 1971 that explicitly forbade the use of certain practices to keep people off welfare, including man-in-the house rules, residency requirements, and regulations denying aid to families with so-called employable mothers.[36]

Taken together the changes inaugurated by these federal initiatives affected welfare policy in two important ways. First, they forced a fundamental restructuring of the way in which welfare benefits were calculated in Texas. Second, they sparked an explosion in the welfare rolls. Each must be considered in detail to appreciate fully the way the War on Poverty affected welfare policy in Texas in the late 1960s and early '70s.

In the early years of the AFDC program in Texas, eligibility and benefit levels were determined on an individual basis. Caseworkers took into account the costs of a minimum-needs budget given a variety of factors including place of residency, size of family, and the price of food, shelter, and certain incidentals. There also was a maximum dollar amount that could be received by anyone under the program. A number of attempts were made to standardize some of the cost calculations that went into determining eligibility and benefits from 1948 through the late 1960s. But they were far from successful. Uncertainty continued to plague the AFDC program throughout the 1950s and '60s. While there were five increases in the amount of state money allocated to the program from 1943 to 1969, the maximum grant figure actually had to be reduced seventeen times from 1954 to 1969.[37]

The Social Security Amendments of 1967 were enacted by Congress to try to bring some uniformity to the AFDC program throughout the nation. It was particularly aimed at states like Texas. Among other things, it required that in the determination of eligibility for benefit levels, states had to ignore $30 per month plus work expenses as well as one-third of additional earnings. The amendments also required that each state establish a standard of need for measuring who is eligible for benefits and for determining how much assistance will be given in light of that standard. Significantly, the amendments only compelled states to recognize what the needs of the poor were in an objective way and to provide a welfare benefit based upon an understanding of that need. After computing the standard of need, states were free to adjust the actual welfare payment to only a fraction of the standard of need in order to meet other budgetary constraints. The goal of the legislation thus was a modest one. As Justice Harlan noted in *Rosado* vs. *Wyman*, the amendments forced "a State to accept the political consequence of such a cutback and [brought] to light the true extent to which actual assistance falls short of the minimum acceptable."[38]

In 1967 amendments had a significant impact upon the AFDC program in Texas. In order to meet new federal requirements, Texas implemented a new standard-of-need formula based upon the federal poverty index on May 1, 1969. This raised the index used to calculate need in Texas by 11%. Texas also ended the maximum grant system and put into place a percentage reduction formula for determining benefits. Thus while the state would calculate the minimum budgetary needs of a poor family, welfare payments would only cover a portion of those needs depending upon the funds made available to DPW by the legislature. Other reforms made by DPW included making special exemptions for earned income as an incentive to work in AFDC and lowering the minimum grant in all welfare programs to $1 to enable maximum participation on Medicaid.

Besides causing a restructuring of the way in which welfare benefits were calculated in Texas, federal government initiatives in the late 1960s also caused an explosion in the welfare rolls that continued through 1972. In total, AFDC caseloads in Texas increased almost fourfold between 1968 and 1972. The families of AFDC in Texas rose from 23,509 in 1967 to 120,254 in 1973. The number of children rose from 79,914 in 1967 to 325,244 in 1973.[39]

Serious problems accompanied the changes in the AFDC program in the late 1960s and early 1970s. For 1968, the constitutional ceiling on welfare spending stood at $60 million. The legislature had appropriated $48.2 million for OAA, $1.4 million for AB, $4.25 million for APTD (Aid for the Permanently and Totally Disabled), and $6.15 million for AFDC. Such funding levels were inadequate in light of rapidly rising participation rates. DPW ultimately found itself caught between a rock and a hard place. Expanding welfare rolls continued to push expenditures up against the constitutional ceiling. As had been the case in previous years, it appeared that there was not enough money to pay all promised welfare benefits. The outcome was inevitable. On September 1, 1968, benefits to the families participating in the AFDC Program were cut.

The legislature's first attempt to deal with the funding problems in AFDC failed. On November 5, 1968, voters rejected a constitutional amendment proposed by the legislature seeking to raise the welfare ceiling to $75 million. Statewide support for the proposal was weak. The proposal only passed in 16 of the state's 254 counties. The legislature did successfully transfer an additional $350,000 into the program in the first week of the 1969 legislative session and thus prevented a second reduction in benefits from taking place. Despite a general consensus in the legislature that something had to be done to alleviate the financial strains confronting the AFDC Program, there was considerable controversy over exactly what it should be. The Senate proposed a constitutional amendment that would have eliminated the ceiling entirely. In its version, the House proposed an $80 million ceiling on welfare expenditures, enough to fund welfare spending in Texas for approximately four years. The Senate reluctantly accepted the measure after considerable debate and an election was called for August 5, 1969.[40]

The reaction of welfare recipients to the cuts and the failure of the November constitutional amendment was swift in coming. For the first time in the history of the program welfare recipients refused to take the changes without a fight. On November 25, 1968, a three-day sit-in was sponsored by the Dallas chapter of the National Welfare Rights Organization and supported by the Students Non-Violent Coordinating Committee at a Dallas regional office of the DPW. On May 1, 1969, there was another sit-in at a Houston regional office. One hundred and forty kids and mothers affiliated with the Houston National Welfare Rights Organization and two VISTA volunteers participated. From June 16 to June 19, there was another sit-in in San Antonio.[41]

The problems facing DPW were compounded in May when a federal court judge issued an injunction against DPW asserting that unless there was an improvement in AFDC benefit provisions in Texas, federal funds for the program would be cut off.[42] The amendment to raise the ceiling to $80 million was ratified on August 5. The results became apparent almost immediately. For the first time in the history of the program substantial increases became possible in the AFDC

Program. Prior to the passage of the amendment in May, the average payment per family had been $76.07. After passage, it was increased to $122.65.

DPW had hoped that the passage of the constitutional amendment in 1969 would enable it to meet 75% of the standard of need in the AFDC Program. But rising participation rates were already pushing welfare expenditures up against the ceiling by mid-1970. DPW announced plans to reduce benefits from 75% of budgeted need to 66%. Governor Preston Smith was able to avoid reductions through an emergency transfer of funds to the DPW.[43]

At the same time Smith was busily digging up more funds for AFDC, a special committee headed by William P. Hobby, president and executive director of the *Houston Post,* was appointed by Lt. Governor Ben Barnes to study welfare problems in Texas and to recommend reforms to the legislature. The committee's final report, *Breaking the Poverty Cycle in Texas,* was a remarkable document calling for an end to the traditional ways in which Texas has dealt with its poor. According to the report,

> Events which have ushered in the seventies have signaled the urgent need for careful evaluation of ways to balance state and national expectations and resources. Public welfare no longer can be viewed as a minimum charitable human reaction to the needs of an undefined few who are less fortunate . . . .
>
> Texas must realize that this is no longer a landed frontier where survival and well-being are the products of individual faith, will and effort alone. It will take resources and ingenuity to make this truly a land of opportunity. Those who are living in poverty have not individually created their poverty any more than those who are prosperous have individually produced their wealth. The fine line between success and failure represents one of the most sensitive and complex unsolved phenomena of this era of space, conglomerates and megalopolises. The future of the state and this nation may rest upon the effectiveness with which the political and economic leadership recognizes and provides for the needs of the less fortunate.[44]

In many respects, the report was the highwater mark of demands for welfare reform in the early 1970s. Yet the proposals made in the report went largely unheeded. There were a number of reasons for this. Traditional suspicions about welfare reform continued to surface. Support for welfare reform in the Senate was limited. In the House, it was almost nonexistent. Meanwhile, Governor Smith's commitment to maintaining and improving welfare programs in Texas was a limited one. While expressing sympathy for the plight of the poor in Texas, Smith added, "At the same time, we must consider the interests of other citizens who are struggling to stay off public welfare rolls in rising inflation and for whom additional taxes might well be the burden that breaks their backs."[45]

One other factor played a major role in inhibiting any state efforts at comprehensive welfare reform: the belief that the federal government would take over full responsibility for the AFDC Program through some sort of negative income tax program. But the hopes of those favoring comprehensive welfare reform at the national level were dashed as a peculiar coalition of conservatives and liberals prevented Nixon's Family Assistance Plan from passing the Senate.[46] Some important changes did take place at the national level in welfare policy in the early 1970s. Old Age Assistance, Aid to the Blind, and Aid to the Permanently and Totally Disabled programs were nationalized under the federal government's new Supplemental Security Assistance Program beginning in 1974. Also in 1972, the federal Food Stamp Program was implemented throughout the entire state. But responsibility for handling the problems of the AFDC remained with the state governments. And problems there were in Texas.

By the mid-1970s, three factors began to seriously affect the implementation of the AFDC program in Texas: federal demands to reduce error rates on the welfare rolls, state budgetary demands to keep AFDC state expenditures down, and, perhaps most importantly of all, state budgetary demands to keep Medicaid costs down. Unwilling to risk further demonstrations from welfare recipients whose checks would be cut if participation rates remained high, Texas politicians encouraged DPW to take an alternative route to control expenditures: slashing the welfare rolls.[47]

The number of people on AFDC peaked in late 1972 and early 1973. By the middle of 1974, a long-term decline had set in on the numbers on the welfare rolls. The monthly average number of children on the rolls in 1973 was 325,244 and the monthly average number of families was 120,253. By 1979, these had dropped to 213,804 children and 91,850 families. This represented a decline of 34.3% in participating children and 23.6% in participating families. Total state and federal spending on the program meanwhile declined from $163.5 million to $115.2 million. This represented a drop of almost 30%.[48]

While the number of participating children and families in the AFDC program in Texas declined sharply in the late 1970s, there was a very different pattern nationwide. Instead of collapsing, participation in the AFDC program nationwide tended to level off from 1974 to 1979. In 1974, a monthly average of 3.3 million families and 7.9 million children participated in the AFDC program nationwide. This rose to 3.6 million families and 7.9 million children in 1976, and declined to 3.6 million families and 7.2 million children in 1979.[49]

The cutbacks on the welfare rolls were felt hard particularly among poor children. In 1975, the average monthly number of poor children on AFDC in Texas was 286,572, approximately 35.25% of all children in Texas living below the poverty line. By 1979, this number had dropped to an average monthly number of 214,267 children, approximately 30% of all children in Texas living below the poverty line. While the percentage of poor children on AFDC fell to under 21.6 in 1982, there were increases to 21.8 in 1983 and 23.6 in 1984.[50]

A number of factors clearly lay behind the sharp drop in AFDC participation in Texas. New federal regulations, changing economic circumstances, and the desire on the part of recipients to improve their lot in a time of skyrocketing inflation played a part in driving people off the rolls. But probably even more important than these was the desire on the part of DPW to tighten eligibility requirements in the state.[51] Some rather striking statistics tend to bear this out. As Figure 10–5 reveals, the number of AFDC applications accepted in Texas between 1971 and 1976 fluctuated between 45,000 and 56,000. In contrast, the number of AFDC grants terminated by DPW rose steadily from 24,417 in 1971 to 62,644 in 1976. Significantly, during this period there were sharp increases in two categories of reasons given by DPW for terminating recipients. In 1971, 2.5% of terminations were due to people failing to keep appointments. This figure rose steadily to 5.8% in 1976. Similarly, in 1971, 2.4% of terminations were due to a refusal to provide information or to follow an agreed-upon plan. This increased to 11.0% in 1973, and to 16.4% in 1974, but fell back to 5.1% in 1975, and 5.7% in 1976. In addition, a new category began to figure prominently in the termination of individuals from the welfare rolls: failure to return the new forms required by the state to verify eligibility. In 1975, failure to return eligibility forms accounted for 12.9% of those terminated from AFDC. This rose to 13.6% in 1976.

There are clearly a number of ways of interpreting these statistics. According to DPW, they represented a systematic effort on the part of the department to root out fraud and error from the welfare rolls in Texas.[52] But there is another way to look at these numbers. They also can indicate the "chilling effect" created by new department policies to curtail welfare program participation. Rather than reflecting an intensifying desire on the part of DPW to serve those in need, these statistics also can indicate an increasing willingness to throw individuals off the rolls for technical reasons, whatever other substantive reasons might exist for their termination.

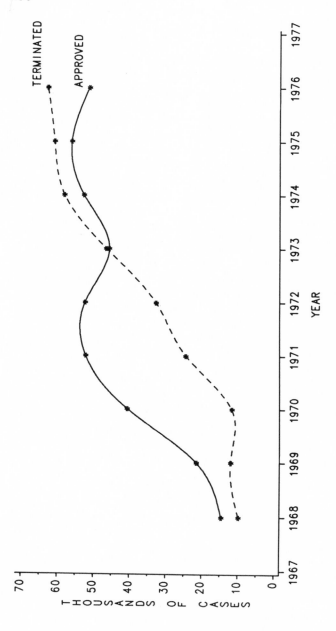

Figure 10-5. Aid to Families with Dependent Children. Grants Terminated and Approved.

Not everyone was pleased with the efforts on the part of the legislature or DPW to cut back welfare in the 1970s. Major religious organizations like the Baptist Christian Life Commission along with other groups like the League of Women Voters and the AFL-CIO began to lobby in defense of the programs sponsored by the newly renamed Department of Human Resources. They also began to lobby heavily to protect the department from serious cutbacks in personnel. Their successes were limited, although important. Demands for serious cutbacks in DHR's operating expenses were mitigated by strong lobbying efforts throughout the Briscoe and Clements administrations. More significantly, they successfully lobbied for the establishment of a special nonrecurring grant to AFDC children in 1978.

Throughout the 1970s, the average monthly benefit per participant was hovering around $32. Most legislators were willing to admit that this grant was woefully inadequate in light of the inflationary spiral of the 1970s. Yet they were unwilling to pass the general grant increases requested by the DHR year in and year out. Such an increase not only would have pushed up welfare spending to the constitutional ceiling of $80 million, it also would have expanded the population eligible for the AFDC program and thus for state Medicaid dollars. There were two attractive features about the nonrecurring grants. First, they would not be counted as income by the federal government because their timing was unpredictable. Because they did not increase the basic AFDC grant, the grants thus did not make any new people eligible for either the AFDC or the Medicaid programs. They also did not affect federal food stamp allocation. They thus would not make new people eligible for either AFDC or Medicaid, and they would not affect federal food stamp allocation. Second, they allowed the legislature to control carefully the money actually going to AFDC recipients.[53]

In 1978 and 1979, special grants of $60 were paid to AFDC children. Groups in favor of liberalizing welfare payments successfully lobbied to increase the grants to $80 in 1981, and to $110 in 1982. No one felt at the time that these special grants were the final solution to the AFDC payment problem. As Phil Strickland, the main lobbyist for the Christian Life Commission, has explained, "The bonus payment was not a good-long term solution. But it was the only way to break the $32 impasse on AFDC payments."[54] And break the impasse it did. Gradually in the late 1970s, an informal coalition in favor of welfare reform began to emerge that wanted to challenge the existing limits to welfare spending in Texas. It recognized that the $80 million ceiling would soon be reached and it wanted to make sure that something more substantive was accomplished than simply raising the ceiling a few million dollars.

The coalition's effort to reform the AFDC Program in Texas basically went through two stages. In the first stage, it sought to change the constitutional ceiling. Reformers recognized that they were in a dilemma of sorts. On the one hand, they did not want it to *appear* that they were asking for too much. Doubling or even eliminating the ceiling was probably not politically feasible. They doubted that either the legislature or the public at large would buy such a wholesale change of direction in welfare policy. On the other hand, they did not want to propose a ceiling that was so low that they would have to return to the legislature and the electorate in a few years to raise it again.

The resolution to this dilemma was intriguing. A constitutional amendment was proposed that changed the ceiling from $80 million a year to $160 million for the 1982–83 biennium. After that the two-year ceiling would be 1% of the state budget. While the amendment provided that the state budget would be determined by statute, it was clear that the budget was to encompass all state and federal monies budgeted by the state during the biennium. The amendment also eliminated the requirements that state assistance could not exceed federal assistance and that forbade state-sponsored welfare programs that had no federal matching funds.[55]

In the fall of 1981, Phil Strickland of the Texas Christian Life Commission and Lt. Governor Hobby helped to form a broad-based nonpartisan group called Citizens Concerned about Children. Their objective was simple: passage of Proposition 2, the constitutional amendment to raise the ceiling to 1% of the state's budget. The group sought to forge a common ground upon which substantive reform of the AFDC Program in Texas could be based. By making the issue of welfare reform nonpartisan and by getting everyone to sign on, the group hoped to close out any opposition that might form over the amendment.[56]

The campaign waged by Citizens Concerned about Children was finely crafted and expertly executed. Fifty thousand dollars was raised and spent in championing Proposition 2. Support for the group came from a diverse set of sources including religious and other non-profit organizations, organized labor, and the corporate community in Texas. Most of the major papers in the state supported the amendment. In the end, the campaign was an enormous success. Proposition 2 was ratified overwhelmingly in November 1982.[57]

Changing the constitutional ceiling was only the first stage in reformers' attempts to liberalize welfare benefits in Texas. The amendment only raised the ceiling of the amount that could be spent. The legislature still had to appropriate funds to the program and DHR had to establish benefit formulas based upon this level of funding. The second stage thus involved lobbying the legislature to increase the actual funds available for AFDC payments. This proved to be a difficult task.

Two factors worked to complicate any discussion of liberalizing benefit payments in the AFDC Program in Texas in 1983. The Reagan budgetary cuts reduced spending on federal domestic programs by about $35 billion. While most of these cuts were in grant aid to state and local governments, funding levels for programs like AFDC and Food Stamps also were affected. It is estimated that AFDC rolls in Texas were reduced by about 15% by the Reagan initiatives.[58] Ironically, this had the unintended consequence of making liberalization of the benefit levels in Texas easier because suddenly less state money was needed to meet current state commitments. However, there was a countervailing force that made liberalization more difficult. Projected tax revenues had collapsed by 1983 leading to new calls for holding the line on state spending.

Unlike the early 1970s, welfare reformers both inside and outside the legislature were not to be denied. During the regular session in 1983, the legislature created a new sliding scale for funding that allowed benefit levels to increase from approximately $32 per person per month plus the bonus (currently $110 a year per child) to $48 per person per month with no ceiling, a net increase of approximately $5 per person per month. In addition, during the special session of the legislature, DHR was exempted from having to return unused funds to the treasury and given the power to raise benefit levels further if funding remained available. On September 26, 1984, the Texas Board of Human Resources raised benefit levels once again to $53.

For proponents of welfare reform in Texas, the victory was only a temporary one. As Phil Strickland noted afterwards, "In light of the reality that the average payment in the United States is $100, an increase to $53 can't be seen as a great step forward. It is, however, a positive and needed action."[59] At the same time that levels were being increased to $53, plans were already being formulated by groups like Texans for Children, the successor to Citizens Concerned about Children, to lobby for a further liberalization of Texas' AFDC Program. For some, the goal was $60 per person per month. For others, it was $70. While the average monthly grant ultimately rose to $57.57 in 1986, those in favor of expanding welfare benefits were not particularly satisfied, much less proud, of Texas' initiatives on behalf of the poor. Most recognized that additional demand would have to be made in future legislatures if the needs of the poor were to be met.

Welfare Policy Today

It is difficult to assess definitively the long-term significance of the welfare reforms that have been instituted in Texas since late 1982. It is possible that the federal government could nationalize the AFDC Program, as was suggested by the Nixon, Carter, and Ford administrations throughout the 1970s. It is possible that the federal government could nationalize Medicaid and place full responsibility for AFDC and food stamps in the hands of the states, as was proposed by the Reagan administration in 1981. Any such actions would make most of the reforms that were enacted in 1982 and 1983 quite beside the point. But such scenarios are unlikely. The question of welfare policy in America has emerged in a new light in most policymaking circles in the mid-1980s. Stimulated by studies like Charles Murray's *Losing Ground,* many liberals and conservatives have discovered (or rediscovered) a "culture of poverty" in America that, it is argued, is nurtured by existing welfare programs. To date, little consensus exists on what should be done to correct the situation. Some conservatives, like Murray, advocate a drastic slashing of federally sponsored welfare programs, an effort meant to give people an incentive to escape poverty. Others of a more liberal persuasion have argued that new federal programs need to be devised to make up for the deficiencies of the existing ones. But while there has been considerable smoke surrounding the debate over welfare reform recently, there has been little fire. Few national political leaders appear to be willing today to risk the dangers that have befallen others seeking comprehensive welfare reform. It is far more likely that national welfare policy will continue to limp along in its present state of disarray with a few changes perhaps being made at the margins.[60]

The most immediate threat to the welfare reforms put into place in Texas in the early 1980s lies not in Washington, but in Austin in the form of the budget crisis brought on by the collapsing price of oil. One can easily imagine a situation in which demands to keep taxes low are coupled to demands to cut the fat out the state government. This could lead, as it has in the past, to a slashing of benefits and a systematic attempt on the part of DHS to cut back the welfare rolls. Cutting state welfare expenditures was one of the first things mentioned as political leaders tried to grapple with the budget crisis during the Special Session in the summer of 1986. However, there are a number of reasons for believing that cutting welfare benefits and keeping them low will not be as easy in the late 1980s as it was in previous years. A number of important changes have taken place in the policymaking environment that point to the beginning of a new era in welfare policymaking in Texas.

First, the 1982 elections put into statewide office a group of moderate Democrats who were willing to listen to and to support cautiously calls for welfare reform. This concern over the needs of the poor in Texas can be seen along a number of fronts: in the welfare reforms instituted in 1982 and 1983, in the appointment of a commission to study the problems of indigent health care in Texas, in the liberalization of the Medicaid Program to cover two-parent families, and in the appointment of three activist members to the Texas Board of Human Services, a first in the history of the board. Meanwhile, most conservative Democrats, like Speaker of the House Gib Lewis, have simply been either unwilling or unable due to both political and personal problems to mount a serious challenge to welfare reform proposals.

Second, the Department of Human Services has begun to play a new role in the policymaking process. In years past, DHS allowed others in Austin and Washington to define the thrust of welfare policy in Texas. Part of this was due to the fact that the department was constrained by state statute regarding the outreach programs that it could engage in. Part of it was also due to the attitude on the part of the legislature as to what the function of DHS actually was. One former board member actually characterized his job as being that of a "shipping clerk," a position forced upon him by a legislature that strictly limited who could get welfare from the state and how much they could get.[61] A shipping clerk mentality clearly no longer dominates the board or the department as a whole. Indeed, since being appointed to office the new board has helped push some new changes that have helped to redefine the role of the department in welfare policymaking, including an elimination of the prohibition against outreach programs and the institutionalization of a strategic plan for the department. It also has been responsible for redefining the standard of need criteria for the first time since 1969 and for championing increases in departmental outlays before the budget committees in the legislature.

A third reason to believe that the conditions under which welfare policy has been made in Texas have changed lies in the fact that there are active and effective lobbyists speaking on behalf of the poor for the first time. While there were groups in the past such as the Texas

Social Welfare Association who spoke out in favor of welfare reform, none of them had the political resources, the political base, or even the political savvy of current lobbyists from such organizations as the Christian Life Commission, the League of Women Voters, the United Way, and the Poverty Education and Research Center. With such lobbyists to act as spokesmen for the poor, it is unlikely that the needs of the poor can be ignored as often or as easily as they have been in the past.

There are, however, still important constraints that will affect any additional attempts to reform welfare policy. The budgetary constraint is an obvious one. DHS estimates that the 1% ceiling could support a $70 AFDC grant if the legislature were to appropriate adequate funding. But declining tax revenues may ultimately force welfare reformers to choose not only between welfare programs and nonwelfare programs such as education or transportation, but between welfare programs themselves. Being forced to choose between increasing the AFDC benefit and liberalizing coverage under Medicaid is something few politicians, bureaucrats, or lobbyists want to be forced to do.

But a budgetary concern is only one of the constraints that may affect the future of welfare policy in Texas. A much more important constraint may well prove to be the changing complexion of party politics. Over the past few years, welfare reform has been raised as a nonpartisan issue. Reformers have sought to provide the facts about welfare policy in Texas to politicians and the public alike, believing that those facts would speak for themselves. As benefit levels increase and the welfare rolls expand due to the reforms already in place, the issue of welfare reform is likely to become much more partisan, separating Democrats from Republicans and further dividing the state Democratic party. The outcome of a partisan debate over welfare reform would not necessarily be all bad, for it would force politicians and citizens to consider questions that have been ignored for far too long in Texas: What are a society's obligations to its poor? to its elderly? to its disabled? to its children? What is the best way to structure a welfare program that provides individuals with the best incentives and opportunities to escape poverty? These are questions that Texas has failed to address in the past. They are questions that it must address for its future.

Notes

1. U.S. Department of Commerce, Bureau of the Census, *Statistical Abstract of the United States 1984, (104th ed.)* (Washington, D.C.: Government Printing Office, 1984), 472; (hereafter *Statistical Abstract; 1980 Census of the Population: Texas)*, Section 1 (Washington, D.C.: Government Printing Office, 1980), 119.

The federal poverty index is based solely on money income. It does not take into account the in-kind benefits that welfare recipients might receive through such programs as food stamps, Medicaid, or public housing. The index is based on the U.S. Agriculture Department's 1961 economy food plan and takes into account the different consumption requirements of families based upon their size and composition. The poverty thresholds are updated every year to take into account changes in the cost of living. For a more detailed discussion, see *Statistical Abstract 1984*, 447.

2. *Statistical Abstract 1984*, 472.

3. *1980 Census*, 119.

4. Ibid.

5. Michael Martin, "Texas at a Glance: Poverty," *Fiscal Notes* (November, 1983): 15.

6. "State Closes Books on Fiscal Year," *Fiscal Notes* (November, 1985):1–8.

7. "Welfare Cutbacks Studied," *Dallas Morning News* (May 22, 1986). See also "Welfare Grants below Average, Official Says," *Dallas Morning News* (February 27, 1985); and Terry Peters, "AFDC Grants Increased—to 21.6% of Poverty," *Texas Research League Analysis* (October, 193): 3–4.

8. Department of Human Resources (September 25, 1984).

9. Payments can go to two-parent families in Texas if the reason for the deprivation of the child or children is the physical-mental incapacity of the father.

10. Interview with Jeff Skarda of the Gulf Coast Legal Foundation, Houston, Texas, September 14, 1984. See also W. Norton Grubb, "The Price of Local Discretion: Inequalities in Welfare Spending within Texas," *Journal of Policy Analysis and Management* 3 (1984):359–72; W. Norton Grubb and Julia Green Brodie, "Spending Inequalities for Children's Programs in Texas," *The Annals of the American Academy of Political and Social Science* 461 (May, 1982):53–62.

11. Richard Michel and Patricia Willis, "Participation Rates in the Aid to Families with Dependent Children Program, Part II: State Rates in 1975," Working Paper 1387–03, Urban Institute, January, 1981. Cited in Grubb, "The Price of Local Discretion, 362–63"; *Statistical Abstract 1984*, 394.

12. Department of Human Resources (October, 1984). See also Texas Department of Human Services (DHS) *Annual Report 1985*, 15.

13. Grubb, 364.

14. DHS, *Annual Report 1985*, 3; and Department of Human Services, *Annual Report 1986*.

15. "Welfare Grants below Average."

16. Barbara McCormick, "Aid to Families with Dependent Children," *Texas Focus* (August, 1982):1.

17. "Per capita income" is an indicator used to measure the general economic well-being of a people. It is derived by dividing the personal income of people living in a particular area by the area's population: Dan Casey, "Texas Per Capita Income Approaches U.S. Average," *Fiscal Notes* (August/September, 1980): 4–6; *Statistical Abstract 1986*, 440.

18. This attitude was reflected in a variety of proposals made to the legislature by *Texas Business* magazine in early 1983. Regarding welfare expenditures, it stated: "We oppose increased spending for welfare and other social services. Current benefit ceilings must be maintained. Texas, at all costs, must avoid becoming a welfare mecca." See, for example, "Recommendations to the Texas Legislature," *Texas Business* (February, 1983):39–57.

19. For a fascinating discussion of the power wielded by the Establishment, see George Norris Green, *The Establishment in Texas Politics: The Primitive Years 1938–1957* (Westport, Conn.: Greenwood Press, 1979); and James W. Lamare, *Texas Politics: Economics, Power, and Policy* (St. Paul, Minn.: West Publishing Company, 1981).

20. Telephone interview with Molly Ivins, February 7, 1984.

21. A large portion of taxes paid in Texas are earmarked for specific purposes. In 1981, the General Revenue Fund comprised only about 30% of all state revenues: Beryl E. Pettus and Randall W. Bland, *Texas Government Today* 3rd. ed. (Homewood, Illinois: Dorsey Press, 1984), 408.

22. Ibid., 397.

23. Some counties in Texas continue to maintain countywide assistance programs.

24. Two contemporary studies that examine the plight of the poor in the late 1930s are Bureau of Research in the Social Sciences, *Texas' Children: The Report of the Texas Welfare Survey* (Austin: University of Texas at Austin, October 1, 1938); Texas Social Welfare Association, *A Study of Basic Social Needs* (Austin: November, 1940).

25. Federal Emergency Relief Administration, *Unemployment Relief Census* (October, 1933), 4, 7, 34. Cited in Ralph W. Steen, *Twentieth Century Texas: The Land and the People* (Austin: Arthur Steck Company, 1942), 25.

26. Texas Relief Commission, *Relief and Rehabilitation in Texas* (Austin: April, 1935). Cited in Bureau of Research in Social Sciences, *Texas Children*, 597, ff.3.

27. For a further discussion of the Townsend Movement and its impact upon federal policy toward the aged, see William Graebner, *A History of Retirement: The Meaning and Function of an American Institution, 1885–1978* (New Haven, Conn.: Yale University Press, 1980), ch. 7. For a fascinating contemporary insight into the issues surrounding old-age pensions in Texas, see the articles by Dale Miller in *Texas Weekly*, August 12, 1933, June 30, 1934, and July 7, 1934.

28. To keep the programs afloat $3,727,095 was borrowed from 1936 to 1939: Texas Department of Public Welfare (DPW), *Annual Report, 1949,* 21–22; Texas Social Welfare Association, "Call for Legislative Action," Publication No. 45.1 (Austin: TSWA, January 15, 1945), 5.

29. Steen, 31–36; DPW, *Annual Report, 1949,* 22; TSWA, "Call," 5. AB did not experience the financial problems that OAA and AFDC did.

30. It should be added that the pay increases that did Murchison in were being forced upon him in part by the federal government. This information was provided to me by Bluford Hestir and Travis Hanes of the Department of Human Resources. Hestir is currently supervising a project engaged in collecting information for an in-house history of the department.

31. Texas Social Welfare Association, "Call for Legislative Action," 5.

32. Interestingly, this meant that for years Texas was unable to supplement federal welfare programs such as Supplemental Security Income. This provision was deleted with the 1982 constitutional amendment.

33. See DPW, *Annual Report,* for the appropriate years.

34. Texas Research League, *Public Assistance for the Aged, Disabled and Blind,* Report No. 4, A Study of Texas State Welfare Programs Series (Austin: Texas Research League, June, 1962), 3.

35. See Census Bureau, *Statistical Abstract,* for the appropriate years on the ranking of Texas welfare programs nationwide.

36. For an excellent discussion of these issues at a national level see James T. Patterson, *America's Struggle Against Poverty 1900–1980,* (Cambridge: Harvard University Press, 1981), ch. 11.

37. For a further discussion of the way eligibility and benefits levels were determined beginning in 1969, see Lottie Lee Crafton, *Aid to Families with Dependent Children, National and Texas,* Report prepared for the Department of Public Welfare (Austin: Center for Social Work Research, School of Social Work, August, 1976).

38. *Rosado* vs. *Wyman* 397 U.S. 397 (1970).

39. DPW, *Annual Report* for the appropriate years.

40. See "Welfare Vote Set for August," *Texas Observer* (May 9, 1969).

41. Legislators opposed to welfare reform in the nation and in the state had a field day when it became known that VISTA workers had supplied transportation to the June demonstration in federally owned cars.

42. See "Texas Welfare Crisis," *Texas Observer* (August 1, 1969).

43. See "The Welfare Crisis," *Texas Observer* (March 6, 1970).

44. *Breaking the Poverty Cycle in Texas,* a report of the Senate Interim Committee on Welfare Reform (Austin: 1970), 1. See also *Poverty: Time for a State Policy,* report of the House Interim Committee on Poverty of the 63rd legislative session (Austin: 1973–74); *Poverty in Texas,* report of the Texas Department of Community Affairs (Austin: 1972).

45. Smith is cited in "The Welfare Crisis," *Texas Observer* (March 6, 1970).

46. See Patterson, ch. 12.

47. Interview with Tom Suehs of Budget and Planning, Department of Human Resources, Austin, Texas, September 25, 1984.

48. DPW, *Annual Report*, for the appropriate years.

49. *Statistical Abstract 1982–83*, 443; *Statistical Abstract 1984*, 393.

50. Department of Human Resources, Budget and Planning, (Austin: September 28, 1984).

51. DPW, *Annual Reports* for the appropriate year.

52. See DPW, *Annual Report: 1976*, 27. For an outsider's understanding of the state of welfare in Texas in the mid-1970s, see Jane Kronholtz, "Texas Skimps on Aid to Poor, Saves Money; But Some Call it Cruel," *Wall Street Journal* (November 11, 1976).

53. See chapter 4 of the Committee on Human Services Report in *A Compilation of Interim Reports of the 68th Texas State Legislature*, Vol. 3 (Austin: 1982).

54. Interview with Phil Strickland of the Baptist Christian Life Commission, Dallas, Texas, September 13, 1984.

55. For a discussion of the constitutional amendment, see Texas House of Representatives, House Study Group Special Legislative Report, "The 1982 Constitutional Amendments," No. 83 (Austin: 1982).

56. Interview with Phil Strickland, September 13, 1984.

57. For a listing of the individuals and groups backing the coalition, see chapter 4 of *Compilation*.

58. Texas League of Women Voters, "Act Now: Increase State Appropriations for Human Services," Human Resources Advocacy Paper (Austin: League of Women Voters, January, 1983); John Kamensky, "The Reagan Revolution Hits Texas," in Eugene W. Jones, *Practicing Texas Politics*, 5th ed., (Boston: Houghton Mifflin, 1983), 514.

59. Virginia Ellis, "Welfare Payments Boosted," *Dallas Morning News* (September 26, 1984).

60. This is the conclusion reached by many, including liberals like Joseph Califano and conservatives like Martin Anderson. For a discussion of the stalemate in welfare policymaking, see Patterson, *America's Struggle*, Epilogue.

61. Interview with Tom Suehs, September 25, 1984. Letter from Bluford B. Hestir, Texas Department of Human Resources (October 11, 1984).

EPILOGUE

*Anthony Champagne and
Edward J. Harpham*

This book has examined the changes that Texas is facing in the late twentieth century. The shift away from an energy-based economy, ongoing demographic changes, and a fundamental restructuring of the political party system have placed Texas at a crossroads in its history. Grappling with the problems surrounding water and energy policy, highway construction, prison reform, education, and welfare policy in this new environment ultimately will cost money and require new allocations of resources. A fundamental question remains, however, whether or not the state possesses the political capacity needed to address these problems coherently.

The 1987 regular session of the state legislature did little to build confidence in the ability of the state to address the problems of a rapidly changing political economy. Nothing was done to alleviate the long-term water problems facing the state. No real efforts were made to free the state from its dependency upon declining energy industry or to rethink its highway policy. While a drive to weaken the reforms in public education passed by the previous session was beaten back, little was done to expand upon those reforms. No systematic attempt was made to confront the problems of higher education and its erosion in comparison to other state university systems. Prison reforms were passed, but only in reaction to federal court orders. Welfare spending continued to come under attack as one place where money could be saved even as Texas' welfare spending in comparison with other states' continued to fall. However inadequate the policy initiatives were in these areas, the real failure of the 1987 legislative session lay in something much more fundamental—in the inability to pass a budget for the next biennium. It was projected by the state comptroller's office that by August 31, 1989, there would be a $5.8 billion state budget deficit if taxes were not raised or spending was not cut. By the end of the session a stalemate had set in among key political leaders that effectively undercut any positive responses to many of the problems of the state.

This political stalemate was a direct reflection of many of the underlying social, economic, and political changes discussed throughout this book. The ongoing plight of the energy industry, an emerging Republican party, and a divided Democratic party have all worked to fragment political authority in the state. But this fragmentation of political authority does not alone account for the failure of the political system to respond to the problems facing the state. Key political leaders in both political parties continue to refuse to believe that the Texas of today differs in any fundamental way from the Texas of years gone by, or that the type of political leadership needed to guide Texas in the future might differ at all from that found in its past.

There are many political leaders throughout the state who sense that Texas stands at a crossroads but have no real vision of where they want to go or how to get there. At times it appears that they would prefer to let the state flounder in the present than to strike out in a new direction with a new sense of purpose. It is difficult to imagine that political bluster alone can curtail the demands for new services that are arising out of the Texas political economy today or blunt the need for additional funds to provide these services. Political bluster can, however, damage the credibility of the state as a good place to do business or to live in the late twentieth century.

To be sure, there are some leaders who believe that the state must be willing to expand and improve upon its efforts in a variety of policy areas. Some continue to argue that we must expand state efforts to improve the quality of public and higher education in the state through more spending. Others continue to work for an improvement of the welfare system in meeting the needs of a growing poor population in the state. Such leaders appear to recognize that Texas government must spend and raise more money if it is to meet the challenges facing the state. Yet even supporters of additional taxes primarily talk of increases in and expansions of the state sales tax, a regressive tax that by no means insulates the budget from the ups and downs of the Texas economy. Although a corporate tax or an income tax could be used to erase the projected $5.8 billion deficit and to put the entire state budget on a more sound footing, neither is being seriously considered in political circles. There are solutions to the budgetary crisis in the state. But like the solutions to the problems discussed in this book, they will only come through the foresight and courage of political leaders who are willing to fight for them.

THE CONTRIBUTORS

Margaret Barton taught Economics and Political Economy at The University of Texas at Dallas from 1979 to 1985. She is currently privately employed in Washington D.C. She has published numerous articles in such journals as the *Bell Journal of Economics* and *Political Methodology*.

Ronald Briggs is Professor of Political Economy at The University of Texas at Dallas. He has published widely in such journals as *Geographical Analysis, Transportation Quarterly*, and *Professional Geographer*. His current research interests focus upon the impact of changing commuting patterns upon urban development.

Anthony Champagne is Professor of Government and Political Economy at The University of Texas at Dallas. He is the author and editor of numerous books, including *Congressman Sam Rayburn*, and has published widely in professional journals. His current research interests focus upon judicial reform and Texas politics.

Philip DiSalvio is Assistant Professor of Public Administration at Seton Hall University. His current research interests focus upon the effect of cutback management techniques in higher education.

Edward J. Harpham is Associate Professor of Government and Political Economy at The University of Texas at Dallas. He is the author and editor of numerous books and has published in such journals as the *American Political Science Review, Western Political Quarterly*, and *Social Science Quarterly*. His current research interests focus upon the development of the American welfare state and the history of political economy.

Donald A. Hicks is Professor of Sociology and Political Economy at The University of Texas at Dallas. He is the author of numerous articles and books, including *Advanced Industrial Development* and *Technology, Regions, and Policy*. His research interests focus upon the processes of industrial-urban change.

Martin T. Katzman is Economics Professor of Environmental Sciences at The University of Texas at Dallas and is Senior Economist at Argonne National Laboratory. He has been a consultant for the U.S.

Department of Energy and the Texas Governors' Office of Nuclear Waste. He has published widely in professional journals and is the author of numerous books including *Cities and Frontiers in Brazil* and *Solar and Wind Energy*. His current interests focus upon risk analysis.

Harry Mika is Assistant Professor of Sociology at Central Michigan University. His current research focuses upon the historical detention process and custodial organizations.

Joe E. Moore, Jr. is Professor of Environmental Sciences at The University of Texas at Dallas. He was Executive Director of the National Commission on Water Quality. He has been an aide to two Texas Governors and the court appointed master in environmental cleanup lawsuits in Detroit and Dallas.

Patricia Osborne has studied Environmental Sciences at The University of Texas at Dallas and currently teaches Sociology in the Dallas Community College System.

David Plank is Assistant Professor of Educational Administration at the University of Pittsburgh. He has served as a consultant for the Dallas Independent School District. His current research interests focus upon educational policy.

Lawrence J. Redlinger is Professor of Sociology and Political Economy at The University of Texas at Dallas. He has published widely in professional journals and is the co-author of *Making Spies*. His research interests focus upon the problem of social order, with a particular focus on social control and regulation, organizations, and the relationship between politics and markets.

Glenn Robinson is Assistant Professor of Government and Political Economy at The University of Texas at Dallas. His research interests focus upon Texas politics.

INDEX